James Donaldson

A Critical History of Christian Literature and Doctrine

From the death of the apostles to the Nicene Council. Vol. 3

James Donaldson

A Critical History of Christian Literature and Doctrine
From the death of the apostles to the Nicene Council. Vol. 3

ISBN/EAN: 9783337301408

Printed in Europe, USA, Canada, Australia, Japan

Cover: Foto ©Lupo / pixelio.de

More available books at **www.hansebooks.com**

A CRITICAL HISTORY

OF

CHRISTIAN LITERATURE

AND DOCTRINE

FROM THE DEATH OF THE APOSTLES TO

THE NICENE COUNCIL.

BY

JAMES DONALDSON, M.A.

VOL. III.

THE APOLOGISTS Continued.

London

MACMILLAN AND CO.

1866

OXFORD:
BY T. COMBE, M.A., E. PICKARD HALL, AND H. LATHAM, M.A.
PRINTERS TO THE UNIVERSITY.

CONTENTS.

BOOK III. THE APOLOGISTS *Continued*.

CHAPTER IV.—TATIAN.

                                      PAGE

I. *His Life.* His country. His profession. His conversion. His Christian life. His heretical life. His heretical opinions. Misrepresentations. His opinion of Marriage; of another God; of Adam. Explanation of his heresies 3

II. *His Writings.* His Oration; its genuineness and date. His other works. His Harmony. His heretical work, On Perfection according to the Saviour . . . 20

III. *Estimate.* His character. His references to persecution. His attitude towards heathenism. His treatment of philosophers. His rejection of all human studies. His defence of Christianity . 27

IV. *Abstract of the Oration to the Greeks* . . 34

V. *Doctrines of Tatian.* On God; his immateriality; peculiar notions of creation. *The Logos. The Spirit,* use of the term; peculiar doctrine of Spirit. *Devil and demons;* their nature, their continuance, and ultimate state. *Man;* his nature. Freewill. Salvation. Christians; their mode of life. Resurrection. *Scriptures. Morality* . . . 40

VI. *Literature.* Manuscripts and editions   60

CHAPTER V.—THEOPHILUS.

	PAGE
I. *Life.* His descent; date of death	63
II. *Writings of Theophilus.* Genuineness of the Books addressed to Autolycus; their completeness. Other works of Theophilus	64
III. *Estimate.* His style. His treatment of heathenism. Defence of Christianity	69
IV. *Abstract of Theophilus to Autolycus*	72
V. *Doctrines of Theophilus* in regard to *God,* the *Trinity,* the *Logos,* the *Spirit, Angels, Devil and Demons, Man, Salvation, Christianity,* the *Future State,* the *Scriptures*	83
VI. *Literature.* Manuscripts, editions, and translations	105

CHAPTER VI.—ATHENAGORAS.

I. *His Life.* Information derived from the fragment of Philip of Sida—from the inscription on the MSS. as to the date	107
II. *The Works of Athenagoras.* His genuine works. The Novel attributed to him	114
III. *The character of Athenagoras and his writings.* Their superior literary style. Explanation of the persecutions of the Christians. His treatment of mythology and of philosophy. His Platonism. His defence of Christianity	115
IV. *Abstract of the Apology of Athenagoras.* Abstract of the Treatise on the Resurrection of the Dead	125
V. *The Doctrines of Athenagoras* in regard to *God,* the *Logos* and the *Spirit, Angels,* the constitution of *Man,* Sin, and Salvation, the *Future State,* the *Scriptures, Morality*	142
VI. *Literature.* Manuscripts, editions, and translations	176

Chapter VII.—Hermias.

I. *Life and Writings* 179
II. *Literature* 180

Chapter VIII.—Hegesippus.

I. *Life.* His descent. The period at which he lived . . 182
II. *Writings.* His 'Notes' or 'Recollections.' His agreement in doctrine with the Churches in Greece and Italy. An account of his Fragments: on the death of James; appointment of a successor to James; interview of the relations of our Lord with Domitian; the martyrdom of Simeon; the seven heresies of the Jews. The Muratori Fragment; an account of it; discussion of its authorship; its character; its date. The Latin History of Josephus or Hegesippus 184

Chapter IX.—Dionysius of Corinth.

I. *His Life* 214
II. *His Writings* 214
  Pinytus, Philippus, Modestus, Soter, and Musanus . . 218

Chapter X.—Melito.

I. *His Life* 221
II. *His Writings.* Eusebius's list of them. Fragments preserved. Fragments and Apology attributed to Melito 223

Chapter XI.—Apollinaris.

I. *Life* 240
II. *The Writings of Apollinaris.* The Works mentioned, and the Fragments given by Eusebius. Other Works attributed to Apollinaris; that on the Passover. Doctrine connected with the name of Apollinaris . . . 240

CHAPTER XII.—THE LETTER OF THE CHURCHES IN VIENNA AND LUGDUNUM.

I. *The Authorship.* The Letters of the Martyrs. The date of the persecution. The authorship of the Letter of the Churches. Objections considered . . . 205

II. *Literature* 262

III. *Translation of the Letter* 263

IV. *Doctrines of the Letter* in regard to *God, Christ, the Spirit,* the *Devil, Christians,* a *Future State,* the *Scriptures, Morality* 280

BOOK II.

THE APOLOGISTS.

THE APOLOGISTS.

CHAPTER IV.

TATIAN.

I.—LIFE.

THE ancient writers who have mentioned Tatian are numerous[a], but nearly all of them simply repeat the information which we find in his own Discourse to the Greeks. The exceptions to this are Irenæus, Rhodon, and Epiphanius.

Tatian tells us that he "was born in the land of the Assyrians." "These things, O Greeks," he says, "I, Tatian, who philosophize according to the barbarians, have put together, having been born in the land of the Assyrians, and having been taught first your beliefs, and secondly those which I now profess to proclaim[b]." What he means by the land of the Assyrians is somewhat uncertain, for the name Assyria was applied by the Greeks and Romans[c] not merely to Assyria proper, but also to Syria; and we have instances of the word so used in a writer who was a native of Samosata[d]. Moreover, Clemens Alexandrinus[e], referring to Tatian, calls him a Syrian, and this statement is repeated by several of the later writers, as Epiphanius. Many have therefore

---

[a] See the lists in Worth's edition of Tatian, and in Daniel's Tatianus der Apologet, p. 2.
[b] c. 42.   [c] See Dr. Smith's Dictionary of Geography, art. Assyria.
[d] Lucian de Dea Syria, c. 1. It is questionable, however, if this piece is really Lucian's.   [e] Strom. iii. c. 12. p. 547 (Pott).

been inclined to regard him as a Syrian. The probability, however, is that Tatian would be precise in such a statement; the more so, as he uses Assyria elsewhere to denote Assyria proper. This matter is comparatively of little importance, though it is of some moment to know that he actually came from the East. For the circumstance that he was born a barbarian, and that the Greeks would always be inclined to taunt him with his birth, may have had no small influence on his opinions and modes of thought. Such an influence we see prominent enough in the works of another Eastern, Lucian, who frequently drags in his Syrian birth to show that he was not ashamed of it[f].

We know nothing of the time of his birth, or of his parents, or of his early training. He states that he was brought up in heathenism ($\pi\alpha\iota\delta\epsilon\upsilon\theta\epsilon\grave{\iota}\varsigma$ $\delta\grave{\epsilon}$ $\pi\rho\hat{\omega}\tau o\nu$ $\tau\grave{\alpha}$ $\dot{\upsilon}\mu\acute{\epsilon}\tau\epsilon\rho\alpha$[g]), and he had grown up and become famous before he adopted the Christian religion. Considerable discussion has taken place as to what was his profession before he embraced Christianity. His own words are, "These things I have expounded, learning them from no one, but wandering over many lands. I on the one hand acted as sophist in your matters, and on the other hand fell in with many arts and devices. At last I came to the city of the Romans, and staying there I became acquainted with the varieties of statues which have been brought from you to them; for I do not, as the custom with many is, try to strengthen my own positions by the opinions of others; but I wish to commit to writing all the things which I myself shall clearly understand. Wherefore, bidding farewell to the great boasting of the Romans and the cold talking of the Athenians, to beliefs that do not cohere, I laid hold of the barbarous philosophy according to us[h]." The words which have been made matter of discussion are $\sigma o\phi\iota\sigma\tau\epsilon\acute{\upsilon}\sigma\alpha\varsigma$ $\tau\grave{\alpha}$ $\dot{\upsilon}\mu\acute{\epsilon}\tau\epsilon\rho\alpha$, which we have translated literally above. Some[i] take the $\sigma o\phi\iota\sigma\tau\epsilon\acute{\upsilon}\epsilon\iota\nu$ to

---

[f] Adversus Indoctum. c. 10. See the note of Solanus, and especially that of Francklin, in his translation.   [g] c. 42.   [h] c. 35.

[i] See Valesius in Euseb. Eccl. Hist. iv. 16. He has been followed by a considerable number of scholars.

mean that Tatian was a philosopher. Of course it may admit of this meaning—but it likewise has the other meaning, and that too more frequently, of 'acting as a rhetorician.' So Rufinus understood the word in Eusebius (magistrum egit eloquentiae); and so did Jerome j. The most conclusive proof, however, that Tatian meant by σοφιστεύειν the work of a rhetorician is, that he has generally used the term in connexion with composition and styles of writing. In the passage now before us, the many 'arts and inventions' can scarcely refer to anything else than the 'rhetorical artifices k' of the sophists. The great boasting of the Romans (μεγαλαυχία), and the cold reasoning of the Greeks (ψυχρολογία), also refer to the characteristic styles acceptable in Rome and Greece l. In another passage ridiculing the niceties of the dialects of Greece, he says m, "For this reason we bade farewell to the wisdom which is with you, even although I was one of considerable celebrity in it. For according to the comic poet, 'these things are the superfluous shoots, and the babblings, the museums of swallows, the corrupters of art n.'" And then he goes on to assert that rhetoric was used only for unjust purposes o. If further proof were required, we should have it in the character of the age. The rhetoricians were exceedingly numerous at this period. They travelled from one country to another, attracting the young to their schools, lecturing on all kinds of subjects, and generally succeeding in filling their pockets with money. Lucian at first was one of these p; and from what he tells us of himself we may gather some notion of the life of Tatian. It is not unlikely, how-

---

j "Tatianus qui primum Oratoriam docens non parvam sibi ex arte rhetorica gloriam comparaverat." De Viris Illustr. c. 29. Jerome's notice is borrowed entirely from Eusebius, whose notice is a combination of the passage in Tatian now quoted, with another to be immediately quoted.

k Otto's explanation.

l Some think that Tatian hits at particular rhetoricians with these expressions. m c. 1. n Aristoph., Frogs, 92.

o See Daniel, p. 17; Otto on c. 35, note 1.

p See History of Greek Literature, by Donaldson, vol. iii. p. 218; and Life of Lucian, prefixed to Lehmann's edition.

ever, that before his conversion he had relinquished the rhetorical profession, and, like Lucian, had betaken himself to pure literature, or perhaps was undetermined. The reason for this supposition is that in the passage above quoted the only reason assigned for his bidding farewell to the wisdom of the Greeks is his discontent with the whole theory of purity of diction prevalent in his days. He could see no *real* difference as to purity between a Doric word and an Attic word; and therefore he abandoned the arts of the rhetoricians.

The rhetorician turned himself to every subject of study. He was a combination of our literary man and lecturer. Tatian applied himself diligently to the study of mythology, history, poetry, art, and chronology. His references to Greek writers are more numerous than those of any early Christian writer except Clemens Alexandrinus. He could not help in the course of his studies coming in contact with the various philosophies of his times; but in his case, as in that of Lucian, Eastern antipathies prevented him from seeing the good side of Greek speculation. The intensity of his character would probably also have inclined him to the Stoics; but he too frequently discovered amidst their grand doctrines the most detestable practices and hypocrisies; and accordingly, while his own ideas border most nearly on those of the Stoics, he lashes them and the Cynics in no measured language. It is not unlikely that for some time he had felt himself unable to accept any philosophy, and if we may guess from the tone of his book it is probable that his life was none of the best. He seems to have known every filthy statue on the face of the earth. He describes the various movements of a mime with a minuteness which shows that he at one time enjoyed the theatre; and he says nearly as much himself, " I saw one often, and seeing I wondered, and after wondering I despised him[q]." He asserts, too, that he attended athletic performances, and he seems to have been present at the gladiatorial fights[r]. Perhaps we should not be far wrong in guessing that the contempt

[q] c. 22.   [r] c. 23.

which followed his wonder of those things is indicative of the whole course of his heathen life. He grew tired of everything, he sank into a state corresponding to but more bitter than that of Lucian, in which he could not believe anything, and in which all the world seemed to him to be going wrong.

While in this state, as we suppose him to be, he fell in with the Hebrew Scriptures, and was converted. The reasons of his conversion deserve consideration. One of them was the simplicity of the style. The language was so different from the inflated, bombastical stuff with which "the crow-speaking mortals"[s] around him were dunning his ears. His own words must be quoted: "Seeing these things (the difference of legislation in various countries), having also partaken of the mysteries and having tried the modes of worship among all, modes of worship which are carried on by means of effeminate and androgynous beings, finding also among the Romans Jupiter Latiaris delighting in the gore of men and in blood from the slaughter of men, and Artemis not far from the great city[t] (Rome) professing the form of the same actions, and one deity in one place and another in another busy in the production of evil-doing, going into myself, I asked how I might discover the truth. And while I was considering the serious beliefs, I happened to fall in with some barbaric writings, older in comparison with the Greek beliefs, and more divine in comparison with their error: and I happened to yield belief to these both on account of the modesty (τὸ ἄτυφον) of the diction and the illiterate character (τὸ ἀνεπιτήδευτον) of the writers, and the easy comprehension of the creation of the whole, and the foretelling of future events, and the excellence of the commandments, and the government by one being of the whole. My soul thus being God-taught, I understood that the one set of beliefs carry destruction along with them, but that the others destroy the slavery

---

[s] c. 15.

[t] There can scarcely be a doubt that by the "great city" Rome was meant, though among early scholars this was a subject either of mistake or disputation.

which is in the world, free us from many rulers and myriads of tyrants, and grant us not that which we did not receive, but that which, having before received, we were prevented from holding under the power of error[u]." Tatian's information with regard to himself ceases at this point. He does not tell us where he was converted, nor who was the instrument, if any one was. Daniel[v] has supposed that many to whom the change of his opinions was known, counselled him to conceal his beliefs. But this supposition is based on what seems to me a false interpretation of a single passage. "Even," he says, "though Epicurus, the despiser of the gods, hold the torch [lead the way], yet I no longer conceal from princes the comprehension of God which I now have. Why dost thou counsel me to belie the mode of life I have agreed to? Why, saying that thou despisest death, dost thou advise me to avoid it through art[x]?" Here Tatian refers to the conduct of the philosophers who not believing in the existence of the gods, at the same time paid respect to the public gods to escape from punishment or to avoid the outrages of the mob. In this connexion he had already mentioned Diagoras the Athenian, whom the Greeks had punished for his disclosure of the mysteries. And his appeal, "Why dost thou counsel me?" is a mere rhetorical appeal, not to any individual man, but to any one of the numerous sects that thus heartily despised the heathen religion but still openly respected it[y].

Irenæus tells us that Tatian was a hearer of Justin. He speaks as if he knew very little about him. His words are: "They oppose the salvation of the first man (πρωτοπλάστου), and this was now found out with them. One Tatian was the first to introduce this blasphemy. He was a hearer (ἀκροατής) of Justin. As long as he was with him he brought out no such thing: but after his martyrdom, removing from the

---

[u] c. 29. Tatian in this last portion of the passage refers to his 'Doctrine of Spirit,' afterwards explained.   [v] p. 17, note.   [x] c. 27.

[y] Daniel has laid stress on another passage quoted already (c. 42), but the reading κρύπτειν instead of κηρύττειν, I think with Otto, is unquestionably bad.

Church, elated and puffed up by the conceit of a teacher, as if he were better than the rest, he established a mode of teaching of a peculiar character, mythologizing some invisible æons like those from Valentinus, and proclaiming marriage to be corruption and fornication like Marcion and Saturninus; and from his own brain (παρ' ἑαυτοῦ) making opposition to the salvation of Adam[z]."

The statement that Tatian was a hearer of Justin's is confirmed by two allusions to Justin in the work of Tatian. In the one passage he speaks of Justin as the " most admirable" (θαυμασιώτατος[a]), and in the other he speaks of Crescens as plotting not only against Justin but against himself[b]. The statement of Irenæus is repeated again and again[c]. There is not the slightest reason, however, for the supposition that Justin was the means of his conversion, or that the hearer was very pliant in taking in the opinions of Justin. On the contrary, his Oration contains the clearest proofs that his mind was of a considerably different cast from that of Justin's, and that accordingly his notions were widely different.

The only other fact we know with regard to Tatian's ante-heretical life is given us in Eusebius[d]. The historian informs us that Rhodon, addressing Kallistion, said that he had been a scholar of Tatian's at Rome, and that Tatian had then been busy at a work which was to give an interpretation of what was indistinct and concealed in the Scriptures. He calls himself "a herald of the truth," and we can have no hesitation in inferring from this assertion of Rhodon's, and the energetic character of Tatian, that he continued for some time a diligent teacher and student of the Christian religion at Rome. There is no reason, however, for the supposition that he especially employed himself as an antagonist to the Cynics, and Crescens in particular. The few passages which

---

[z] Irenæus, Adv. Haer. lib. i. c. 28, p. 1; Euseb. Eccl. Hist. l. iv. c. 29.
[a] c. 18.   [b] c. 19.
[c] In the spurious part of Tertullian de Præscr. in Epiphanius, Jerome, Philastrius, &c.; see Daniel, p. 34.
[d] Hist. Eccl. l. v. c. 13.

have been supposed to allude to controversies with Crescens do not admit such a meaning[c]. Nor is it anything but a mere guess that reckons Tatian the teacher of Clemens Alexandrinus, described by him simply as ὁ μὲν τῆς 'Ασσυρίας. If Tatian had been the man, Clemens would have been sure to name him.

There is no clue to any dates in connexion with Tatian, except what we get in his Oration and in the remark of Irenæus that his heretical opinions broke out after Justin's death. The Oration, as we shall see, contains clear proofs that it was written in the reign of Marcus Antoninus. Irenæus's statement that "the doctrine was *now* discovered among them," has been supposed by most to imply that Tatian had introduced the heresy shortly before Irenæus wrote his work, the most probable date of which is 174 or 175. The words as they stand apply only to the Encrateis, who might have adopted the doctrine a considerable time after Tatian promulgated it. But since Justin died after the accession of Marcus Antoninus, and since Eusebius places his heresy at 172, the statement of Irenæus should perhaps be regarded as evidence in favour of some such date. I see no reason, however, in Irenæus's use of aorist verbs for the supposition that Tatian must have been dead when he wrote. Nothing is known of his death, and the only piece of information which is given us with regard to his heretical life is subject to very grave suspicion. Our authority is Epiphanius. He gives us nearly the words of Irenæus, but inserts statements of his own of a peculiar character. He tells us, as we have seen already, that Justin suffered martyrdom in the reign of Hadrian, that Tatian behaved himself well while Justin was alive, but that after his death he removed from Rome to the East, and that he first set up his school in Mesopotamia about the twelfth year

[c] The passages supposed to refer to Crescens have been already quoted. One of them is that which, as we have seen, refers to a mime; the other is the appeal, "Why dost thou counsel me to belie my mode of life?" See Daniel, p. 43; Longuerue, p. 8; Nourry, c. 3.

of the Cæsar surnamed Pius, that his new views met with favour first in Antioch, and that they spread over Cilicia and Pisidia f. All of these assertions that relate to dates are on the face of them false. How far are we to believe the other statements? There is great probability that Tatian would leave Rome and preach his new opinions among his old friends at home. Irenæus's ignorance of him goes also to render it likely that he had gone far away from Rome. But we could not regard the information as trustworthy unless we had some idea of the source from which Epiphanius learned what none of the previous writers assert with regard to him.

The heretical opinions which Tatian embraced were three. They are all given by Irenæus, and in fact most of the subsequent writers simply repeat and amplify his statements. This is the case with Jerome, Epiphanius, Philastrius, Theodoret, John of Damascus, and the Alexandrian Chronicle. Some of these writers do not get their information directly from him, but from Eusebius, who quotes the words of Irenæus. Hippolytus gives the substance of Irenæus thus: "Tatian, having himself been a disciple of Justin the martyr, held opinions not like those of his teacher, but, attempting something new, said that there were some invisible æons, mythologizing them like those of Valentinus. Marriage, he says, is corruption, like Marcion. And he maintains that Adam is not saved on account of his having been the leader (ἀρχηγόν) of disobedience g."

It is necessary, before stating all that is known of his heretical opinions, to exhibit some of the mistakes which the later writers, such as Epiphanius, made with regard to them. The head and source of all these lies in their making him the founder of a school. Thus he is called by some the founder the Encratites (or Abstinents), or of the Tatiani, Severiani, &c. Now there cannot be a doubt that Tatian set up a separate school of his own, but it is very questionable whether

---

f Epiph. Pan. lib. i. tom. iii. Hær. xlvi.
g Hæresium Refut. lib. viii. 16.

he united himself with any sect then existing, or whether after his death, or even in his life, his pupils adhered to his opinions and his alone. There can be no doubt of this much, that Irenæus mentions the Ἐγκρατεῖς as existing apart from Tatian, and simply introducing one opinion of his which was in harmony with the rest of their sentiments, and that Hippolytus describes the Encratites as differing from Christians in no point of doctrine[h], but simply in the rigidity of their life and practices, while he does not mention Tatian in connexion with them. Eusebius[i] in like manner says expressly that the heresy was strengthened by Severus and hence those who adopted it were called Severiani.

From this confusion of Tatian with sects various opinions were attributed to him which the earliest writers do not mention. Thus Epiphanius affirms that he used the mysteries in imitation of the holy Church, but employed water only in the service[k]. In like manner Jerome speaks of him as "not merely condemning marriage, but also the food which God created for use[l]." And like statements are made by the pseudo-Augustine, Theodoret, and the Alexandrian Chronicle. There is much in the character of Tatian to make it probable that he held such opinions, but unfortunately the only early writer who makes mention of the matter is Tertullian, who was not careful in laying an opinion at the door of the right owner. In his tract De Jejunio adversus psychicos[m], he remarks with regard to 1 Tim. iv. 3, that the apostle "condemns beforehand those heretics who were to command perpetual abstinence to the destruction and contempt of the works of God, such as I find with Marcion and Tatian." Perhaps Tertullian does not mean to assert here positively that either Marcion or Tatian inculcated perpetual abstinence, but that some of their followers did. Jerome however, after his own fashion, took the passage from Tertullian without

---

[h] τὰ μὲν περὶ τοῦ θεοῦ καὶ τοῦ Χριστοῦ ὁμοίως καὶ τῇ ἐκκλησίᾳ ὁμολογοῦσι. Hær. Refut. lib. viii. 20.   [i] Hist. Eccl. l. iv. c. 29.
[k] Pan. lib. i. tom. iii. Hær. xlvi. c. 2.
[l] Adv. Jovin. lib. i. c. 3, tom. ii. p. 239.   [m] c. 15.

acknowledgment, and says expressly "that the apostle marks out Marcion and Tatian[n]." There is also one passage of Jerome's which at first sight appears to base this view of Tatian's opinion on trustworthy documents. He says in his commentary on Amos ii. 12, "But ye gave the Nazarites wine to drink, and commanded the prophets, saying, 'Prophesy not.' From this passage Tatian, chief of the Encratites, strives to build up his heresy, asserting that wine ought not to be drunk, since the law commanded the Nazarites not to drink wine, and they are now accused by the prophet of giving wine to the Nazarites;" and towards the end of the same passage he speaks "of those heretics who had been rigorous in their abstinence, fastings, dryeatings, cliamenniis[o], of whom are Tatian and Manichæus." Jerome in thus speaking seems to have before his eyes a work of Tatian's, and we should therefore be inclined to rely on the statement. But Jerome himself appears to say that only one book of Tatian's was known to him[p], and that was the oration which has come down to us. He must therefore have derived his information from some later writer, and as we do not know who he is, no reliance can be placed on the statement.

There is still another misrepresentation of the later writers from which we must free ourselves. They generally represent Tatian as in company with Valentinus and Marcion. Irenæus simply says that he formed opinions like theirs, but he does not intimate any personal connexion with these heretics or any derivation of his opinions from them. He does indeed call him in one place "the connexion of all heretics[q]," and this is taken to mean that his system was a mixture of various heretical opinions. If this be correct, we have simply the same statement that we had before. Clemens Alexandrinus has been thought by some to state that Tatian came from the school of Valentinus, but a glance at the passage will

---

[n] Adv. Jov. lib. ii. c. 16, tom. ii. p. 351.
[o] What this means I do not know.
[p] De Vir. Illustr. c. 29.
[q] "Connexio quidem factus omnium hæreticorum," lib. iii. c. 23, 8.

show that the statement is made not in reference to Tatian but in reference to Cassian.

This supposed connexion of Tatian with the Gnostics is probably the reason that Jerome had for reckoning him among the Docetes. And not merely does he reckon him among them, but he speaks of him as the introducer of the doctrine (qui putativam carnem Christi introducens[s]). Perhaps he means that he was the first to apply the doctrine of the Docetes as a reason in favour of the impurity of marriage[t].

All the writers of the Church speak in the strongest terms of reprobation of the opinions of Tatian. Even Origen describes his opinions as most impious. Jerome, however, is the only one that attacks the moral character of Tatian[u]. He had evidently no grounds for such vituperation, but we need not wonder at it when we see how he treated his contemporaries.

The best ascertained point of Tatian's heresy is his reprobation of marriage as being an act of corruption. All the writers bear witness to this. Almost all the writers add that he regarded marriage as on a level with fornication. It is curious that Hippolytus says simply that he regarded marriage as a corruption. We cannot doubt, however, that Tatian maintained that marriage ought to be avoided, but we should have hesitated as to whether he acknowledged in precise words that marriage was actually a sin in all cases had not a passage come down to us saying as much. He discussed this question of marriage in a work "On Perfection according to the Saviour," in which he would no doubt refer

[r] Clem. Alex. Strom. iii. c. 13, p. 553. The point depends on what word the article refers to. ὁ δ' ἐκ τῆς Οὐαλεντίνου ἐξεφοίτησε σχολῆς.

[t] Hier. Comment. in Gal. vi.   [s] See Daniel, p. 265.

[u] It may seem strange to some that Jerome should have attacked Tatian at all on the score of marriage, since his own opinions were so near his. The Scylla and Charybdis of heresy were very near each other. Tatian was a heretic because he pronounced marriage a corruption, and Jovinian was a heretic "because he asserted that there was no difference [in merit] between married women and virgins, and between abstainers and those who feasted simply." Pauli De Hær. c. 47. It is against this Jovinian that Jerome launched forth his strongest bolts.

to Christ's remaining unmarried as being of higher virtue than if He had married. The only argument which He used in establishing his position, of which we know anything, is given us by Jerome. He tells us that he appealed to Gal. vi. 8, "If any one sows in the flesh, of the flesh he shall reap corruption," applying these words to sexual intercourse[v]. In a fragment still remaining to us of the work on the Perfection of the Saviour, he shows that his theory harmonizes with the words of Paul in 1 Cor. vii. 5, "Defraud ye not one the other, except it be with consent for a time, that ye may give yourselves to fasting and prayer; and come together again that Satan tempt you not for your incontinency." "Consent," he says, "is suitable to prayer, but the communion of corruption destroys prayer. Altogether therefore, by way of shaming a man through the permission, the apostle drives him away from it; for permitting them to come together on account of Satan and incontinence, he showed that the man who would obey would be serving two masters; by consent he would be serving God, by dissent incontinence, and fornication, and the devil[x]." Some have supposed that Tatian is the person intended when Clemens Alexandrinus says, "Some one runs down birth, speaking of it as corruptible and perishing, and some one distorts, alleging that the Saviour said with regard to the begetting of children, 'Treasure not up on earth, where moth and rust destroy.' And he is not ashamed to add to these the words of the prophet, 'All ye shall become old as a garment, and moth shall eat you up.'" "In like manner," Clemens adds shortly after, "they introduce the saying (which refers to the resurrection), 'The sons of that age neither marry nor are given in marriage.'" The 'they' here the same scholars[y] take to be Tatian and his school. All this, however, is matter of pure conjecture,

---

[v] Comment. ad Gal. c. 6.

[x] Clem. Alex. Strom. iii. c. 12, p. 547. I have adopted Otto's emendation of συμφωνία for συμφωνίαν in the commencement.

[y] Olshausen, Kirchhofer; Otto Fr. ii. p. 166. Clem. Alex. Strom. iii. c. 12, pp. 550, 551.

and the last quotation Tatian could scarcely adduce unless he believed that the resurrection had taken place already.

The second heretical doctrine which Tatian adopted was that of the existence of another God besides the God of all. It is noteworthy that Irenæus and many others simply say that he introduced invisible æons or ages. The extent of our knowledge with regard to these æons is contained in the word 'invisible.' Clemens Alexandrinus and Origen, who knew the works of Tatian, give us more light as to his real opinions. He found great difficulty in reconciling the deeds ascribed to God in the Old Testament with the character of God as revealed by Christ and his apostles; and the permission of polygamy especially staggered him. "Tatian," says Clemens, "separates the old man and the new, but not as we say, looking on the old man as the law and the new as the gospel. So far we agree with him in making the division, but not in the way he wishes when he destroys the law as being the law of another God, but the same man and lord renewing the old no longer permits polygamy, for God required it when there was need of increasing and multiplying, but now He introduces monogamy[z]." The only instance that has come down of the application of his notion that the God of the Old Testament was different from that of the New, is his explanation of Gen. i. 3, "Let there be light." These words, he maintained, were a prayer and not a command; and he went so far as to declare that the God was in darkness when He thus prayed for the light[a].

The third point of his heresy was a refusal to believe that Adam was saved. The only light we have on his reasons for this belief is a statement by Jerome that he appealed to the words of the apostle Paul, 1 Cor. xv. 22, "In Adam we all die."

These are all the facts we know with regard to Tatian's heresy. It will be seen that, as the opinions stand, they do

---

[z] Clem. Alex. Strom. iii. c. 12, p. 548.
[a] Origen, De Oratione, c. 24. (Lommatzsch, tom. xvii. p. 188.) Clem. Alex. Ecll. ex script. prophett. 38. (Vol. iv. p. 44 Klotz.)

not form any system, nor do they give any insight into their origin. With the oration before us, however, we shall not find it difficult to account for most of his aberrations.

Tatian, as we have seen, was a man of strong individual character and of great self-reliance. We have already quoted a passage in which he expresses his determination to relate only what he himself knew and had thoroughly comprehended. This self-reliance was carried too far. He was too much inclined to look upon all things around him as mean, inferior, and base. His eye was not open to the great and good of past times; and accordingly, in his treatment of all philosophers and poets of the ancient world he is contemptuous, ready to believe the worst stories about them, and totally incapable of seeing anything good in them. Besides this, he was thoroughly sick of the world as he found it. He saw nothing but wretchedness, licentiousness, and all forms of sin on every hand. In this state of mind he comes upon the Old Testament, and his whole soul, longing for something to love, finds in the simple language and earnest exhortations of the prophets something to captivate his heart, while the prediction of future events satisfies his reason. He comes to the Christians; he recognises in them men of a noble character, of high and exalted ideas, of fixed principles; and for a time he finds rest. But the discontent which had become habitual with him before, breaks out again. Christians are not so good as they ought to be; the writings of the apostles are higher in their tone than those of the Old Testament; and altogether his ideas with regard to Christianity change as his studies go on. Very likely, too, he felt the Christian life within him getting cold, especially after death put a stop to his intercourse with Justin, and his temptations to indulge in the vice to which he seems to have had a depraved liking, may have grown strong on him. He went to an extreme at a bound. All sexual intercourse is unlawful. Man is made of soul, body, and spirit. The spirit is the immortalizing, perfecting element in man. Where the spirit is not, where only body and soul act, there is corruption. But sexual intercourse is such an act; and consequently, if one indulges in such a propensity of pure body and soul (ψυχή) he is sowing in the flesh, and will of the flesh reap corruption. His reason and his wish would thus go hand in hand. It is needless to say that such a mode of reasoning is liable to great objections, and would necessarily involve him in contradictions, but he would be very far from seeing them. It is possible to suppose that even without any ascetic tendency he might have reasoned from his notions of man's composition that marriage was unlawful. But there was Tatian's character in addition to this; and he seems to have carefully studied the writings of the apostle Paul with especial sympathy for anything that was in favour of stern living. Thus, "he said that women were punished on account of their hair and ornament by the power which is appointed over these, which gave to Sampson his power in his hair, and which punishes those who rush to fornication on account of the ornament of their hair[a]." The whole of this passage is evidently based on 1 Cor. xi. 10, "For this cause ought the woman to have power on her head because of the angels." Hence also arose his speculation on the old man and the new—in fact on the relation of the Law to Christianity. Jerome[b] asserts that Tatian rejected some Epistles of Paul; and it has been conjectured, not without some support from the context, that the rejected Epistles were those in which marriage is spoken of as honourable, such, for instance, as those to Timothy.

We have already seen how Tatian's rejection of marriage would make the polygamy of the Old Testament a stumbling-block. It seems likely that he regarded the old man spoken

---

[b] Ecll. Prophett. 38, 39. Clemens Alexandrinus in the same passage tells us, "that he said that there were punishments of blasphemies, babblings, and incontinent words, and that they were punished and chastised by word (reason)." He evidently refers to a system of punishments going on in the world, carried out by angels or powers, by which each wrong act was punished by something of a like nature. The text reads εἴπομεν, Maranus, εἶπε μέν.

[a] Jerome, Præf. in Comment. in Epist. ad Tit. He held the genuineness of Titus, according to Jerome. Otto, fr. xi.

of by Paul as the mere conjunction of body and soul; that the God of the Old Testament was the God of body and soul; that He therefore did not think marriage wrong; that the law was his work; and that Christ came to give men back the Spirit. It is easy to see how Tatian would fix such ideas on Justin's doctrine of the Logos, especially when Tatian saw nothing good in heathenism. Any one, besides, would feel difficulty in settling what parts of the Old Testament spoke of Christ and what of God; and Tatian's criterion would simply be that those passages which spoke of the Spirit were the inspiration of Christ, while those that referred to mere body and soul would be the sayings of the God of the Old Testament.

The position of æons in Tatian's mind seems to me an insoluble problem. In the Oration he had already come to the conclusion that time was merely a conception of the human mind. "Why do you divide time," he says, "saying that one part of it is past, one present, and the other future? How can the future ever pass away, if the present exists? Just as those who, sailing, think in their ignorance, as the vessel rushes along, that the mountains are running, so ye know not that ye are running past, and the age ($αἰῶνα$) standing as long as He who made it shall wish it to be [c]."

How he came to believe that Adam was not saved is a matter which can be conjectured with much more ease and much greater probability. The passage which Jerome adduces as containing his argument is, in fact, a satisfactory reason for it, if it be understood in a particular way: "We all die in Adam," not "we all died in Adam;" but we Christians and heathens, in as far as we die, all die in Adam. If Adam is thus, as it were, the principle of death now, it is impossible that he could be saved. He cannot be *now* the principle of death himself, and at the same time in the enjoyment of life; and no doubt Tatian would join this with all that is said of the psychical man in the same chapter. The first man Adam

---

[c] c. 26, p. 163 A.

was born a living soul—no spirit. He had thus the elements of corruption, and nothing more. The last Adam, Christ, was a life-giving Spirit: He was the source of spirit to men, and therefore of incorruptibility. The first man was of the earth earthy—destined to die, the source of death to all—the last man was heavenly. The earthly and those who are merely earthly must perish—the heavenly alone can live. Tatian could not see how Paul could believe that he who was mere soul and body and remained the source of this defective nature to others, could by any possibility be capable of salvation. Whether Tatian regarded Adam as allegorical or not may be a doubtful matter. It seems to me that he did not—that he looked upon him as real and permanent. But at the same time there seems to be in his thoughts a curious blending of allegory and reality, which is difficult for us to realise.

Commentators have busied themselves very much in attempting to trace the philosophy of Tatian to some source. Some maintain that he drew many of his opinions directly from the Gnostics[d], while others imagine that the Jewish Cabbala furnished him with many ideas. It will be seen from the exposition which we have given that to us he appears to have derived his philosophy from his own temperament, from the general spirit of the age, and especially from peculiar stress laid on particular parts of the Epistles of Paul.

II. TATIAN'S WRITINGS.

Eusebius tells us that Tatian "left a great number of writings." Of these only one now remains—the Oration to the Greeks. We have the names of several, either mentioned in his own Oration or by subsequent writers. The following is a list of them:—1. A Work (περὶ ζώων); 2. The Apology or Oration to the Greeks; 3. A work on Perfection according to the Saviour (περὶ τοῦ κατὰ τὸν σωτῆρα καταρτισμοῦ); 4. A Harmony

---

[d] Longuerue, Dissert. pp. x., xi.

of the Four Gospels (τὸ διὰ τεσσάρων). Some other works have also been attributed to him: viz. 1. One on the Nature of Demons; 2. On the Difficulties in the Scriptures (προβλημάτων βιβλίον); 3. An Explanation of some of the Apostle Paul's Epistles; 4. A Chronicon.

The most important of all Tatian's works is his Apology or Oration to the Greeks. There can be no doubt that the work which has come down to us is the same as that known to the early writers. It is mentioned by Clemens Alexandrinus, who informs us that Tatian, in his address to the Greeks (ἐν τῷ πρὸς Ἕλληνας), had shown accurately that the philosophy of the Hebrews was older than that of the Greeks[e]. Origen thus speaks of the work: "And there is also in circulation the Address to the Greeks of Tatian, who was younger (than Josephus), giving a most learned account (πολυμαθέστατα ἐκτιθεμένου) of those who have made inquiries with regard to the antiquity of the Jews and Moses." Eusebius mentions it[f]: "Of his works the one best remembered by many is his famous Address to the Greeks, in which, rehearsing the periods upwards, he proved that Moses and the Hebrew prophets were earlier than all those who were famous among the Greeks. This seems to me to be the best and most useful of all his writings[g]." Clemens Alexandrinus, Origen, and Eusebius all speak of this work as highly valuable for its chronological services. In fact, Tatian seems to have been the first to have given a full and satisfactory demonstration of this point to the ancient world; and accordingly Eusebius, in his Præparatio Evangelica, has made large extracts from this work, and thus there is no room for doubting its genuineness. As we have seen already, the Oration of Tatian seems to have been the only work of his known to Jerome. He calls it, in imitation of Eusebius, "florentissimus liber."

It is impossible to fix the exact date of the Apology, but as all ancient writers, except Epiphanius, agree that he

---

[e] Strom. i. c. 21, p. 378.
[f] Contra Cels. lib. i. c. 16. p. 40. (Lommatzsch.)
[g] Hist. Eccl. lib. iv. c. 29.

flourished in the reign of Marcus Aurelius, the probability is that his Apology was written in his time. The internal evidence is in favour of this date. We place no reliance on the supposition that Justin was dead when Tatian wrote. On the contrary, we think it not unlikely that Justin was alive when Tatian wrote his Apology; for the Apology is the work of the man before he had been long habituated to Christian thought and intercourse, and therefore while he was still listening to Justin's teaching. The internal evidence in regard to the time in which the Apology was written is found in two passages. In one he mentions that philosophers received yearly large sums of money from the king of the Romans [h], a statement peculiarly applicable to Marcus Aurelius; and in the other he mentions Peregrinus, under the name of Proteus, a name which we know was not given him at least until Peregrinus had become very well known [i].

The place in which the Apology was written is not known. From the circumstances mentioned already there is a considerable probability that it was written in Rome, and there is nothing in the work itself contradictory of the supposition. Maranus indeed has supposed that in the passage quoted already, where he states he came to Rome at last [k], it is implied that he had by the time he was speaking left Rome. But such an inference is groundless.

We need scarcely refer to the notion that the Oration was written after Tatian had become a heretic [l]. Our exposition of the theology of Tatian will show that he did not regard the God of the Old Testament as different from the Everlasting God, and there is no reference either to marriage or Adam which shows that he had then fallen upon the opinions pronounced heretical.

Tatian mentions in his Apology his work on Animals. His words are, "Man is not, as the crowspeakers dogmatise, a

[h] c. 19. [i] c. 25. See Aulus Gellius, N. A. xii. 11.
[k] Præf. pars. iii. p. 106. He also appeals to what is said about Crescens, "qui in magna urbe nidum posuerat."
[l] Maranus. Præf. pars iii. p. 106, refutes this notion at length.

reasonable animal, receptive of mind and science; for it will be shown that according to them even irrational existences are receptive of mind and science. But man alone is the image and likeness of God; I mean man not when he does things like the animals, but when he has advanced far away from humanity, even up to God Himself. But about this matter we have treated more accurately in our work on Animals[m]." This is all we know about the work. It is plain that it must have been written after he had become a Christian; indeed, after he had formed his own notion of Christian psychology, or of man as body, soul, and spirit. No remnant of the work has come down to us in any shape.

Tatian is supposed by some to make mention of another work in the following sentence: "I shall show, in a work against those who have discussed divine things, what the learned among the Greeks have said with regard to our mode of life and the history of our laws, and how many there are and who they are who have mentioned them[n]." Difficulty has been experienced with the words πρὸς τοὺς ἀποφηναμένους τὰ περὶ θεοῦ, especially by early editors[o]. But scholars are now agreed that the words refer to those Greeks who inquired into the nature of God, and made positive affirmations with regard to Him. Tatian merely promises to write a book here; whether he ever wrote it is unknown.

We are in the same ignorance with regard to another work. We have quoted the passage already. "Rhodon," says Eusebius, "affirms that a book of problems had occupied Tatian; through which (problems) Tatian having promised to present what was indistinct and concealed in the holy writings, Rhodon himself in his own writing promises that he will exhibit the solutions of his problems[p]." The words used by Eusebius are, φησὶ δὲ καὶ ἐσπουδάσθαι τῷ Τατιανῷ

---

[m] c. 15. Worth defines Tatian's idea of ἀνθρωπότης here as "omne illud in homine, quod ipsi juxta cum reliquis animalibus commune est." Note on this chapter, with him chapter 24.

[n] c. 40.

[o] Gesner. See Maranus, Praef. pars iii. p. 105. and Otto, in loc.

[p] Eccl. Hist. lib v. c. 13.

προβλημάτων βιβλίον. The probability is that the word ἐσπουδάσθαι does mean that the work was actually written, but it by no means compels one to the supposition. And perhaps Tatian was simply collecting all the instances he could get of difficulties in the Old Testament, in the hope of being able to solve them. There is not only no reason to suppose that Tatian was a heretic when he was preparing this book, but the mention of him by Rhodon as having been his teacher, gives us a guarantee that Tatian was still a teacher in the Church.

The notice of this work is of considerable importance, for it tells us that Tatian was a diligent and careful expounder of the Old Testament; and perhaps he was the first to comment on the Old Testament by itself, and occupy himself simply with the explanation of its meaning.

Tatian also employed his powers on the New Testament. He was the compiler of a harmony of the Gospels, the nature of which has been a matter of the keenest discussion, all the keener that we have no satisfactory description of it. The first writer who mentions it is Eusebius[o], who says, "The first leader of them, Tatian, compiling some connexion and collection I know not how of the Gospels, named it a Diatessaron (τὸ διὰ τεσσάρων), which is even now in circulation among some." Eusebius, it is plain, neither saw it nor knew the nature of it. Jerome says nothing of it. Epiphanius remarks, "The Gospel by the four (τὸ διὰ τεσσάρων εὐαγγέλιον) is said to have been made by him, which some call the Gospel according to the Hebrews[p]." Epiphanius also had not seen it. Theodoret is the only one who saw it and described it. He says, "He composed the Gospel which is called the Diatessaron, cutting off the genealogies and the other things which show that our Lord was born of the seed of David according to the flesh. This book was used not only by his own party, but by those who followed the apostolic doctrines. They did not perceive the mischief done to the Covenant (Testament), but used the book in their simplicity as being

[o] Hist. Eccl. lib. iv. c. 29.   [p] Haer. xlvi.

concise. I found more than two hundred such books honoured in the churches among us, and, collecting them all, I put them aside and introduced the Gospels of the four evangelists[q]." Theodoret's information cannot be depended on. It is not unlikely indeed that Tatian's Harmony should be found in the diocese of Theodoret, which was in Syria; but many such harmonies must have been composed, and it would require a critical eye to distinguish between the genuine Harmony of Tatian and those of others. Theodoret's hint as to the heretical interpolations seems very questionable. It would be strange indeed if the simple people did not discover it. The omission of the genealogies, if it had taken place in Tatian's Harmony, could be accounted for on the supposition that the Harmony was intended to be more concise than the four Gospels in full, and was adapted for spiritual edification. And then we must remember that the Harmony of Tatian was confounded with the Gospel according to the Hebrews; and it is not beyond the reach of possibility that Theodoret should have made some such mistake.

In fact, there is no reason to suppose that Tatian composed his Harmony when a heretic, and there is nothing in the Gospels which would have been regarded by him as contradictory of his opinions. The Gospels say nothing about Adam; and his opinions about another God and marriage it would be as easy to reconcile with the Gospels as with Paul's letters.

From the turn of Tatian's mind the conjecture may be hazarded that Tatian's Harmony had no doctrinal aim, but was an attempt to bring the facts of the life of Christ into chronological order.

There are two Harmonies extant, for which claims have been raised as being Tatian's Diatessaron. The one begins with the opening words of John, " In the beginning was the Word;" and the other with the words of Luke, " Since many have attempted." Dionysius Bar-Salibi, Bishop of Amida, living about 1207, asserts that Ephrem Syrus wrote a commentary

[q] H. F. i. 20.

on the Diatessaron of Tatian, and that the Diatessaron began with the words, " In the beginning was the Word." Victor of Capua, in the sixth century coming upon a Harmony, concludes, without the slightest attempt to weigh evidence, that he had before him the identical Harmony of Tatian, and not of Ammonius. His Harmony begins with, " Since many have attempted." Scholars have waged war on these two authorities; which are in fact no authorities at all. For the truth is that we know no more about Tatian's work than what Eusebius, who never saw it, knew; and consequently we should not be able to identify it, even if it did come down to us[r], unless it told us something reliable about itself.

Tatian also applied his mind to the explanation of the Pauline Epistles, as we have seen already, and it is probable that he published a work on the subject. Eusebius remarks, " They say that he dared to alter ($\mu\epsilon\tau\alpha\phi\rho\acute{\alpha}\sigma\alpha\iota$) some expressions of the apostle, as correcting the composition of the words[s]." Eusebius himself evidently did not know what Tatian had done. It was natural for later writers to suppose that Tatian had interpolated and corrupted the Pauline text. But there is no good reason for such a supposition[t]. We have seen that Tatian's heresies rested on his interpretation of the Pauline letters. It is likely that in explaining the statements of Paul he paraphrased the words, and probably this is all that he did. An instance of this we have in the words he uses in referring to 1 Cor. vii. 5, where he changes " that Satan may not tempt you" into "on account of Satan." The work on the Pauline Epistles, if it was written at all, in all probability was heretical.

The only work which we know for certain was heretical was, On Perfection according to the Saviour. This work has often been called the forerunner of the De Imitatione Christi, falsely attributed to Thomas à Kempis. But Tatian's work

[r] See the whole controversy in Daniel, p. 89, and the writers referred to by Heinichen, on Euseb. Hist. Eccl. iv. 29.   [s] Hist. Eccl. lib. iv. c. 29.
[t] See Mill, in his Prolegomena to the New Testament, quoted by Daniel, p. 115.

dealt much more closely with Christ's character than that of Kempis. Its nature has been already intimated.

Epiphanius mentions that the Encratites used only a part of the Old Testament. Some modern critics have concluded that the selection must have been made by Tatian.

Rufinus[u] says that Tatian compiled a Chronicon. No one knows anything of it. Malalas indeed calls both Clemens and Tatian chronographers, but there is no reason to suppose that either the one or the other wrote a chronicle. The facts relating to the dispute between Peter and Paul, for which their authority is adduced, may have been stated in some of the many volumes now lost.

III. ESTIMATE OF TATIAN.

I have already given, in some measure, a portraiture of the cast of Tatian's mind in my account of his life. He was a man of very considerable power, earnest, one-sided, gloomy, rash, rather self-conceited, and passionate equally in his likes and in his dislikes. He held his own opinions visibly in the teeth of the whole world, and he held them with all the greater dogmatism that he had not taken long time to make up his mind, and did not deliberate calmly on his reasons. He was keenly alive to praise and blame, and insults seem to have stung him to the quick. He was more moved by impulse than by reason, though he was not without very considerable powers of philosophising.

Tatian's Oration is not strictly an apology. It is an address to the Greeks, written with the desire to show them that barbarian philosophy and teachings had something in them that was worth their attention. Unfortunately he is extravagant in his praise of all that is barbarian, and heaps unmerited abuse on even the best exertions of the Greeks.

Tatian takes little notice of the persecutions of the Christians, or of the slanders heaped on them. He affirms that the hatred of Christians arose from a prejudice which

[u] Hist. Eccl. lib. vi. c. 11.

was adopted without examination, that they were unjustly accused merely for their name[x]. He hurls the accusation of the eating of human flesh back on the Greek gods and heroes[y], and shows the inconsistency of the Greeks in excommunicating the Christians as atheists[z].

His references to the Greek mythology are generally in the way of strongest denunciation. He recognises, however, in the origin of polytheism a spark of the divine Spirit. "It [the soul]," he says, "possessing as it were a spark (ἔναυσμα) of its [the Spirit's] power, and not being able to see the perfect things on account of its separation (from the Spirit), in seeking after God, fashioned in its error many gods, following the devices of the demons[a]." He identifies the gods of the Greeks completely with the demons; and says of them, "These ye worship, O Greeks, made of matter." Given to matter, therefore, the gods were essentially low and grovelling, and led men into all kinds of wickedness and grossness[b]. They themselves indulged in all kinds of vices, as the stories of the Greeks themselves affirm. Tatian enumerates many of them, especially their love adventures[c], and holds them up to ridicule. He maintains also that the gods must be mortal, for they no longer produce[d].

Tatian's objections generally take a practical turn. He views the influence of a belief in the gods on the life of men, and he thus finds the strongest reasons for condemnation of the whole system in the absurdities and fatalism of divination, and in the profligacies of the theatrical spectacles exhibited in honour of the gods.

Astrology is especially the contrivance of the demons, and Tatian tries to show how utterly false the whole system is, and that it is not the stars but free-will that has destroyed men[e]. He regards charms also as a special activity of the demons, by which men are misled into foolish deeds and fearful crimes[f].

[x] c. 27, p. 164 A. [y] c. 25, p. 162 D. [z] c. 27, p. 164 B.
[a] c. 13, p. 152 D. [b] c. 12, p. 151 D. [c] c. 8, p. 147 C D.
[d] c. 21, p. 160 A. [e] cc. 8, 9, 10, 11. [f] cc. 17, 18.

He condemns also the teachings of the theatre. He affirms that they present the gods in the basest characters, and contaminate the minds of the spectators with the most fearful pollutions [g]. There is no reason to suppose that the statements of Tatian are exaggerations; on the contrary, the remains of the drama bear ample witness to the truth of his affirmations. But Tatian does not rest here, but finds special fault with the poets for " deceiving the audience by means of assumed characters [h]," and the actors for pretending to be what they were not [i].

Tatian states that his attention to the true nature of heathenism was partly aroused by his finding that human sacrifices were offered up to the gods [k].

Tatian treats the philosophers with the utmost contempt, accusing the whole of them of vain boasting. He condemns the whole Greek literature, rhetoric, poetry, and philosophy, as borrowed [l]. And when he comes to deal in particular with philosophers, he utters not a syllable in their praise, but hurls abuse on Diogenes and Aristippus, Plato and Aristotle, Heraclitus, Zeno, Empedocles, and Crates, telling some stories, generally false, to their disadvantage [m], and appealing to these as principal proof of the failure of their speculations to benefit themselves. "Many are the reasons of offence in them," he says, "for the one hates the other; they oppose rival opinions, selecting for themselves exalted positions on account of their arrogance [n]."

Tatian inveighs in the strongest language against the philosophers of his own day. He blames them for accepting salaries from the Roman emperor [o]. He contemptuously describes their mode of dress and their habits [p], and exhibits their inconsistencies and vacillations [q]. His language is not

---

[g] c. 22, 160 C.
[h] c. 22, p. 161 B. Otto translates σχήματα ' figurati sermones ;' Maranus, 'gestus.'
[i] c. 22, p. 160 D.
[k] c. 29, p. 165 A.
[l] c. 1.
[m] cc. 2, 3.
[n] c. 3, p. 144 B. Comp. c. 32, p. 168 A.
[o] c. 19, p. 157 D.
[p] c. 25, p. 162 B.
[q] c. 25.

dissimilar to that of Lucian, but he has not one word to say in favour of any of them. He is especially severe against Crescens and the Cynics, as might have been expected in the circumstances.

There is no real grappling with the opinions of the philosophers. He opposes strongly and forcibly the opinion of the Stoics, that the world was to receive a new shape by a natural conflagration[q]. He abuses Democritus for his theory of antipathies, and in as many words sends him to eternal fire for his nonsense[r]; and he again and again affirms that he cannot help *laughing* at favourite theories of this or that philosopher. He inveighs strongly against the attempt to allegorise the stories of the gods as ending in blank atheism[s].

Indeed, he seems to have set his face against all human studies. "What good," he says, "can one get from Attic style, and the sorites of philosophers, and the probabilities of syllogisms, and the measures of the earth, and the positions of the stars, and the courses of the sun? Employment in such inquiries as these is the work of a man who lays down opinions (δόγματα) as laws to himself[t]." In another passage he says, "With us there is no desire of vainglory and no diversity in our opinions. For separated from the common and earthly creed (λόγου), and obeying the commandments of God, and following the law of the Father of incorruption, we reject everything that depends on human opinion[u]." Tatian here does not refer to opinions merely on religious questions, but on all questions. Accordingly he condemns the fictions of the poets and investigations into the history of music as useless[v]. He heaps abuse on Sophron, and calls Æsop, as being a writer of fiction, the false talker (ψευδολόγος); and in one mass seems to characterise poetesses as abandoned women[x]. He doubted altogether the propriety of using drugs in the cure of diseases. He seems to have supposed that the use of matter implied subservience to the demons, and was a deification of matter.

[q] c. 6. [r] c. 17, p. 155 D. [s] c. 21, p. 160 A. [t] c. 27, p. 164 C.
[u] c. 32, p. 167 B. [v] c. 24, p. 162 A. [x] c. 34, p. 169 D.

"Why," he says, "do you not approach the more powerful Lord, instead of curing yourself as a dog cures himself by means of grass? ... Why do you make gods of the things which are in the world?" His language indeed is not plain. And Maranus has tried to rescue Tatian by affirming that he did not blame the right use of drugs, but the application of drugs which had potency only through their charming power, and that he wished in all cases that the praise should be given to God. But I think that a careful study of chapters seventeenth and eighteenth will leave a strong impression on the mind that Tatian went farther than this, and believed that cures were to be immediately effected by God alone without the employment of matter. "If one is cured by matter, trusting to it, much more will he be cured by having recourse to the power of God[z]." And after he has finished the discussion, he says, "Even if ye be cured by drugs (I grant you this by way of concession, κατὰ συγγνώμην ἐπιτρέπω σοι), you ought to assign the cure to God[a]." It is plain here that he did not believe that they were cured by drugs; and by drugs (φαρμάκοις) he means any kind of medical drug, and not mere charms.

He goes so far in his desire to find fault, that he blames grammarians for speaking of time as present, past, and future, time itself being in reality steady, and we ourselves sailing as it were along its immoveable banks[b].

Tatian contributes but little to the defence of Christianity. His great service consists in his having earnestly sought for a satisfying and influential religion. He had felt the truth of what he proclaimed, and the power of the truth over him is all the more manifest that his natural temper seems to have been far from the best. Those passages which contain his own experiences would certainly make a deep impression. When he tells how he tried all the forms and rites of the Greek religion, he would be sure to arrest attention. And when he narrates his falling in with the Bible, and gives a

---

[z] c. 18, p. 157 B. Comp. p. 157 A. [a] c. 18, p. 157 A.
[*] c. 20, p. 158 D. [b] c. 26, p. 163 A B.

glowing description of the morals of the Christians, the very fact that such a restless nature had found satisfaction somewhere would give weight to his words[c].

His argumentation divides itself into two parts. In the first he expounds his doctrine of God, the Spirit, and the Logos. He does this evidently in the belief that these doctrines will naturally commend themselves to his hearers. For he does not give any reasons for his beliefs. He asserts boldly that he derives them from a source higher than human wisdom. In speaking of his doctrine of spirit he says, "In affirming these things we are not making assertions on mere tradition (ἀπὸ γλώττης[d]), or on probable reasonings and sophistic combinations, but we employ words (λόγοις) of some diviner utterance, and those of you who wish to know this, make haste to learn it[e]." There cannot be a doubt that Tatian was wrong in supposing that he found his whole doctrine of matter and spirit, God and Logos, in the Old Testament. It was not even the same as that of many of his fellow-Christians. And there cannot be a doubt, farther, that he was equally wrong in insisting on a belief in these speculations as essential to Christianity, based though these speculations were on passages of Scripture, and especially on Pauline modes of thought. But such mistakes were inevitable. Believing the Bible to be divine, he supposed it to contain the whole truth. He looked down on all human studies, and used the Old Testament in acquiring his knowledge of terrestrial, paradisaical, and heavenly geography, as well as of divine truths[f].

His other great argument is that the writings of Moses were older than those of the Greeks, and that whatever truths the latter had got were borrowed from the former. He proves the antiquity of Moses with uncommon learning. And

---

[c] Pressensé, sec. ii. vol. ii. p. 399 ff., refuses to acknowledge any good in Tatian's oration. "This harangue was more calculated to irritate than persuade."

[d] Worth translates, "non summis, ut aiunt, labiis."

[e] c. 12, p. 152 A.   [f] c. 20, p. 159 B.

then he boldly states his inference: "We must believe him who has the advantage in respect of age rather than the Greeks who drew from the fountain his dogmas, certainly not in full knowledge of their meaning; for many sophists among them, under the influence of a meddling, inquisitive disposition, attempted to adulterate the truths which they learned from Moses and those who philosophise like him; in the first place, that they might be thought to have some claim to originality, and secondly, that they might give a corrupt representation of the truth as a kind of mythology, hiding what they did not understand by means of a fictitious mode of composition[g]."

As might be expected, Tatian does nothing to conciliate the favour of the Greeks. He places the Christian religion—which he designates 'our philosophy[h],' 'the conduct of life according to us' (τῆς καθ' ἡμᾶς πολιτείας[i]), or 'the conduct of life according to God' (τῆς κατὰ θεὸν πολιτείας[k])—in direct and absolute antagonism to heathenism. He says that "it is not holy to compare our knowledge of God with that of those who wallow in matter and mud[l]," and that in a case where Justin had condescended to use Greek modes of thought. He bursts out again and again into threats against the Greeks for laughing at the Christian doctrines. To take one instance, he says of Democritus, "He who boasts of the magician Ostanes, will be delivered up to the devouring power of eternal fire in the day of the end [of the world]. And you also, if you do not cease your laughter, will have the benefit of the same punishments as the cheats[m]." Daniel has remarked that Tatian nowhere mentions the love of God in his work, but great stress cannot be laid on such a fact as this, as he was really not preaching, but rather defending himself.

A critic cannot help being somewhat severe with a man like Tatian. But it is not to be forgotten that his life may have been more victorious than many a one that would look much better. It is difficult to realise the temptations and

[g] c. 40. p. 173 A B.   [h] c. 31, p. 166 A.   [i] c. 40, p. 173 B.
[k] c. 42, p. 174 B.   [l] c. 21, p. 160 C.   [m] c. 17, p. 155 D.

VOL. III.

struggles through which he had to pass, the earnest longings of his soul which were often disappointed, and the many bitternesses that his keenly sensitive and not very well balanced mind would bring upon him. No doubt such men are often of eminent service in the Church, with all their faults, and sometimes partly by means of these very faults.

IV. ABSTRACT OF THE ORATION TO THE GREEKS.

Do not bear a hostile mind to barbarians, O Greeks; for what practice has not received its origin from barbarians? Divination, sacrifice, astronomy, letter-writing, and many such arts are borrowed from barbarians. There is no good reason for boasting of your superiority in diction. You have various dialects, so that I am not able to say whom I should call a Greek. And you mix your language with barbaric words. You have set up your rhetoric for unjust purposes, and your poetry that you might put together the loves of the gods[s]. Your philosophy is equally a failure; witness the character of Diogenes, Aristippus, Plato, and Aristotle[t], Heraclitus, Zeno, Empedocles, Pherecydes, Crates. These philosophers oppose each other, and arrogantly claim the highest places for themselves[u]. Why then, O Greeks, do you oppose us? If the king orders me to pay taxes, I am ready to do it. Only when he orders me to deny God do I refuse obedience. God is without beginning, and cannot be bribed. But I shall give a full explanation of our beliefs[x]. Tatian now explains the doctrine of the Logos. The whole chapter is translated in the account of his doctrine[y]. There will be a resurrection, and God will be the judge of men. The doctrine of the resurrection is in harmony with reason[z]. The Logos made men and angels with freewills. He foreknew the future, and thus warned them against wickedness, and praised righteousness. But when they made a god of the first-born, who was the wisest of them, the power of

[s] c. 1. [t] c. 2. [u] c. 3.
[x] c. 4. [y] c. 5. [z] c. 6.

the Logos excluded the leader of this folly and his followers from living with him. Man became mortal, and the firstborn is made a demon, and those who imitated him became a host of demons[a]. Men formed the occasion of revolt to the demons. They devised astrology for them also, and thereby induced a belief in fate. But did not the demons themselves fall under fate as well as men? And besides, how could we honour those whose opinions are often contradictory to each other, and whose practices are abominable[b]? In their astrology they use the names of animals with which they are compelled to live, since they have been driven from heaven. Moreover, the placing of the names of certain gods and goddesses in the stars is absurd and full of contradiction, while no good reason can be given for omitting certain other gods[c]. The gods also are transformed. Thus Zeus becomes a dragon. And some mortals also are turned into gods of stars. Where were their stars before they died? Moreover, you sacrifice a sheep, and worship it in the shape of a star[d]. How shall I welcome life according to fate? I care not for the honours which the stars are supposed to confer; and we have all the same sun. Rich and poor are alike subject to death. It is not fate but our free-will that has ruined us. We have become slaves on account of sin[e]. There are two varieties of spirit; soul, and that which is greater than soul. The whole creation is material, but with some parts more beautiful than others. The demons also are made of matter, and possess a material spirit. And there is spirit in the stars and animals, and other such things[f]. The soul is not immortal by itself, but mortal. It dies if it know not the truth. But it does not die, even though it be dissolved, if it acquire the knowledge of God. Living alone it tends towards matter. Married to the spirit, it mounts to the regions of the spirit. The spirit lived originally with the soul, but the soul would not follow it, and therefore the spirit left it. The Spirit of God is still with those who are just[g].

[a] c. 7. [b] c. 8. [c] c. 9. [d] c. 10.
[e] c. 11. [f] c. 12. [g] c. 13.

But ye, O Greeks, have followed demons, supposing them to be possessed of power. The demons, however, have got possession of your minds, by imposing on you through ignorance and appearances. They themselves do not die easily, but their life is a perpetual death, and, when they shall be punished, they will die like men. Their sins are greater than those of men, on account of the immeasurable extent of their life[h]. The soul consists of many parts, and is not simple. Man alone is the image and likeness of God; but only if the soul be joined to the Spirit of God. If God does not dwell in him, then he is superior to animals only in respect of his articulate speech. The demons have no flesh. They are the effulgences of matter and wickedness, and therefore they cannot repent. But man can repent and conquer death by a death which is through faith[i]. The demons that give commands to men are not the souls of men. They revel in misleading the souls whose tendency is downwards. Their power lies in their influence over matter. Reject matter, and the demons are conquered. Diseases also arise from matter; but the demons make men believe that they are the causes, whereas they attack only when disease has seized the man[k]. The opinion of Democritus, that disease (πάθος) is destroyed by antipathy, is not correct. There are attacks made by demons, and "the man who is diseased, and the man who says he is in love, and the man who hates, and the man who wishes vengeance, get these demons to help them." The charms applied in these cases have no power in themselves, but the demons have defined the use of each. How absurd is the supposition that, though when alive I could accomplish very little, yet when dead, a bone of me should be a powerful charm[l]! Medicine is of the same contrivance. If any one is cured by trusting to matter, much more will he be cured by giving attention to the power of God. The demons do not cure, but make prisoners of men. They attack the members of some one, then publicly bring him forth, and fly from him, leaving him in his old state[m]. Be

[h] c. 14. [i] c. 15. [k] c. 16. [l] c. 17. [m] c. 18.

instructed by us, who know about these things. Your philosophers cannot teach you how to despise death rightly. We must despise death through the knowledge of God. What is divination? The notions in regard to it are full of inconsistencies. Thus Apollo foretells, but Apollo did not know the future in the case of Daphne [n]. Even if ye be cured by drugs, you ought to ascribe the cure to God. The world still drags us, and on account of weakness I seek out matter. But the perfect spirit is the winging of the soul. When sin came, the spirit left, and the first men were driven out from a land different from ours and an arrangement better than this here. This land we know of through the prophets [o]. For we are not fools in saying that God appeared in human form. There is no reason why you should laugh at such a statement, seeing that your own stories are full of the appearances of gods in the shape of men. But your stories are nonsense. If you speak of the origin of the gods, then you prove that they are mortal. Why does not Hera bring forth now? Do not allegorise your stories; for if you do, then the divinity of the gods vanishes. Either they are gods and have the character which is usually ascribed to them, or they do not exist at all [p]. Of what sort are your teachings? Are not your public assemblies justly the subjects of ridicule? I myself frequently saw an actor. He put on a false character. He was sometimes this person, sometimes that; and in his one person he brought out all the evil deeds attributed to the gods, and thus taught every species of wickedness. The theatres are full of evil practices [q]. I saw men bearing about a burden of flesh [athletes] who had prizes and garlands for their insolence and striking. That, however, is the most harmless form of the evil. There are those who sell themselves to be murdered; and the rich man buys the murderers [gladiators]. These men fight for nothing, and no one assists them in their distress. The man who goes to the gladiatorial spectacle and returns home without seeing one killed, returns disappointed [r]. What profit can we get from plays or investigations

[n] c. 19.   [o] c. 20.   [p] c. 21.   [q] c. 22.   [r] c. 23.

about music[s]? What good have your philosophers done? Many of them are mercenary. They contradict one another, while we agree, teaching that God is bodiless, and will be our judge, and that soul and body will be rendered immortal together. What harm do we do you, O Greeks? The stories told of us are false, but true of some of your gods[t]. Give up, then, making a boast of language which is derived from others. Your books are like labyrinths. Why do you divide time into present, past, and future, when time cannot be divided, and the present never can become the past? The book-writers are the source of your babbling, dividing wisdom, and attaching the names of men to each part. Ye thus destroy yourselves, warring against one another [u]. Why do you fight with me when I am simply choosing my own opinions? You would not condemn a robber merely on account of his name. You blame us for speaking against the gods, while your own writers—Diagoras, Leo, and Apion—have spoken equally strongly. Why do you advise me to conceal my mode of life? Why do you urge me to avoid death if you really despise death? And what is the use of your investigations about the course of the sun, the position of the stars, syllogisms, &c.[x]? Your law-making also is blameworthy; for while it ought to be one and the same everywhere, it is as various as there are cities [y]. I also shared in the mysteries, and tried all sorts of worship, but seeing gods delight in human sacrifice and urging on to every iniquity, I sought truth somewhere else. Being in this state I fell in with the Scriptures. I thus became God-taught [z]. I wish now to cast error away as being the trifles of childhood. Wickedness is dissolved when we trust the words of God. You, O Greeks, should not mock us because we are called barbarians [a]. I shall now prove that 'our philosophy' is older than the practices of the Greeks. Moses is allowed to be the founder of the barbarian philosophy. Homer is the oldest of the Greeks. Tatian here mentions the various Greek writers who wrote on

[s] c. 24.   [t] c. 25.   [u] c. 26.   [x] c. 27.
[y] c. 28.   [z] c. 29.   [a] c. 30.

the date of Homer, and he gives their various opinions. These opinions cannot be true [b]. With us there is no desire of vainglory. We speak the truth. It is a good thing if your credulity can be limited. Ye laugh at us, though you will one day weep for it. You throw away your admiration on trifling objects and despise us who are really good [c]. You mock us, saying that we talk nonsense among women and youths, virgins and old maids. But you have disgraced yourselves by the many statues which you have raised to women, especially to women of questionable character, such as Sappho [d]. Indeed, statues generally teach lessons of immorality, and are made rather in honour of the bad than of the good. Tatian adduces many instances [e]. These statues I have seen myself. I write down only what I know through my own personal investigations. I have digressed, however, and shall return to what I promised to prove, that the writings of Moses are older than those of Homer [f]. Suppose that Homer lived in the time of the Trojan war, I shall show that Moses was much older. I shall appeal to Chaldean, Phenician, and Egyptian witnesses. My Chaldean witness is Berosus the Babylonian, whose character is guaranteed to us by Juba, a writer on the Assyrians [g]. There are three Phenician witnesses—Theodotus, Hypsicrates, and Mochus—also Menander of Pergamus [h]. The Egyptian records are very accurate. Ptolemy of Mendes has interpreted them. After him comes Apion the grammarian. They both say that the sojourn of the Israelites in Egypt took place in the reign of Amosis, who was contemporary with Inachus, king of Argos. Inachus reigned twenty generations before the capture of Troy [i]. In proof of this Tatian gives the names of the successors of Inachus down to Agamemnon, in whose reign Troy was taken. All the most illustrious deeds of gods and men in Greek history were performed after the time of Inachus. Prometheus, for instance, lived in the time of the fifth Argive king. Tatian gives many instances [k]. Moses was therefore earlier than the

[b] c. 31. [c] c. 32. [d] c. 33. [e] c. 34. [f] c. 35.
[g] c. 36. [h] c. 37. [i] c. 38. [k] c. 39.

ancient heroes, wars and gods. He ought therefore to be believed rather than the Greeks, who borrowed from him and perverted what they borrowed [l]. Moses is not only more ancient than Homer, but than all the other poets—Linus, Philammon, and suchlike. They preceded the Trojan war at the utmost only by three, or two generations. He was anterior to those reckoned wise, such as Minos, Lycurgus, Draco, and Solon, long anterior to the seven wise men [m]. These things I, Tatian, who philosophise according to the barbarians, have composed [n].

V. DOCTRINES OF TATIAN.

God.—The teaching of Tatian with regard to God is remarkable for the clear expression of the immateriality of God. This doctrine is stated negatively and positively. 'The Perfect God' is said to be 'fleshless [o]' and 'bodiless [p].' "God is a spirit, not pervading matter [as the Stoics thought], but the maker of material spirits and of the shapes in it. He is invisible and intangible, having Himself been the Father of things sensible and invisible [q]." "He has also no constitution in time, being without beginning, and being Himself alone the beginning of the whole [r]."

Tatian maintains that God alone possesses goodness by nature or inherently [s]. He asserts that nothing wicked was made by God [t].

He attributes the creation of the world to God, and recognises two stages—that of the putting forth of matter by God in a state of shapelessness and inapplicability, and the preparation of the world out of this matter by separation [u]. He believed that the world was dissoluble and dissolving [v]. "God we know through His creation, and comprehend his invisible power by his works [w]."

[l] c. 40.   [m] c. 41.   [n] c. 42.   [o] c. 15, p. 154 B.
[p] c. 25. p. 162 C.   [q] c. 4, p. 144 C.   [r] Ibid.   [s] c. 7, p. 146 C.
[t] c. 11, p. 150 D; conf. c. 17, p. 156 C   [u] c. 12 p. 151 A.
[v] c. 25, p. 162 C.   [w] c. 4. p. 144 D.

He maintains that God alone ought to be worshipped: "Man ought to be honoured in a human way, but we must fear God alone, who is not to be seen by human eyes, nor is He comprehensible by art. When ordered to deny Him only, obey will I not, but I will die rather that I may not be proved a liar and ungrateful[x]." "But we must not bribe the unnameable God, for He, being in need of nothing, must not be accused by us as if He were in need[y]."

Salvation is God's free gift[z], and through knowledge of Him we attain it. God is to raise us from the dead and to be judge[a].

Tatian seems to have experienced considerable difficulty with the idea of creation. He could not believe in the eternal independent existence of matter, because that would carry along with it the existence of two eternal substances of equal power. But then came the question, How could matter exist if it had not been? The way in which Tatian answered this question was peculiar. He did not say, as a modern might have said, that the thought of the world was in God, but he maintained that all things were with God, not actually but potentially; that He was the substance of all things Himself. And thus he came very near, if not exactly, to the theory of emanation, matter itself not indeed existing separately from the Divine mind, but being inclosed in the Divine power, and at the proper time 'cast forth' ($\pi\rho o\beta \epsilon \beta \lambda \eta \mu \acute{\epsilon} \nu \eta$) by the Maker of all. His words are, "For matter is not beginningless, as God, nor on account of its being beginningless is it of equal power with God; but it is begotten ($\gamma\epsilon\nu\nu\eta\tau\acute{\eta}$), and has come into existence not by any other, but has been put forth by the Maker of all alone[b]." The representations with regard to the existence of all things with God before their creation are brought under our notice in Tatian's doctrine of the Logos.

[x] c. 4, p. 144 C.   [y] c. 4, p. 145 A.   [z] c. 32, p. 167 B.
[a] c. 25, p. 162 D; c. 18, p. 157 B; c. 6, p. 146 A.
[b] c. 5, p. 145 C; comp. c. 12, p. 151 A. Sir William Hamilton's explanation of our conception of creation throws light on Tatian's idea. See his Discussions, p. 620.

The Logos.—There is only one passage in which Tatian speaks of the Logos; but it is one of considerable difficulty, almost every sentence of it being liable to different interpretations[c]. It runs as follows: "God was in the beginning, but we have understood that the beginning was a power of reason. For the Lord of all, Himself being the substance of all, was alone in as far as the creation had not yet taken place, but as far as He was all power and the substance of things seen and unseen, all things were with Him: along with Him also by means of rational power the reason which was in Him supported them. But, by the will of his simplicity, the reason leaps forth; but the reason, not having gone from one who became empty thereby, is the firstborn work (ἔργον) of the Father. Him we know to be the beginning of the world. But He came into existence by sharing (μερισμός), not by cutting off; for that which is cut off is separated from the first; but that which is shared, receiving a selection of the work, did not render Him defective from whom it was taken. For as from one torch many fires are lighted, but the light of the first torch is not lessened on account of the lighting of many torches, so the Logos (Reason) going forth from the power of the Father did not make Him who begot Reason Reasonless. For I myself speak, and ye hear; and yet through the interchange of speech (logos), I who talk to you do not become empty of speech. But putting forth my own voice I have chosen to arrange the matter in you which is not arranged. And as the Word begotten in the beginning begot in his turn our creation, He Himself fashioning the material for Himself, so I, being begotten again in imitation of the Logos and having comprehended the truth, put into order the confusion of related matter[d]."

[c] Daniel gives fully the various attempts of scholars on this passage and the endeavours out of it to defend or impugn the orthodoxy of Tatian, p. 150. In Worth's edition of Tatian we have Longuerue, p. xii., positively asserting that Tatian is heterodox, and quoting a scholiast who was of the same opinion, while in another part we have Bull's attempt to prove him quite sound, p. 143.

[d] c. 5. p. 145 A B C.

We proceed to explain this difficult chapter. A scholiast supposes that the words "God was in the beginning," refer to the words of the apostle John, "In the beginning was the Word," but it is difficult to suppose that Tatian would identify the Father with the Logos. It is far more likely that Tatian has direct reference to Gen. i. 1, that he infers from the words "In the beginning God created the heavens and the earth" that God was in the 'beginning,' and then taking ἀρχή, 'beginning,' to mean 'governing principle,' an interpretation which we shall see again in Theophilus, he explains the beginning itself as a power or exercise of the Logos. The statement, then, is that God was when a beginning was formed, and the beginning arose through an exercise of the divine reason. In the next sentence Tatian asserts that God Himself is the substance, that which stands under and supports all things (ὑπόστασις), and God was so for ever. How Tatian succeeded in freeing himself from the thought that God was the All, might be a question if it were not that the whole style of his thought prevented him from seeing any difficulty in his own assertion. He distinguished between God and his creation, and in the most distinct manner asserts that God alone, and not his creatures, is to be worshipped. He here merely ventures a little beyond his depth without having any fixed idea whither he was going. In the next part of the same sentence he speaks of the Logos, and as we have translated his words, they mean that before all things were created, while they yet merely existed in God's power, they were supported by the Logos or Reason in God which displayed itself solely in a rational power: in other words, all things were potentially existent in God, and they were, as such, supported by the Logos of God also existing potentially in God. Another translation gives us very nearly the same meaning: "Being with Him, the Logos Himself, who was in Him, subsisted through the rational power." The statement here is that the Logos in God was a potential one, and there is no assertion of any activity of the Logos in regard to the potential existence of the All[e]. Perhaps this translation gives on the whole better sense, though the intransitive use of ὑπέστησε is at least peculiar. The next sentence states that the Logos leaps forth. The expression 'leaps forth' is peculiar, and reminds one of those who resolved the Logos into occasional exercises of the rational power of God[f]. We have no reason, however, to attribute this opinion to Tatian, and he afterwards uses the more common expression προέρχεσθαι. The expression 'by the will of his simplicity' seems to me to mean, by the will of a being who was as yet simple, undivided, and unshared. The reference I take to be to the μερισμός which took place. Some regard the expression as merely "the simple will." "The going out of the Logos from God was for God no necessity, but an act of pure free-will [g]." Whatever interpretation is given to τῆς ἁπλότητος, the βουλήματι clearly expresses that the leaping forth of the Logos was an act of God's will. The words οὐ κατὰ κενοῦ χωρήσας appear to me to intimate what Tatian afterwards explains, that God did not lose any of his reason by sharing it with his Logos. Some take the κατὰ κενοῦ to mean 'in vain,' with not much advantage to the sense, but in greater harmony with Greek construction. The illustrations which Tatian gives of the μερισμός, 'sharing,' of the Logos have already passed under our notice in Justin. There is one part of his sentence, however, on which various meanings have been put. The words τὸ μερισθὲν οἰκονομίας τὴν αἵρεσιν προσλαβόν seem to me to mean that that which is shared, though it receives a choice of a new service, yet does not make the original source needy.

---

[e] Bull's defence of Tatian's orthodoxy rests mainly on his ingenuity in translating this passage. He translates, 'per rationalem vim et ipse et verbum quod in ipso erat, substitit,'—'Through rational force both He Himself, and the Word which was in Him, subsisted.' Then he asks Petavius, if God subsisted by rational force, how can any one say that the Logos subsisted merely in force (δυνάμει) when the very same terms are applied to God? But for Bull's translation we should have expected ὑπέστησαν, and the whole context is against it. Def. Fid. Nic. sect. 3, c. 6; Worth, p. 148.

[f] See the exposition of Justin Martyr's Doctrines, vol. ii. p. 220.

[g] Daniel, p. 155.

Thus a lamp lighted from a torch may serve quite a different purpose from the torch, but does not diminish the light of the torch. It seems to me that the statement is a general one, not a particular. Many, however, have taken it to refer only to Christ, and the clause then states two facts—that He derived his being by sharing, and received in addition the management of the world. Others suppose the οἰκονομία to refer to the divine nature [h]; and the meaning to be that that which is shared belongs to the same nature from which it receives the share. "The confusion of cognate matter" is, as Worth has noted, his fellow-men whom he is addressing.

The activity of the Logos in the production and guidance of man is given in a continuation of this passage. "The heavenly Logos," he says, "being [i] a spirit from the Father and Logos (Reason) from the rational power, in imitation of the Father who begot Him made man the image of immortality, in order that, as incorruption is with God, in the same way man receiving a share of God might have immortality. The Logos, then, before the creation of men, becomes the fashioner of angels." The activity of the Logos on man after his creation is thus described: "The power of the Logos having with itself the faculty of foreknowing what was going to happen, not by fate but by the sentiment of those who chose with free-will, foretold the results of things to come, and He became a hinderer of wickedness through prohibitions and a praiser of those who should remain good [k]." When man yielded to the temptations of the devil, then the power of the Logos shut out both the devil himself and those who followed him from intercourse with him.

The only point that remains to be noticed is that Tatian speaks of the Logos as the being that directed the prophets

---

[h] See Daniel, p. 158 ff, for a full discussion of the meaning of οἰκονομία. Also Otto, in loc.

[i] 'Being a spiritual being, as proceeding from the Father, who is Spirit.' This seems to be the meaning of πνεῦμα γεγονώς.

[k] c. 7, p. 146 B C D.

in prophesying. Tatian does not connect the Logos with Christ, his subject not leading him to speak of Christ at all. He once speaks of the 'suffering God¹,' and asserts "that God appeared in the shape of man ᵐ." It is probable that Tatian would put the same meaning on these expressions as Justin would, and that he believed the Logos, though God, could suffer and could make Himself apparent to man.

Spirit.—Tatian almost invariably mentions Spirit in connexion with the nature of man. We have already seen that he regarded God as a spirit, and that he spoke of the Logos as a spirit from the Father. Besides these, Tatian recognises two spirits, one called a material spirit, the other called the Holy Spirit, the Spirit of God, the perfect Spirit, and the heavenly Spirit. Tatian speaks of these spirits principally in connexion with man.

The material spirit is "that which pervades matter ⁿ." "The world possessing according to the power of Him who made it some things more brilliant, and other things unlike these, has partaken of a material spirit by the will of Him who fashioned it º." God is therefore the fashioner of these "material spirits ᵖ." Though Tatian thus uses the plural in reference to the spirit pervading matter, he takes care to show that he regards the spirit as only one. "There is a spirit," he says, "in the stars, a spirit in angels, a spirit in plants and waters, a spirit in men, a spirit in animals, but while it is one and the same it possesses varieties in itself ᑫ." The demons received their constitution from matter and possessed the spirit which is from it ʳ. In man both spirits made their appearance. "We know," he says, "two varieties of spirits, of which the one is called the soul, the other is greater than the soul and is the image and likeness of God, and both of these spirits existed in the first human beings, so that they are

---

¹ c. 13, p. 153 A.   ᵐ c. 21, p. 159 C.   ⁿ c. 4, p. 144 D.
ᵒ c. 12, p. 151 C.   ᵖ c. 4, p. 144 C.   ᑫ c. 12, p. 152 A.
ʳ c. 12, p. 151 C.

in one respect material, and in another superior to matters." "The spirit at first lived with the soul, but the spirit left it when the soul no longer wished to obey it [t]." This spirit was the "share of God [u]" noticed already, that which had in it incorruption. Accordingly, "when the more powerful spirit has been separated from man, he who was made in the image of God becomes mortal [x]." "The perfect spirit is the winging of the soul, and the soul when it cast the spirit away on account of sin flew as a nestling, and fell on the earth, for removing from its heavenly fellowship it desired participation in things inferior [y]." The great work of the soul now is to have its fellowship with the spirit renewed. "When the soul lives alone," he says, "it tends downwards towards matter, dying along with the flesh, but when it possesses union with the Divine Spirit it is not helpless, but ascends to the places to which the spirit guides it; for its habitation is above, but the origin of the soul is below [z]." "It is our duty now to seek back what we have lost, and to join the soul to the Holy Spirit, and to bring about a union with God [a]." The spirit is thus the representative of God in man. "God wishes to dwell in man through the spirit acting as ambassador [b]." Tatian also attributes to this spirit prophetic powers. "The Spirit of God," he says, "is not with all, but with some who live justly. Being brought down and being intermixed with their soul, it through prophecies proclaimed to the other souls that which was concealed, and those souls which obeyed wisdom attracted to themselves the spirit allied to them, while those who did not obey but rejected the minister [the Spirit] of the suffering God showed themselves fighters with God rather than worshippers of God [c]." He attributes the invention of gods also to a spark of the spirit still remaining in the soul. "Possessing," he says, "as it were a spark of the power of the spirit, but on account of its separation

[s] c. 12, p. 150 D.
[x] c. 7, p. 147 A.
[a] c. 15, p. 153 D.
[t] c. 13, p. 152 D.
[y] c. 20, p. 159 A.
[b] c. 15, p. 154 C.
[u] c. 7, p. 146 C.
[z] c. 13, p. 152 C D.
[c] c. 13, p. 153 A.

not being able to see clearly those things which were perfect, while seeking God the soul fashioned many gods, in its mistake following the devices of the demons[c]." In harmony with all that is stated already, Tatian remarks that the soul was saved by the spirit[d].

The scholiast's note on the meaning of πνεῦμα deserves attention. He defines spirit as "a constitution given by creation, or a power which God sowed in matter, and thus produced in this visible world the different natures of land animals, of water animals, of birds, zoophytes and plants[e]."

Devil and Demons.—Tatian does not mention the devil by name, but there is one passage in which he, without doubt, speaks of him. He says of the first human beings, that "when they followed one wiser than the others on account of his being firstborn, and declared him god, even though he rose up against the law of God, then the power of the Logos debarred him who began the folly and those who followed him from living with Him (the Logos)[f]." "This firstborn becomes a demon on account of his transgression and ignorance, and those who imitated him, that is, his appearances (φαντάσματα), became an army of demons and were delivered over to their folly on account of free-will[g]." This is the only allusion to the devil; he is here called the firstborn, and his fall is connected with the fall of man.

The demons are said to have been cast out of heaven[h], and to have lived with animals after having been expelled from the life of heaven[i].

The demons chose men as the objects in whom to exhibit their revolt from God. They thus devised the system of astrology to induce men to believe in a fate[k], and they chose the animals with which they [the demons] lived, to be as it were the alphabet and foundation of their scheme[l]. They act also upon men by magic and by the healing of diseases.

The charms have no natural power. But the demons have determined for what each particular charm is to be used, and then "when they see their assistance received by men, they take hold of the men and make them slaves to themselves [m]." In this way "they turn men away from the worship of God by making them trust grasses and roots [n]."

The demons are equally deceptive in their cures. "Demons," he says, "do not cure, but by art carry men captive, and the most admirable Justin rightly said that they were like robbers [o]." The plan they take is this: "They attack the members of some persons, then through dreams they manage to make their glory known to them, then they order such publicly to come forth, and in the sight of all, after having enjoyed worldly honours, they fly from the sick persons, put an end to the disease which they had caused, and restore the men to their former state [p]."

Tatian describes more minutely the action of the demons on men in chapter 16. He says, "The demons revelling over men in their wickedness, by diverse and deceitfully-planned contrivances turn away their minds, which have already begun to tend downwards, that they may not be able to elevate themselves to the journey in the heavens. But the things which are in the world have not escaped our notice, and the divinity becomes comprehensible to us since the power which renders souls immortal [the Spirit] has come to us. Now the demons are seen even by those destitute of the Spirit of God, since they sometimes show themselves to men, that they may be thought to be of some importance, or that, since they are friends having evil hearts, they may do them some injury as if they were enemies, or that they may afford opportunities to those like them of paying honour to themselves. For if it were possible for them, they would have dragged down heaven itself along with the rest of creation. But now this they by no means do, for they are unable; but, by means of the inferior matter,

---

[m] c. 17, p. 165 B.   [n] Ibid. p. 165 C.
[o] c. 18, p. 157 C.   [p] Ibid.

they war against matter which is similar to themselves. If one wishes to conquer these, let him expel matter. For armed with the breastplate of the heavenly Spirit, he will be able to preserve everything embraced by it. There are then diseases and dissensions of the matter which is in us: but the demons themselves ascribe the causes to themselves when they occur, attacking whenever disease seizes hold of a man. Sometimes, also, by the storm of their folly they shake the constitution of the body. These being struck by the word of God's power, in fear depart, and the sick man is healed."

One of the motives mentioned in this passage for the activity of demons is that they might have honour paid them. Tatian several times alludes to the desire they have for worship: "They were eager to become robbers of divinity[p]." He accordingly identifies them with the gods worshipped by the Greeks[q], and he speaks of the "demons with their leader Zeus[r]," as if he regarded Zeus as the devil.

Tatian divides demons into two classes, those who attached themselves to the grosser forms of matter, and those who turned themselves to the purer. "The demons, having received their constitution from matter and possessing the spirit which proceeds from it, became licentious and gluttonous, some of them turning to that which was purer, while others chose the defective portion of matter and lived a life similar to it[s]." They had the spirit of matter in them. They were born of matter. They were even more, "They are the effulgences of matter and wickedness[t]." Tatian does not explain what he means by this expression, but it is probable that he thought of Christ as the effulgence of God; and as the being of Christ had no will, power, or thought that was not the Father's, so the demons had no activity of their own which was not identical with the activity of

[p] c. 12, p. 151 D.   [q] Ibid.
[r] c. 8, p. 147 C.   [s] c. 12, p. 151 D.
[t] c. 15, p. 154 C.

matter and wickedness[u]. If this be the case, then it is easy to understand his statement, which he seems to regard as an inference from the passage now quoted, that the substance of the demons did not admit of room for repentance. The human race had a spark of the spirit remaining, the divine spirit had completely abandoned the demons.

Though thus entirely material, yet they have no flesh. The putting together of their bodies, though it "be of matter," is "spiritual, like the constitution of fire or air[v]." On account of their fleshlessness, "they do not die easily; but living, they carry on practices of death, for they die as often as they teach sins to those who follow them[x]."

Their bodies also are invisible to those who possess merely the soul and not the divine spirit, "for the inferior cannot comprehend the superior[y]." They may, however, make themselves visible to the psychical for their own purposes[z]. They generally impose on men by unreal appearances. They deceive "souls, that are left alone[a], by means of ignorance and unreal appearances" (φαντασιῶν)[b]. And they imitate the unreal appearances (φαντάσματα) of the devil[c]. A complete view of their bodies is easily obtained by those who are guarded by the Spirit of God[d].

The continuance of the demons is thus accounted for: "The Lord of all has permitted them to revel until the world, receiving an end, be dissolved, and the Judge appear; and all the men who desire the knowledge of the perfect God shall receive through the revolt of the demons a more perfect testimony by means of the contests in the day of judgment[e]." Tatian states here that the revolt of the demons has the effect of trying in a satisfactory manner the virtue of those who know God. The meaning is the same if we translate according to Otto's punctuation, "the men who, notwithstanding

---

[u] See Worth's note on the passage. [v] c. 15, p. 154 C.
[x] c. 14, p. 153 B.   [y] c. 15, p. 154 C.   [z] c. 16, p. 155 B.
[a] That is, souls from which the Spirit has gone away. See below.
[b] c. 14, p. 153 B.   [c] c. 7, p. 147 A.   [d] c. 15, p. 154 C.
[e] c. 12, p. 151 D.

the revolt of the demons, desire the knowledge of the perfect God."

Their ultimate state is also described. At present the demons do not die like men, but when they shall be punished, they will be able to die like men: for "they will not partake of eternal life." "The demons abusing their present life to sin, dying continually even in the course of their living, shall have again the same freedom from dying which they had before, but as far as the condition of it is concerned it will be like that of men who have deliberately done whatever the demons ordered them to do during their lifetime[f]."

Man.—The principal beliefs of Tatian with regard to man have already been adduced in noticing his opinions on the Logos and Spirit. Tatian recognised in man body, soul, and spirit. The spirit, or highest nature, had a principle of immortality in it, but at the fall man lost it. He was then cast forth, "not from this earth, but from a land of much better arrangement than this." This land he seems to place above the heavens: for he says, "The heaven is not boundless, but limited and finite; but those parts which are above it, namely the better ages, having no changes of seasons by which various diseases are produced, and partaking of a completely perfect temperature, have the day abiding and a light which is inaccessible to men here[g]."

Tatian says almost nothing of any other consequence of the fall of man. He mentions that "if there is anything destructive in things produced, this has taken place on account of our sin[h]."

Man having lost the divine spirit, was left only with soul and body. The soul, left to itself, naturally tends downwards: for it is intimately connected with matter: and "matter wishes to get the mastery over the soul[i]." The connexion between body and soul is so intimate that the one is dissolved with the other. "The soul is the bond of the flesh, and the flesh

[f] c. 14. p. 153 C D.
[h] c. 19. p. 158 D.
[g] c. 20. p. 159 A.
[i] c. 15. p. 154 C.

contains the soul[k]." That is, the soul gives life and activity to all the parts of the body, and thus enables it to have one economy, to serve for one great end. The flesh, on the other hand, is that in which the soul resides. He accordingly regards the "soul as consisting of many parts[l], not one single substance: it is compound, so that it can be seen only through the body: for soul would never appear without a body, nor does flesh rise again without the soul." He therefore rejects that notion of man which describes him as "a rational animal, capable of induction and science." The true definition of man is "the image and likeness of God," but this definition applies only to the "man who does not do things like animals, and who has been advancing beyond humanity up to God Himself;" in other words, only to the man who has the divine spirit. If God does not dwell in a man through the spirit, then that man has no advantage over the wild beasts except in his articulate voice. He is no longer the likeness of God, but his mode of life is like that of wild beasts[m].

Though Tatian thus speaks of the soul as if it were purely material, there is one passage in which he seems to ascribe to it the power of knowing the truth. The passage itself, however, almost prevents us from interpreting the language exactly; and we must suppose that he wished us to understand his words with his explanations of the spirit in our minds. The passage is a very famous one, and runs thus: "The soul is not immortal by itself, but mortal. It is also capable of not dying. For it dies and is dissolved with the body when it does not know the truth, but it rises again afterwards with the body at the end of the world, receiving death as a punishment in immortality. Again, however, it does not die, even though it be dissolved for a time, when it has acquired full knowledge of God.

[k] c. 15, p. 154 B.

[l] Worth translates πολυμερής as meaning 'one of many parts,' and altogether there is much ingenious but not satisfactory meddling with this passage. See Daniel, p. 203.

[m] c. 15, p. 154 A B C.

For by itself it is darkness and there is no light in it. And this is that which is said, 'The darkness comprehends not [does not take hold of] the light.' For the soul did not of itself save the spirit, but was saved by it, and the light comprehended [took hold of] the darkness. Truly the light of God is reason (Logos), but the ignorant soul is darkness. On this account when it lives alone it tends downwards to matter, dying along with the flesh; but possessing an alliance with the divine spirit it is not helpless, but mounts up to the places to which the spirit leads it [n]." The first part of this passage has been interpreted various ways [o]. The real meaning seems to depend on the word 'die.' Tatian evidently means that the soul dies when it is sinful, that it becomes mortal then. There is nothing but soul and body: and therefore when the body dies, it must die, it has no longer any work to perform: that which it kept together is dissolved and it therefore dies. But when a man consists of body, soul, and spirit, on his body becoming dead, the connexion between body and soul is broken, but then the spirit comes to its assistance and it mounts up to those places to which the spirit guides it.

Tatian lays special stress on the doctrine of free-will in man. Describing angels and men, he says, "Both forms of creation came into existence free, not having a nature of goodness which alone was with God, but the form was perfected by men through the freedom of the choice, so that the wicked man should be justly punished, as having become injurious on his own account, and that the just man might be praised deservedly on account of his good deeds, not having transgressed the will of God in the exercise of his free-will [p]." "We were not born to die," he says, "but we die on our own account. Free-will has destroyed us. We who were free have become slaves; we were sold on account of sin. Nothing evil was made by God; we ourselves have brought out wickedness; and we who brought it out are

[n] c. 13. p. 152 B C D. [o] See Otto's note on the passage.
[p] c. 7. p. 146 C.

able to reject it again [q]." Tatian takes care to note that the prophecies of the Logos took place not according to fate, but because He foreknew the minds of the free agents [r]. He also exhibits the absurdity of the doctrine of fate, especially in its connexion with the stars [s]. God made the world "for our sake [t]."

Tatian says little of the salvation of man. In a passage already adduced he asserts man's power to gain what he had lost; and he has again and again asserted that the great object of man's aims is to unite his soul with the Divine Spirit. This union is sometimes represented as life, and generally the subjective state of man's mind in this life is represented by the words the 'knowledge' or 'comprehension' of God. "I see," he says, "that it is the same sun that shines on all, and that there is one death against all, whether they live in the midst of pleasure or in the midst of poverty [u]." Then, after a little, he adds, "Why dost thou, frequently desiring according to fate, frequently die? Die to the world, rejecting the madness in it; live to God, rejecting the old birth through the comprehension of Him [x]." Tatian opposes to the power of comprehending God worldly comprehension, "above which," he says, "the things of our instruction are [y]." And in another passage he remarks that "it is not holy to compare our comprehension with regard to God with those who wallow in matter and mud [z]." Tatian, as we have seen, varies the expression by speaking of a knowledge of the truth.

Tatian also speaks of faith, especially in connexion with the resurrection. He recognises a relation between faith and knowledge. "He who believes shall know [a]." And he attributes both to faith and to knowledge the same effect—the conquest of death. "Men," he says, "after the loss of immortality have conquered death by a death which is through faith, and through repentance (μετάνοια) a calling has been freely granted to them according to the word that says,

[q] c. 11, p. 150 D. [r] c. 7, p. 146 D. [s] c. 8, p. 147 B.
[t] c. 4, p. 144 D. [u] c. 11, p. 150 B. [x] c. 11, p. 150 BC.
[y] c. 12, p. 152 B. [z] c. 21, p. 160 C. [a] c. 19, p. 158 D.

'Since they were made somewhat inferior to the angels.' It is possible, then, for every one that has been conquered to conquer again, rejecting the constitution of death [b]." Again, addressing the Greeks, he says, "If ye say that death ought not to be feared, sharing in our opinions, die not on account of human insane desire of glory like Anaxarchus, but become despisers of death on account of the knowledge of God. For the constitution of the world is good, but the mode of life in it is bad [c]."

Sometimes the comprehension of God is spoken of as a comprehension of the truth. Thus, in a passage already quoted, it is said, "I being born again in imitation of the Logos, and having made the comprehension of the true [d]."

The attribution of spiritual life to comprehension of God, to what seems an intellectual operation, is seen also in the efficacy which he assigns to the reading of the Old Testament. "While I was thinking earnestly," he says, "I chanced to fall in with some barbaric writings, older than the doctrines of the Greeks, and more divine in contrast with their error, and it chanced that I was persuaded by them on account of the humility of the words and artlessness of the speakers, and the easy comprehension of the creation of all, and the foreknowledge of things future, and the excellence of the precepts, and the unity in the government of the whole. My soul being God-taught, I understood that the writings of the Greeks lead to condemnation, but that these writings break down the slavery in the world, and tear us away from many rulers and ten thousand tyrants, and give to us, not what we have not received, but what, having received, we were prevented by deceit from retaining [e]."

Tatian says nothing of the Church nor of baptism. He evidently makes an allusion to the Thanksgiving, when he says that Christians were misrepresented by the accusation that they ate human flesh [f]. He describes, however, various

---

[b] c. 15, p. 154 D.
[d] c. 5, p. 145 C.
[f] c. 25, p. 162 D.

[c] c. 19, p. 158 A.
[e] c. 29, p. 165 B.

phases of the Christian life. He seems to intimate that the progress of the Christian is gradual. "We know," he says, "that the constitution of wickedness is like that of the smallest seeds; it gets strong by small additions: but it will be again dissolved if we obey the words of God and do not scatter ourselves. For He [God] has got possession of our powers through some secret treasure in digging, which we ourselves were filled with dust, but thereby we afford it the means of remaining firmly together. For he who receives entire possession of it has got under his powers the most valuable riches [g]."

The Christian's life is a separation from the world. Various passages have already been quoted in which Tatian brings forward this idea. "If you are superior to passions, you will despise all things that are in the world [h]." Tatian condemns the heathen games, and pours out his most effective sarcasm on some player whom he had seen. "Who would not," he says, "mock at your public assemblies, which being brought about by the device of wicked demons, turn men to shame [i]." He also, for his own part, rejected the civil service. "I do not wish to be a king; I do not wish to be rich; I have rejected the prætorship: I have hated fornication; I do not make voyages on account of insatiable greed; I do not contend to have garlands; I am freed from glory-madness; I despise death; I am superior to disease of every sort; sorrow does not consume my soul. If I am a slave, I endure slavery; if I am free, I do not boast of my birth [k]." He also asserts that as a Christian he is ready to pay taxes. He recognises the right of the slave-master to service, and he will honour man as a man ought to be honoured [l].

He lays especial stress on the universal adaptation of Christianity to men, and the purity of the Christian life. He says, "With us there is not the desire of vainglory, and we

---

[g] c. 30, p. 165 C D. The treasure is that described in Matt. xiii. 44. See Otto's note.
[h] c. 19, p. 158 C.   [i] c. 22, p. 160 C.
[k] c. 11, p. 150 B.   [l] c. 4. p. 144 B.

do not use diversities of opinions. For being separated from the public and earthly teaching, and obeying the commands of God, and following the law of the Father of incorruption, we reject everything that depends on human opinion. But not only do the rich philosophise, but the poor enjoy instruction for nothing: for the things from God cannot be repaid by any gift in the world. And thus we admit all who wish to hear, be they old women or mere youths; in one word, every age receives honour with us: but all lasciviousness is far removed from us. And when we speak we do not lie [m]." He appeals with especial satisfaction to the chastity of the virgins, who "at their distaff speak the divine utterances [n]."

Tatian mentions a resurrection of all at the end of the world [o], and a judgment. According to his principles he found a difficulty in conceiving of the separation of the soul, or life-principle, from the body; and, as we have seen, he affirms that "the flesh does not rise again apart from soul [p]." "I affirm," he says in opposition to the Stoics, "that the flesh is made immortal with the soul [q]." We have seen already that he thought that the soul of a good man, in consequence of his possession of spirit, did exist somehow or other after death; though from his principle, that soul could not appear without body, the souls of such could not be recognisable. On the other hand, the souls of the wicked must for the time have been entirely dissolved. Tatian's views with regard to the state of the dead immediately after death have been understood in various ways. Dodwell and Daniel maintain that he regarded all souls as dissolved at death [r], as certain Arabian Christians refuted by Origen afterwards believed [s]; while most other commentators try to reconcile his expressions with the more common beliefs of Christian writers. In opposition to the Stoics, he maintained also that the conflagration took place once for all [t], and not after certain revolutions of ages. "Once," as he says in c. 6, p. 145 D, "when our ages

---

[m] c. 32, p. 167 B.   [n] c. 33, p. 168 C.   [o] c. 6, p. 145 D.
[p] See c. 15, p. 154 A.   [q] c. 25, p. 162 D.
[r] See Daniel, pp. 226 239.   [s] Euseb. Hist. Eccl. vi. 37.   [t] c. 25, p. 162 D.

have been finished;" and he affirms that "this resurrection after the end of the whole" will take place "for the sake of judgment entirely on account of the constitution of men alone." "God Himself the Maker is judge." He attributes the resurrection to God's power, and says that he can see no reason why men should not believe such a thing possible, since they had once been nothing themselves, and now were. "If fire," he says, "destroy my flesh, the world contains the matter dissolved in vapour; if I am consumed away in rivers or in the sea, if I am torn by wild beasts, I am laid up in the treasury of a rich Lord. The poor man and the godless knows not what things are laid up, but God, who is king, when He wishes, will restore my substance, visible to Himself alone, to its former state [v]." Body, soul, and spirit are thus coupled together: "The prophets being persuaded that the heavenly spirit would along with the soul possess the covering of mortality, foretold things which the other souls did not know [w]."

Tatian says nothing of the blessedness of those who obey, except what has been adduced already. We have also quoted passages in which he speaks of the punishment of the wicked. He calls the fire 'eternal' in speaking of Democritas: "He shall be delivered up to the devouring of eternal fire (αἰωνίου) in the day of the end;" and he declares to the Greeks that if they do not stop their laughter, they will endure the same punishment as the jugglers [x].

Scriptures.—Tatian does not give any exposition of his ideas with regard to the Scriptures. The principal passage in which he speaks of them has been quoted already. He also speaks of "the most Divine interpretations which, committed to writing as time went on, have made those who gave heed to them entirely God-loved [y]." Worth supposed the word 'interpretation' to refer especially to the Septuagint; but the opinion of Daniel [z] is much more feasible, that Tatian calls the Scriptures themselves interpretations because he regarded the authors as interpreters of God revealing Himself.

[u] c. 6, p. 146 A; c. 25. p. 162 D.   [v] c. 6, p. 146 A B.
[w] c. 20, p. 159 B.   [x] c. 17. p. 155 D.   [y] c. 12. p. 151 C.   [z] p. 138, note.

We have also adduced the passages in which Tatian speaks of the prophets. They had the Spirit of God, they lived piously, and were enabled to reveal to other souls what was hid[z].

As we have seen already, Tatian knew our Gospels, the Acts of the Apostles, and the Epistles of Paul. There is no proof that he knew any other of the New Testament writings[a].

Morality.—Most of the special points of Tatian's morality have been noticed already: his contentment with the existence of slavery, and his praise of virgins as such. He heaps reproaches on a woman who bore thirty children. "What business have I to reckon and regard as wonderful the statue made by Periclymenos of a woman who bore thirty children? For it were noble to abominate one who carried off the chief spoils of much incontinency[b]." There is no reason to suppose that Eutychis, the woman alluded to, was in any way unchaste; and Gesner wisely remarks that for his part he agrees much rather with the divine poet David in Psalm cxxviii.[c]

Tatian also expresses his condemnation of theatres and gladiatorial shows.

VI. LITERATURE.

MANUSCRIPTS.

There are six manuscripts of Tatian, and a seventh has been collated, but its present locality is not known. It is represented however by the first edition, Editio Tigurina, 1546, fol. The editor, John Frisius, when in Venice received a manuscript of Tatian from his friend Arnoldus Arlenius Peraxylus, and took it to Zurich. Of the six manuscripts now known, by far the best is Codex Parisinus 174, (Gallicanus or Regius 1,) preserved in the Royal Library at Paris. It is supposed by Montfaucon[d] to belong to the tenth century.

---

[z] c. 13. p. 153 A; c. 20, p. 159 B.
[a] See Daniel, p. 131, for a full exhibition of Tatian's quotations from the Old and New Testaments.   [b] c. 34. p. 169 C.
[c] See the note in Worth on the passage.
[d] Palaeogr. etc. Paris, 1708. fol. p. 277.

It was partially used by Ducæus; completely collated by Lequien for Worth, who also gave some of the scholia which it contains; and lately, Hase collated it for Otto's edition, which is the first that contains all the scholia. There is another manuscript of Tatian in the Royal Library at Paris, called Codex Parisinus 2376, (Gallicanus or Regius 2,) which contains, besides Tatian, many other writings. Nourry asserts that it was written in 1534, "ut annotatur," by a monk Bessarion in the monastery of St. Antony in Venice. Hase examined the codex for Otto and found no such name, but a note to the effect that "brother Valerian wrote this book in the monastery of St. Antony at Venice in the year of our Lord 1539." This information renders it likely that Valerian made his copy from a manuscript still preserved at Venice in the Library of St. Mark, called Codex Venetus 343. It is said to belong to the twelfth century. Other two copies of Tatian's work made by Valerian are extant. One, Codex Bononiensis, is preserved in the Library of Bologna, and a transcript from it, Codex Ætonensis, which Worth collated while living with the head master of Eton, Henry Godolphin. It is still preserved in the Eton Library. This transcript was made in 1534. The other codex that remains to be mentioned is the Codex Mutinensis, in the Ducal Library of Modena, a beautiful MS. of the tenth century, containing many important works besides the Oration of Tatian. For a full account of these manuscripts see Daniel, p. 78, and especially Otto in his Prolegomena to his edition of Tatian, pp. xiii–xx.

EDITIONS.

The first edition, as has been mentioned already, was published at Zurich in 1546, under the editorship of Joannes Frisius, with emendations from Conrad Gesner. In the same year and place was published a Latin translation of the work by Conrad Gesner. It appeared subsequently in the Orthodoxographa of Heroldus (Basil. 1555, fol.), in Latin in several of the large libraries, and in Greek and Latin in the collected editions of the Apologists, Paris, 1615, 1636, and Cologne or Wittenberg, 1675–1686, and that of Maranus. The Wittenberg edition had a few notes written by Christian Kortholt. In the Auctarium to the Paris Great Library of 1624 appeared the Greek text, with Latin translation and notes by Fronto Ducæus. It appeared also in the Melissa of Antonius, a monk, Venice, 1680. See Νεοελληνικὴ Φιλολογία, by Bretos, Part i. p. 36.

A separate edition of Tatian appeared at Oxford in 1700. Its title gives some idea of its contents: "Tatiani Oratio ad Græcos. Hermiæ irrisio Gentilium Philosophorum. Ex vetustis Exemplaribus recensuit, adnotationibusque integris Conradi Gesneri, Frontonis Ducæi, Christiani Kortholti, Thomæ Galei, selectisque Henrici Stephani, Meursii, Bocharti, Cotelerii, utriusque Vossii, aliorumque suas qualescunque adjecit Wilhelmus Worth, A.M. Oxoniæ, e Theatro Sheldoniano, 1700." Besides the things here specified, it contains a full list of testimonies, Bull's dissertation on the co-eternal existence of the Son, Frisius's dedicatory epistle to the first edition, and Gesner's to the first Latin translation, Nourry's dissertation, the Abbé Louis du Four de Longuerue's dissertation on Tatian, Cave's remarks on Tatian and Hermias, and indices. The edition is altogether very valuable, and Worth contributed much to the understanding of Tatian, though his modesty made him place his emendations in notes rather than in the text.

The only other separate edition of Tatian is by John Charles Theodore Otto, Jenæ, 1851, 8vo. It is unquestionably the best edition. The Prolegomena give a full account of the various manuscripts, editions, and translations, a short chapter on the diction of Tatian, and an analysis of his work. It has the largest collection of the fragments of Tatian. It contains the first complete edition of the Paris scholia, and it is furnished with admirable notes and good indices.

CHAPTER V.

THEOPHILUS.

I. LIFE.

OUR information with regard to Theophilus is derived from his own work, and from the short notice which Eusebius gives of him and his writings. We do not know where he was born, for the words, "The other two rivers, called Tigris and Euphrates, are well known to us, for they border on our regions[a]," indicate that his place of abode rather than his birthplace was in the East. We gather that he was brought up a heathen from the statement which he makes in regard to his conversion. "Do not disbelieve," he says in reference to the resurrection, "but believe; for I also did not believe that this would take place; but now, after I have fully considered, I believe, having at the same time fallen in with the sacred writings of the holy prophets[b]." He here states that he had not been convinced of the reality of the resurrection until he had fallen in with the Scriptures. Nor is the inference nullified by the mode which he adopted, in common with all Christians, of speaking of the personages of the Old Testament, as 'Abraham our patriarch,' 'Abraham our forefather,' 'David our ancestor[c].' Hosmann, indeed, attempted to maintain a theory which would literally suit both classes of passages. He supposed that Theophilus was a Sadducee; that, consequently, he knew little of the Scriptures, and did not believe in a resurrection, but that he was a real Jew. The few passages relating to the matter which occur in the work of Theophilus are not sufficient to bear up such a precise theory.

[a] lib. ii. c. 24, p. 101 C.   [b] lib. i. c. 14, p. 78 D.
[c] lib. iii. c. 24, p. 134 B; iii. c. 25, p. 135 A; iii. c. 28, p. 138 A.

It is possible, but by no means probable[d]. Eusebius informs us that he was the sixth overseer of the Church in Antioch, and that he was appointed to that office about the eighth year of the reign of Marcus Aurelius: "Then [about the eighth year of the reign of Marcus Aurelius] was Theophilus known as being over the Church of the Antiochians, the sixth from the Apostles[e]." The same date is given in the Chronicle as translated by Jerome. There is no trustworthy notice of his death. As we shall see afterwards, Theophilus appealed to a work of Chryseros[f], a freedman of Marcus Aurelius, in which chronological data were given down to the death of that emperor. He must therefore have lived during part at least of the reign of Commodus, the sovereign who is probably meant by the term βασιλεύς in the passage, "How many taxes and tributes she (the mother of the gods) and her sons pay to the king[g]."

II. THE WRITINGS OF THEOPHILUS.

The principal work of Theophilus, and the only one that has come down to us, is his three books addressed to Autolycus. Eusebius thus speaks of it: "Of Theophilus, whom we have pointed out as being overseer of the Church of the Antiochians, there are in circulation the three elementary (στοιχειώδη) writings which are addressed to Autolycus[h]." Jerome mentions them among the other writings of Theophilus[i], and Lactantius evidently refers to the third book when he says, "Theophilus in the book concerning times written to Autolycus[k]."

Their genuineness has been generally acknowledged by modern scholars. Dodwell, however, supposed that the work bore internal evidence that it was written in the reign of the emperor Severus, and therefore he assigned it to a younger Theophilus. This internal evidence is contained in a passage

[d] See Fabricius, Bibl. Græc., vol. vii. p. 101, note q, ed. Harles.
[e] Hist. Eccl. iv. 20.
[f] lib. iii. c. 27, p. 137 B.
[g] lib. i. c. 10, p. 76 C; comp. 76 D.
[h] Hist. Eccl. iv. 24.
[i] De Viris Ill. c. 25.
[k] Instit. Div. i. 23.

in chapter thirtieth of Book third. "They (the Greeks)," says Theophilus, "persecuted those who worship God, and persecute them daily. And not only so, but they even go the length of assigning prizes and honours to those who in harmonious language insult God; but of those who are zealous in the pursuit of virtue and practise a holy life (τοὺς σπεύδοντας πρὸς ἀρετὴν καὶ ἀσκοῦντας βίον ὅσιον), some they stoned, some they put to death, and up to the present time they subject them to savage tortures." There are two statements in this extract to which Dodwell[1] appeals. First, he gathers from it that the book was written while persecution was raging, and second, he maintains that the σπεύδοντας πρὸς ἀρετήν can mean nothing else than proselytes, and ἀσκοῦντας βίον ὅσιον must refer to philosophic ascetes like Origen and his pupils. The only period to which both of these marks will apply is the reign of Severus, during which a persecution raged and Origen and his scholars were alive. In both points Dodwell has forced his inferences too far. In regard to the first, it is well known that, though there was no public and systematic persecution of the Christians during the reign of Commodus, there was a great deal of private malevolence shown to them, and that even in Rome itself the Christian Apollonius was accused before the senate and condemned to death A.D. 186[m]. Then the interpretation of the words σπεύδοντας πρὸς ἀρετήν and ἀσκοῦντας ὅσιον βίον are unwarranted. Both expressions are perfectly applicable to true Christians of any age, and there is nothing in the words in the slightest degree characteristic of any particular period. In opposition to Dodwell, we have the express testimony of Eusebius that Theophilus, sixth bishop of the Church of the Antiochians, was the writer of the work. And the work itself bears internal evidence of having been written in the reign of Commodus. In calculating periods, Theophilus mentions the death of Marcus Aurelius, but says nothing of the death of Commodus. Dodwell replies to this, that the writer ends there because he is quoting from a work of Chryseros.

[1] Dissert. Iren. ii. 44. 50.
[m] See the Præfatio of Wolfius, and Cave, Hist. Literaria, vol. ii. p. 31.

There might be some force in this reply if Theophilus had merely quoted. But he has done much more. He has simply based his calculations on the statements of Chryseros, and always in summing up he concludes with the death of the emperor Verus. If he could have gone beyond that date, he no doubt would have felt himself compelled to do so for the sake of completeness. Especially in summing up the whole age of the world, he would have done his best to make it accurate. His words are, "Taken together, all the years from the creation of the world amount to 5695, with the odd months and days q." He certainly seems here to be giving all the years of the world, and if this were the case, then there is great probability that the third book of Theophilus was written in the year of the death of Marcus Aurelius. Besides this, chronological writers multiplied after the age of Theophilus of Antioch, and there appears to be no good reason why the records of Chryseros should be quoted in preference to any others, except that they had just made their appearance, and consequently were up to the latest date. Moehler gives another reason for an earlier date than the reign of Severus. He [r] calls attention to striking resemblances between passages in Theophilus and Irenæus which had been previously noticed, and he thinks that these passages in Irenæus appear to have been taken from the work of Theophilus. But such an argument is worthless, except there be the most exact resemblance. In the two cases adduced, the resemblance is very slight, and not verbal. In the first [s] we have simply the same figure employed; and in the second [t] there is the same rather peculiar opinion that Adam was created a child and not a full-grown man.

There can be no doubt that the three books of the work were written separately, and transmitted the one after the other to Autolycus. The introductions to the second and third books prove this. The second book commences with

[q] lib. iii. c. 28, p. 138 B.   [r] Moehler, Patrologie, p. 286.
[s] Theoph. i. 5; Iren. adv. Hær. ii. 6. 2.
[t] Theoph. ii. 25; Iren. adv. Hær. iii. 22. 4.

a reference to the first: "When there was previously, O most excellent Autolycus, a discourse between us, while you inquired who was my God, and afforded your ears to our discussion, I expounded to you the nature of my piety." The third commences like a letter, "Theophilus to Autolycus sends joy," and the subject of the treatise is then announced. Whether Theophilus put the three books together afterwards, or whether this connexion is the work of transcribers, we have no exact means of knowing, though it is likely that Theophilus himself put them together[u].

Wolf supposes that there are traces of incompleteness in the present text, one passage being omitted in the first book, and two in the third. The appearances which have led him to this supposition do not warrant such a conclusion when viewed more narrowly. Thus in lib. i. c. 10, he supposes the connexion to be broken; but on examining the passage more accurately, there is found to be an unquestionable bond of connexion[x].

Theophilus seems in Book third to refer to Book first in the words, "Since we have discoursed with regard to them in another" (ἐν ἑτέρῳ[y]); and he unquestionably refers to Book second: "To this Noah there were three sons, as we pointed out in the second volume" (ἐν τῷ δευτέρῳ τόμῳ[z]).

Of the other works of Theophilus little is known. He mentions himself "The first book which relates to histories" (ἐν τῇ πρώτῃ βίβλῳ τῇ περὶ ἱστοριῶν[a]). He mentions also that in some work, probably in this, he had discussed the history of Noah[b]. He mentions elsewhere that he had written a work in which he had spoken largely of the devil[c]. Maranus imagined that he wrote a work called Γένεσις Κόσμου, Genesis Mundi, and that it was the same as the Histories. In the passage, however, to which Maranus refers[d], there is evidently

---

[u] Grabe, Spicilegium, ii. p. 218; quoted also in Wolf's edition of Theophilus.
[x] See Otto's note 1, on c. 11.
[y] lib. iii. c. 3, p. 119 A.
[z] lib. iii. c. 19, p. 129 C.
[a] lib. ii. c. 30, p. 106 B.
[b] lib. ii. c. 30, p. 106 D; c. 31, p. 107 A; iii. c. 19, p. 129 B.
[c] lib. ii. c. 28, p. 105 A.
[d] lib. ii. c. 29, p. 105 B.

F 2

no allusion to a work by Theophilus, but to the book of the Old Testament called Genesis.

Eusebius thus enumerates his writings. "Of Theophilus... there are in circulation three elementary writings to Autolycus, another having the inscription against the heresy of Hermogenes (πρὸς τὴν αἵρεσιν Ἑρμογένους), in which he has used proofs from the Apocalypse of John, and some other instructive works" (καὶ ἕτερα δέ τινα κατηχητικὰ αὐτοῦ βιβλία). Eusebius then refers to the general efforts made by "the shepherds of the Churches" to render void the endeavours of heretics to draw them away from the right path. Then he adds, "That Theophilus along with the rest warred against them, is plain from some work made by him not ignobly against Marcion; which also, along with the other writings that we have mentioned, is still preserved[g]." Jerome repeats the statements of Eusebius, and then adds, "I have read under his name commentaries on the Gospel and the Proverbs of Solomon. They do not seem to me to agree with the elegance and diction of the former volumes[h]." Jerome notices another work of Theophilus in an Epistle to Algasias[i]. "Theophilus," he says, "the seventh overseer of the Antiochian Church after the Apostle Peter, who forming the sayings of the four evangelists into one work, has left to us a monument of his abilities. With regard to this parable he has made the following remarks in his commentaries." Of the commentaries on the Gospel and the Proverbs of Solomon Jerome himself doubted the genuineness, and his testimony, occurring as it does in an epistle, is not sufficient to make us sure of the genuineness of the Harmony.

There is extant a work bearing the name of Theophilus of Antioch, "Four Books of Commentaries on the Gospels," which has been printed in some of the great libraries and in Otto's edition of Theophilus. It exists only in Latin. There is the clearest proof that it was written long after the time of Theophilus, and probably the original was in

[g] Hist. Eccl. iv. 24. [h] De Vir. Illustr. c. 25.
[i] Quaest. vi.

Latin. Quotations from Cyprian and Jerome occur in the work[k].

III. ESTIMATE OF THEOPHILUS.

The work of Theophilus which has come down to us is not an apology for the Christians, like the other apologies of this age. He mentions the accusations which were commonly made against the Christians, and refutes them well. But his main business is to convince Autolycus of the falsehood of heathenism and the truth of Christianity. His arguments have a direct personal bearing on Autolycus, and are often introduced in reply to objections which that learned heathen had made.

The style of the work is clear and not without force. Theophilus himself, in the commencement of the first book, scorns the idea of using elegant language, for he thinks that the sole object of a highly polished style must be the gaining of applause "for miserable men who have been corrupted in their mind." "The lover of truth," he says, "does not give heed to ornamented speeches, but examines the real object of the speech, what it is, and of what kind it is." Theophilus deserves the credit of being enthusiastic in his love of truth. He gets a firm hold of his arguments, and exhibits them in clear, concise, not altogether unornamented language. He seems also to have read a great deal, but he must have been a superficial reader, and hasty in his judgments. He has committed very many blunders, misquoting Plato several times[l]; ranking Zopyrus among the Greeks[m]; and giving a peculiar, if not an inaccurate, account of the death of Pausanias[n].

In writing to Autolycus, Theophilus thought that it was necessary for his purpose to show the folly of heathenism and the truth of Christianity at the same time. His view of heathenism is a dark one. He has sympathy with no part

---

[k] See Permaneder, Patrologia Specialis, vol. i. p. 193; Lumper, vol. iii. p. 143.
[l] lib. iii. cc. 6, 16.   [m] Ibid. c. 26.   [n] Ibid

of it. He looked upon it as a mere worship of idols, for the most part[o]; and these idols he believed to have borne the names of dead men [p]. He almost never alludes to the fact that the heathens supposed that there were real beings above and beyond the mere images of stone, though he mentions the gods as demons when quoting from a Psalm[q].

In his treatment of the philosophers and poets he is equally undistinguishing. All of them were impious. He makes the universal statement that "writers wish to write a multitude of books for vainglory[r]." He then lays down the principle that "writers should themselves be eye-witnesses of the facts which they affirm, or have accurately learned them from those who saw them[s]." He then proceeds to judge Homer and Hesiod, Orpheus, the tragedians, Herodotus and Thucydides, Socrates and Plato, and "the rest of the philosophers," and concludes, "We assert these things to exhibit their useless and godless state of mind. For these all being in love with vain and empty glory, neither themselves knew the truth nor assuredly did they urge others to the truth[t]." The reason of this sweeping condemnation it is easy to see. The truth of Christianity Theophilus makes to depend on his proving that the Old Testament was older than the writings of the Greeks, and that it was inspired. Man could not ascertain the truth for himself. He must get it direct from God, who knew about these things. Now as Socrates and Plato did not pretend to divine inspiration, they were utterly ignorant. Theophilus saw no medium between absolute ignorance and entire knowledge.

But Theophilus could not deny that such men as Plato and Socrates and many of the poets had expressed the truth in regard to many most important points. True, indeed, he tries to show that they were often inconsistent with themselves. But notwithstanding this, there still remained the problem, How could they have got the truths which they, at least

[o] lib. i. cc. 1, 8; ii. c. 2.
[q] lib. i. c. 10. Psalm xcvi. 5.
[s] lib. iii. c. 2.
[p] lib. i. cc. 9, 10.
[r] lib. iii. c. 1.
[t] lib. iii. cc. 2, 3.

occasionally, proclaimed? Theophilus's explanation is that they stole them from the prophets[u]. He was shut up to this conclusion from his distrust of the powers of man to reach truth.

His defence of Christianity is perilled entirely on his success in proving that the Scriptures of the Old Testament are inspired. At the commencement, indeed, of the discussion he has to prove the unity of God and the reality of the resurrection. And he has for this purpose adduced several good arguments. But he soon passes to a consideration of the Old Testament, by the reading of which his own mind was led to believe these doctrines. The inspiration of this book is proved by two arguments. First, the prophets always agree with each other in their teachings[x]. In this respect they form a marked contrast to the Greek philosophers and poets, who differed from each other and were often inconsistent with themselves. And secondly, the fulfilment of the prophecies, which Theophilus looked on as an unquestionable fact, was sure proof that the prophets contained God's Holy Spirit[y].

In exhibiting to the mind of Autolycus the consistency and truth of the doctrines of the Old Testament, Theophilus appeals especially to the account of the creation of the world and man. He unquestionably looked on the Bible as a storehouse of physical facts, as well as of spiritual instructions. And he ridicules in contrast the statements of Plato, who seems to have been wiser than the other Greeks[z]. He also throws contempt on the Greek writers, and especially Aratus, who in ignorance of Scripture ventured to assert that the earth was spherical[a].

This one-sidedness of Theophilus is seen in the very great stress which he lays on the argument that the writings of all the prophets were older than any of those of the Greeks[b]. He commences his arrangement of dates in a solemn manner:

[u] lib. i. c. 14 ; ii. c. 37.
[y] lib. iii. c. 17.
[a] lib. ii. c. 32 ; iii. c. 2.
[x] lib. ii. c. 9 ; iii. c. 17.
[z] lib. iii. c. 16.
[b] lib. iii. c. 23.

"I ask grace from the only God that I may speak the whole truth accurately according to his will, that you and every one who reads this may be guided by his truth and grace[c]."

It is difficult to estimate how the arguments of Theophilus would be received by a heathen. Most of them, it is easy to see, would be far from satisfactory, and many objections to them would naturally arise in minds accustomed to believe in oracles and to despise barbarian literatures.

Theophilus devotes one portion of his work to the exposition of the religious truths and moral precepts given in Christianity, and we may well believe that these, though they have no place in his argument, would more powerfully attract earnest minds than his chronological discussions or his expositions of the book of the Genesis. It is to be noticed that Theophilus does not mention in his discussion any of what we now call the distinctive truths of Christianity. The Old Testament, according to him, contained all the truths which man requires to know.

IV. ABSTRACT OF THEOPHILUS TO AUTOLYCUS.

BOOK FIRST.

Theophilus opens his first book with an attack on the prevalent style of writing for effect, and not for truth. The lover of truth does not give heed to such tricked-out language. He then addresses Autolycus: "Since you, O friend, have astounded me with empty words, boasting of your gods made of stone and other materials, and call me a Christian as if the name were bad, I confess that I am a Christian;" and then he shows that the name has really in itself a good meaning[d], and that the name of God was not disagreeable, and would not be disagreeable to him if he thought justly with regard to God[e]. But if you say, says Theophilus, "Show me thy God;" I would reply, "Show me your man, and I will show you my God." The man must have a pure soul

[c] lib. iii. c. 23.
[d] He does this by identifying χριστός with χρηστός.   [e] c. 1.

before he can see God. Impieties cover him with darkness, so that he cannot see God[f]. You will say to me, "Do you who see God explain to me the appearance of God" (εἶδος). I answer, "God's appearance is indescribable." All names by which He may be called are appellations derived from his own works; and He made all things that his greatness might be perceived through his works[g]. Just as the life-principle of man is invisible, but its existence is perceived through the motion of the body, so God is perceived through his providence and works. So is the presence of a pilot on a ship inferred. So the existence of the sun, though it is too bright to look on. And so is an earthly king known through his orders[h]. Consider His works, the changes of the seasons, the regular march of the stars, the beauty of seed, and plant, and fruit, the generation of animals of every kind, and the supply of food to all creation, and many such operations of God[i]. But you are ignorant of this God on account of the blindness of your soul. God Himself can cure you, however; and if you live righteously you can see God. When God raises up the body immortal with the soul, then will you see God worthily[k]. But you do not believe that the dead are raised up. You are unwilling to take it on trust. But in most occupations in life confidence is the leading principle. There is good reason, therefore, for trusting ourselves to God: first, because He made us; and second, because if you believe that images made by man are gods, how much more ought you to trust the God who made you[l]? The names of your gods are the names of dead men, and those of a disreputable character: Kronos devoured his children, Zeus was guilty of incest and adultery, and his offspring Heracles, Dionysus, Apollo, Aphrodite, and Ares betrayed human weaknesses. But what is said of them is nothing to what is said of Osiris. And why should I speak of Attis, Adonis, Asklepius, Sarapis, and Scythian Artemis? It is your poets and historians who relate these stories, not Christian writers[m]. The Egyptians

[f] c. 2.   [g] cc. 3, 4.   [h] c. 5.   [i] c. 6.
[k] c. 7.   [l] c. 8.   [m] c. 9.

worship beasts. The Greeks know the makers of their gods, such as Phidias. How many Jupiters are there? I should not like to describe the deeds of the mother of the gods nor of her worshippers, nor how many taxes she and her sons pay to the king[n]. I should rather honour the king who gets the taxes than the gods who pay them, but I cannot worship him. I worship God, who really is God and is the true God. A king is not made for being worshipped, but for being lawfully honoured. And we ought, therefore, to honour and pray for Him[o]. As to your laughing at me, calling me a Christian, you do not know what you say. A ship, a tower, a house are not beautiful or useful until they are anointed. Man also is anointed: so is the air and everything under the sky with light and spirit, and we are called Christians because we are anointed with the oil of God. The argumentation of Theophilus depends here on the literal meaning which he attaches to Christos, the Anointed One, and he plays on this meaning, and also on the similarity of pronunciation between χρηστός, 'useful,' and χριστός, 'anointed[p].' As to your denying that the dead are raised, you say, Show me even one dead man raised, that seeing I may believe. But seeing is not believing. Then you believe that Heracles and Asklepius are alive, though they died. God gives many tokens of a resurrection in nature, such as in the changes of the seasons[q]. Therefore believe, submitting to God, lest, if you have disbelieved, you will be at last convinced, tortured in eternal pains. These punishments are mentioned by the Greek poets and philosophers, who stole them from the prophets to give their opinions some authority. Read the prophetic writings, and they will guide you more clearly how to flee eternal punishments, and how to obtain the eternal blessings of God[r].

BOOK SECOND.

Book second commences with a reference to the first. Theophilus speaks to Autolycus. I expounded to you the nature

[n] c. 10. [o] c. 11. [p] c. 12. [q] c. 13. [r] c. 14.

of piety: then we bade each other a hearty farewell. You afterwards urged me to give a fuller account of our doctrines, and I now wish in this writing to demonstrate the foolishness of the worship in which you engage[s]. It seems laughable to me that artists should make gods out of stone and suchlike materials, and that the people who buy them should worship them, and that even the artists should assist in the worship, though they at one time looked on them as mere stone. Those who read mythological stories are in the same plight. They read of the birth of the gods, and of similar events, and straightway forget all this when they worship them[t]. Moreover, if the gods were then in the habit of begetting, why do they not beget now? And how is it that Olympus was inhabited by them in olden times but is now desolate? And why did Zeus dwell in Ida? Why was he not everywhere? Why did he leave Ida? Did he die, or go somewhere else? He died, and his tomb is in Crete[u]. The philosophers are equally at fault in regard to God, some saying that He does not exist, or takes care only of Himself, some that there is no Providence, while the Platonics maintain that not only is God uncreated, but that matter likewise existed from all eternity, thus making matter equal to God[x]. The poets differ widely from the philosophers. For Homer makes Ocean the origin both of the world and of the gods[y], though Ocean is nothing but water, and not a god at all. Hesiod[z] likewise assigns an origin to the gods and to the world itself, and makes most of the gods posterior to the world[a]. Hesiod mentions a creation[b], but he does not say who the creator was[c]. The Greek stories and genealogies also make it manifest that the gods were born and were really men. Theophilus appeals especially to a writer, Satyrus, on the Alexandrian families, who traces the genealogy of Ptolemy Philopater up to Dionysus, and who asserts that the Alexandrian tribes were named from the descendants of Dionysus[d]. Moreover, the Greek

---

[s] c. 1.   [t] c. 2.   [u] c. 3.   [x] c. 4.   [y] Il. xiv. 201.
[z] Theog. 73, 74, 104–115.   [a] c. 5.   [b] Theog. 116–133.
[c] c. 6.   [d] c. 7.

writers, historians, philosophers, and poets disagree in their statements. Some say that matter is uncreated, others that it is created. Some say that there is a providence, some that there is not. Aratus[e], for instance, asserts that all things are full of God, while Sophocles asserts that there is no providence in anything. Homer, Simonides, Euripides, Menander speak of a providence, and even Sophocles elsewhere recognises it. Against their will these poets confess their ignorance. Inspired by demons, they spoke in a deceptive spirit, but sometimes they wakened up in their souls and spoke things in harmony with the prophets, with regard to the monarchy of God, and the judgment, and suchlike[f]. The prophets were holy men inspired by God, and spoke always in harmony with each other[g]. They agreed in their account of the creation. They were able to do this, because it was the Logos who was present at the creation with God, that came down to the prophets and spoke through them[h]. Theophilus quotes the account by Moses of the creation as given in the first chapter of Genesis[i]. No man could adequately explain the greatness of the six days' creation. Some of the heathen writers tried to give a narrative of it, but they seldom hit the truth, and the effect of the little truth which they had was completely marred by its intermixture with error[k]. Theophilus now proceeds to explain the first chapter of Genesis, often verse by verse. He confines himself to a purely material explanation in chapter 13. He then finds in the varieties of plant-life the signs of a resurrection. He likens the world to the sea, the Churches to islands with good harbours, the sects to rocky and dangerous islands[l]. Then on the fourth day the lights were created—the types of a great mystery. For the sun is a type of God, and the moon of man. In like manner the three days before the lights are types of the triad—God, his Logos, and his Wisdom. The brilliant fixed stars are the types of the prophets: the less brilliant are the righteous: the planets are those who rebel

[e] Phænom. 1-9. [f] c. 8. [g] c. 9. [h] c. 10.
[i] c. 11. [k] c. 12. [l] c. 14.

against God[m]. On the fifth, animals made from water were produced. They were blessed by God in order to show the blessings of baptism. The carnivorous birds and monsters of the deep are types of transgressors, the herbivorous of the righteous who do not injure the weaker[n]. On the sixth day quadrupeds and wild beasts were made. They were types of men who were ignorant of God. They were called θηρία, 'wild beasts,' from θηριοῦσθαι, 'to become wild,' not because they were originally wild, but because when man transgressed they transgressed with him[o]. The work of creating man is so great that man himself cannot describe it. The language used in Scripture in speaking of his creation is intended to convey a notion of his dignity. All things were subjected to him, and his food was to be only from the fruits of the earth; and animals were also to live on the productions of the soil[p]. Theophilus now proceeds to give an account of the creation of man, and his location in Eden and his fall, quoting Gen. ii. 4—iii. 19[q]. Theophilus supposes Autolycus to object, "You say that God should not be contained in a place, and how do you say now that He walks in paradise?" Theophilus replies by expounding the doctrine of the Logos[r]. The pains of women in childbirth and the despised condition of serpents are proofs of the truth of the sacred narrative[s]. God had made plants and trees before; but those in paradise were of especial beauty, and elsewhere there were no such trees as those of life and knowledge. Man was to work here: that is, to keep the commandment of God[t]. The tree of knowledge was good, but man was as yet a babe and could not receive the knowledge worthily. Besides, God wished to test his obedience, just as children ought to submit to their parents. It was his own disobedience, therefore, that made him be turned out of the garden of Eden[u]. His expulsion was really a blessing, that he might not remain in sin for ever. In his exile he had to pay the penalty of his sins, and then through death he is refashioned[x]. Man was made neither mortal nor

[m] c. 15.   [n] c. 16.   [o] c. 17.   [p] c. 18.   [q] cc. 19, 20, 21.
[r] c. 22.   [s] c. 23.   [t] c. 24.   [u] c. 25.   [x] c. 26.

immortal. His mortality or immortality was made dependent on his conduct. He brought death on himself, but now he who obeys the will of God can acquire eternal life. When Adam was cast forth from the garden, he knew Eve his wife. She had been made from his side to show that there was but one God, and that their goodwill to each other might be greater. There is a trace of Eve's being deceived by the serpent in the cry 'Evan^z.' Theophilus remarks in this place that the history opens up here and would demand greater space and exposition. He therefore refers his readers to Genesis. He then relates the death of Abel through Cain, who was influenced by the devil[a]. He then gives the descendants of Cain, and relates their inventions, which were long anterior to the time of Apollo and Orpheus. He refers his readers to another work for the history of Noah[b]. After the deluge there was a beginning of cities and kings. Theophilus gives a list of the names contained in Genesis x., and then proceeds to narrate the dispersion, and after that he gives the names of various kings[c]. Theophilus next states how the tribes of men were spread over the whole earth[d]. The philosophers, poets, and historians among the heathens were born long after these events, and therefore could not relate them truly, unless they were inspired. But that they were not inspired is proved by their not foretelling events. The Christians alone have the truth[e]. It is your business, therefore, to examine the sayings of God, spoken through the prophets. They were sent to teach men that there is one God, and to urge them to refrain from every vice[f]. The divine law forbids the worship not only of idols, but of the sun, moon, and stars, and commands us to worship only the one true God in holiness of heart. Moses speaks of the oneness of God, and so do Isaiah and Jeremiah, describing also the creation of the world and the formation of man. All the prophets agree in all things with each other. They also rebuked those who seemed to be wise, on account of the hardness of their heart[g].

[y] c. 27.   [z] c. 28.   [a] c. 29.   [b] c. 30.   [c] c. 31.
[d] c. 32.   [e] c. 33.   [f] c. 34.   [g] c. 35.

The Sibyl, who was a prophetess among the Greeks, also reproaches the human race in the same way. Theophilus here makes a large extract from the Sibylline verses [h]. Some also of the poets have spoken of the punishments of the wicked, as Æschylus, Euripides, and Archilochus; and some have taught that God sees all things and waits till He will judge, as Dionysius, Æschylus, Simonides, Euripides, and Sophocles. They stole these teachings from the law and the prophets [i]. The poets also, such as Timocles, teach God's providence, his care even for the dead as well as the living, and while apparently teaching one thing they have taught another. Thus speaking of a multitude of gods they came to the unity of God: and denying that there was sensibility after death they have confessed it. Thus Homer, Iliad xvi. 856; xxii. 362; xxiii. 71. All these things the man who seeks the wisdom of God will learn. Try, therefore, to have frequent conferences with me, that you may accurately learn the truth, hearing the living voice [k].

BOOK THIRD.

Theophilus to Autolycus. Since you yet, after all our conferences, look upon our religion as nonsense, thinking that our writings are recent, I shall prove their antiquity to you [l]. Writers ought either to have been eye-witnesses of what they describe, or to have learned them accurately from those who saw them. In this point of view the principal Greek writers, Homer, the tragic and comic poets, and the philosophers, are failures [m]. They neither knew the truth nor urged others on to it. Their statements are contradictory. Some have denied the existence of God and providence; and some have attributed horrible crimes and vices to the gods [n]. I should not adduce these stories, did I not see you hesitate in regard to the truth, and too much inclined to believe the false tales told of us, that we hold our wives in common and mingle

[h] c. 36.   [i] c. 37.   [k] c. 38.   [l] c. 1.   [m] c. 2.   [n] c. 3.

indiscriminately, that we have sexual intercourse with our own sisters, and that we eat human flesh. They say also that our doctrines are new, and cannot be proved[o]. They blame us for eating human flesh, while it is themselves that are guilty. The Stoics say that fathers should be cooked and eaten by their sons. Diogenes says that children should sacrifice and devour their parents, and Herodotus relates instances of human beings being eaten[p]. The philosophers are equally at fault in regard to illicit intercourse. Plato taught a community of wives, and Epicurus recommends sexual intercourse with mothers and sisters, even contrary to law. They even predicate such things of the gods[q]. They assert that there are gods, but notwithstanding they reduce them to nothing, some saying that they are composed of atoms, some that they go into atoms and suchlike. Plato makes the gods material; Pythagoras denies a providence; Clitomachus, Critias, Protagoras, and Euhemerus are atheistic. Philemon and Aristo in their verses give a different account of God and providence. Thus some assert that there is a God, and that He takes care of men, and others that He neither is nor takes care of men[r]. They attribute unlawful deeds to the gods, to Jupiter, Juno, Cybele; Jupiter Latiaris who thirsts for human blood; Attis, or Jupiter Tragœdus. So that they attribute to the gods the indiscriminate intercourse and eating of human flesh which they falsely attribute to us[s]. We acknowledge but one God; we know that there is a Providence, and that God teaches us to act righteously. He has given us his law in Exod. xx. 3–8, 11–17. This law was given through Moses to the Jews whom God rescued and led out of Egypt[t]. They were strangers in the land of Egypt. When God led them forth, He commanded, "Ye shall not crush the stranger," &c. Exod. xxiii. 9[u]. Besides giving the law, God sent prophets to teach them. They urge to change of mind. Thus Isaiah lv. 6, 7, xxxi. 6; Ezek. xviii. 21–23; Jer. vi. 9[x]. The prophets also speak of righteousness in the same way as the

[o] c. 4. [p] c. 5. [q] c. 6. [r] c. 7.
[s] c. 8. [t] c. 9. [u] c. 10. [x] c. 11.

law and the gospels. Thus Isaiah i. 16; lviii. 6-8; Jer. vi. 16; Hosea xii. 6; Joel ii. 16; Zech. vii. 9[y]. The holy Word teaches with regard to chastity, that we must not sin even in thought. Thus Solomon in Prov. iv. 25; vi. 27. But more distinctly does the evangelic voice speak, Matt. v. 28, 32[z]. We are taught also to be kind not only to those of the same tribe, but to those who hate us. Thus Isaiah lxvi. 5, and the gospel, Matt. v. 44, 46. Those who do good are not to boast, Matt. vi. 3. And the divine word gives instructions with regard to obeying authorities, &c., 1 Tim. ii. 2[a]. How could those who learn such things be guilty of the indiscriminate intercourse, the incest, and the eating of human flesh, of which they are accused? We do not even visit the shows or the theatres, lest our eyes or ears might be polluted[b]. I will now show you that the Christian religion is not new nor fabulous, but that it is older and truer than all the poets and writers who wrote in uncertainty. Those ancient writers who said that the world was created, varied in their estimate of its age. Apollonius the Egyptian said that 153,075 years had passed. Plato also uttered a great deal of nonsense on this point. Plato spoke from conjecture[c], and longed for a divine instructor. Some of the poets also confessed that they had learned from divine providence. How much more shall we know the truth, who have received it from the prophets! They always spoke in harmony with each other[d]. Plato speaks of a flood, but makes it partial; and there is another story about a flood connected with the names of Deucalion and Pyrrha. Clymenus also is mentioned as being in a second flood. Moses gives the true account of the flood. His writings show that it was not partial[e], and that there was no second flood. There were only eight saved in the ark. All the rest of the human race were destroyed. The remains of the ark are said to exist yet on the Arabic (Armenian) mountains[f]. Moses led the Jews who were expelled from the land of Egypt by king Pharaoh. Here Theophilus

[y] c. 12. [z] c. 13. [a] c. 14. [b] c. 15.
[c] c. 16. [d] c. 17. [e] c. 18. [f] c. 19.

gives a list of the successors of Pharaoh, and the periods during which they reigned[g]. Manetho spoke against Moses and the Hebrews, saying that they were expelled from Egypt on account of leprosy. He is very inaccurate in his account of the chronology; but he is forced against his will to confess two things—that the Hebrews that went into Egypt were shepherds, and that they went forth from Egypt; so that, even from the Egyptian records to which he appealed, it can be shown that Moses and those with him were nine hundred or a thousand years before the Trojan war[h]. With regard to the building of Solomon's temple, there are documents in the Tyrian archives which show that it took place one hundred and thirty-four years eight months before the Tyrians founded Carthage. These documents were written by Hieromus king of Tyre, who corresponded with Solomon. The date is proved by Menander the Ephesian, who gives the successors of Hieromus and the periods of their reign down to the time of the founding of Carthage. The sum of the periods is 155 years 8 months. But the temple was built in the twelfth year of Hierom's reign, therefore 133 years 8 months before the founding of Carthage[i]. From the writings of Manetho the Egyptian and Menander the Ephesian, also from those of Josephus, it is proved that the writings of Moses, and even of the prophets who came after him, were earlier than the writings of the Greek poets, philosophers, and historians. I shall now give a more complete account of the dates, trusting to the books of Moses, who described both the events before the flood and the events after it. "And I pray for favour from the only God, that I may accurately speak the whole truth according to his will, that you and every one who reads this work may be guided by his truth and favour[k]." Theophilus hereupon gives a list of dates, beginning with Adam. Letters are used for figures; and, as is usual in such cases, the readings vary much. Otto's arrangement of the numbers gives the following result. From Adam to the flood 2242 years. From Adam

[g] c. 20.   [h] c. 21.   [i] c. 22.   [k] c. 23.

to the end of the captivity 4954. Theophilus has followed Scripture up to this point. He now calculates from the reign of Cyrus, who was contemporaneous with Tarquinius Superbus. He gives the years of the Republic and the emperors, and finds that from Adam to the death of Marcus Aurelius the years are 5695[1]. This calculation proves the absurdity of Plato's assertion, that two hundred millions of years had elapsed since the flood, and of that of Apollonius mentioned above[m]. Our writings are therefore more ancient and more true than those of the Greeks. Thallus says that Belus and Kronos were contemporaneous, but Belus lived after the Trojan war. Moses flourished before it. Therefore Kronos or Saturn was long subsequent to the time of Moses, according to the testimony of Thallus. Berosus also bears testimony to the truth of the holy writings in several particulars[n]. The Greeks make no mention of the histories that give the truth; first, because they only recently became acquainted with letters, and second, because they sinned, and still sin in not making mention of God, but discussing vain and useless matters. Thus they have not found the truth[o].

V. DOCTRINES OF THEOPHILUS.

God.—In the remaining work of Theophilus there are very precise and definite notions of God. He supposes a man to say to him, "Relate to me the form of God." To this Theophilus answers, "Hear, O man; the form of God is inexpressible and indescribable, and cannot be seen with fleshly eyes. For in his glory He is unfathomable; in his greatness He is incomprehensible; in his height He is inconceivable: He is incomparable in strength, unsearchable in his wisdom, [He is beyond all advice]; He is inimitable in goodness, and his beneficence baffles description. For if I call Him light, I speak of his own creature; if I call Him Logos (Reason), I speak of his governing principle ($ἀρχή$); if I call Him mind, I speak of his thinking; if I call Him spirit,

---

[1] See Otto, Prolegg., p. liv.
[n] c. 29.
[m] cc. 24, 25, 26, 27, 28.
[o] c. 30.

I speak of his breath; if I call Him wisdom, I speak of his offspring; if I call Him strength, I speak of his sway; if I call Him power, I am mentioning his activity; if providence, I but mention his goodness; if I call Him kingdom, I mention his glory; if I call Him lord, I mention his being judge; if I call Him judge, I speak of Him as being just; if I call Him Father, I speak of Him as being all things[p]; if I call Him fire, I but mention his anger. You will say to me, Is God angry? Yes; He is angry with those who act wickedly, but good and kind and merciful to those who love and fear Him; for He is an instructor[q] of the pious and father of the righteous, but He is a judge and punisher of the impious.

"He is without beginning, for He is unbegotten [uncreated], and He is free from all change, inasmuch as He is immortal. And He is called God ($\theta\epsilon\delta s$), because He placed ($\tau\epsilon\theta\epsilon\iota\kappa\epsilon\nu\alpha\iota$) all things on security afforded by Himself, and on account of $\theta\epsilon\epsilon\iota\nu$; for $\theta\epsilon\epsilon\iota\nu$ is running, and moving, and being active, and nourishing, and foreseeing, and governing, and making all things alive. But He is Lord, because He rules over the whole; Father, because He is before the whole; fashioner and maker, because He is creator and maker of the whole; the Highest, because He is above all; Almighty, because He Himself rules and embraces all: for the heights of the heaven, and the depths of the abysses, and the ends of the earth are in his hand, and there is no place of his rest. For the heavens are his work, the earth is his creation, the sea is his workmanship, man is his formation and his image; sun, moon, and stars are his elements, made for signs, and seasons, and days, and years, that they may serve and be slaves to man; and all things God has made out of things that were not into things that are, in order that his greatness may be known and understood through his works[r]."

[p] The text is supposed to be corrupt here. Otto proposes, "I speak of Him as loving."

[q] Maranus remarks that παιδευτής here probably means 'chastiser;' Theophilus referring to the difference of God's punishment of the righteous and the wicked.   [r] lib. i. cc. 3, 4, pp. 71, 72.

This extract contains almost all that we learn of God from Theophilus. There are three points in it however that demand further notice. The first is the approach towards the consideration of God as purely immaterial. Theophilus does not, as some have asserted, maintain the immateriality of God. It will be noticed that in the passage quoted he does not deny that God has an εἶδος, or form, but he simply says that this form cannot be expressed. In another passage he speaks of God as if He were space: " It is the peculiarity of God the Highest and Almighty, and of the being who is truly God, not only that He is everywhere, but that He sees all things and hears all, but is by no means contained in place; for if He were, then the place containing Him would be greater than He; for that which contains is greater than that which is contained. For God is not contained, but is Himself the place of all" (τόπος τῶν ὅλων [s]). In another passage he describes God as " being the place of Himself [t]."

The second point is the distinct enunciation of the doctrine that God may be known from his works. Every man has originally the power of thus seeing God. But no one does see God unless his life be pure. " Show me thy man," says Theophilus, "and I will show thee my God[u]." " When sin is in a man, such a man cannot see God[v]." " God is seen only by those who are able to see Him when they have the eyes of their soul opened[w]." " If thou perceivest these things, [that God made the world, heavens and earth, and clouds,] living chastely, and holily, and righteously, thou canst see God. But before all, let faith and the fear of God have rule in thy heart, and then shalt thou understand these things. When thou shalt put off the mortal and put on incorruption, then shalt thou see God worthily[x]."

The third point is the enunciation of the doctrine of creation. This enunciation is made several times. In opposing the Platonic notion that matter was uncreated, he remarks: " What is there great if God made the world out of existent

[s] lib. ii. c. 3, p. 81 E. [t] Ibid. c. 10, p. 88 B. [u] Ibid. i. c. 2, p. 70 A.
[v] lib. i. c. 2, p. 70 C. [w] Ibid. p. 70 B. [x] Ibid. c. 7, p. 74 B.

materials? For an artist, when he gets material from any one, makes what he likes out of it. But the power of God is manifested in this, that He makes out of things that are not whatsoever He wishes [y]." Theophilus draws out the points of contrast between this creative power of God and the merely constructive power of man [z]. He also expressly mentions his belief that matter was created by God. He thinks that this original creation of matter is pointed out in the words, " In the beginning (or, as he takes it, in the governing principle) God created the heavens and the earth;" and that from this matter " God made and fashioned the world [a]." He asserts that if matter were uncreated it would be unchangeable, and if unchangeable, then it would be equal to God (ἰσόθεος); " for that which is created is mutable and alterable, but that which is uncreated is immutable (ἄτρεπτον) and unalterable" (ἀναλλοίωτον [b]).

Theophilus insists strongly on the belief in and worship of God alone. He says: " We also confess that God exists, but that He is one, the founder, and maker, and fashioner, of this entire universe, and we know that all things are arranged by his providence, but by Him alone; and we have learned a holy law, but we have as lawgiver Him who is really God, who teaches us to act righteously, to be pious, and to do good [c]." Then Theophilus quotes the ten commandments, with the exception of the third and fourth. In fact, one of the great reasons which Theophilus assigns for God's "patiently enduring until He shall judge man [d]," is that He wishes to teach them that there is one God. " The God, and Father, and Founder of the whole did not abandon humanity, but gave a law and sent holy prophets to bear a message to the race of men, and teach them so that each one of us should re-awaken and know fully that there is one God [e]." Theophilus describes the mode of worshipping God. " We must serve Him who

[y] lib. ii. c. 4, p. 82 D. See also lib. ii. c. 13, p. 92 B.
[z] lib. ii. c. 13.
[a] Ibid. c. 10, p. 89 A.
[b] lib. ii. c. 4, p. 82 C.
[c] Ibid. iii. c. 9, p. 122 D.
[d] lib. ii. c. 37, p. 115 B.
[e] Ibid. c. 34, p. 110 B C.

alone is truly God, and Maker of all, in holiness of heart, and in all sincerity of purpose" (εἰλικρινεῖ γνώμῃ [f]).

Trinity.—Before proceeding to the doctrine of the Logos, it is necessary to examine what Theophilus says of a Trinity. He uses the word 'triad' in reference to this subject. He says that the first three days of creation were "types of the triad— God, and his Reason (Logos), and his Wisdom [g]." In explaining the words "Let us make man" he remarks that God spoke "to no other than to his own Reason and his own Wisdom [h]." The peculiarity of this doctrine is that one requires considerable care to distinguish between acts of God's reason and God's wisdom; and yet we have here both Reason and Wisdom hypostatized. Even Theophilus himself could not regularly distinguish them: for we shall find him calling the Logos also the wisdom of God. In the only other passage, however, in which the three are placed together Theophilus plainly identifies the wisdom with the Spirit. "God, through his Logos and Wisdom, made all things; for 'with his word (λόγῳ) the heavens were made firm, and all the host of them by his Spirit [i].'" But, as if to make the confusion complete, we shall find him calling the Logos also the Spirit. Theophilus does not seem to have been startled by any of the difficulties connected with the doctrine of the Trinity. The expression "*his* Logos and *his* Spirit" gives his idea of the relation of the Logos and Spirit to God: and yet their belonging to God did not in his eyes destroy their personality.

The Logos.—Theophilus does not mention the Logos by the name of Jesus or Christ. There is nothing surprising in this, as the subject of his work leads him to speak principally of the creation. The doctrine of Theophilus with regard to the Logos is given mainly in two passages. He distinguishes between the λόγος ἐνδιάθετος and the λόγος προφορικός. He regards the Logos as the organ through whom God created the world, as the inspirer of the prophets, and as the being

---

[f] lib. ii. c. 35, p. 110 D.
[g] Ibid. c. 15, p. 94 D.
[h] lib. ii. c. 18, p. 96 D.
[i] Psalm xxxiii. 6: lib. i. c. 7, p. 74 D.

who appeared to the Old Testament patriarchs. He also identifies the Logos and the Wisdom, and ascribes to them the same functions. The first extract gives most exactly the ideas which Theophilus had of the relation of the Logos to the Father. Theophilus wishes to explain how it is said in Genesis that God walked in the garden. "The God and Father of all cannot be contained, and is not found in a place, for there is no place of his rest. But his Logos, through whom He made all things, being his power and his wisdom, taking up the person (πρόσωπον, 'mask' j) of the Father and Lord of all, went to the garden in the character (προσώπῳ) of God, and conversed with Adam. For the divine writing itself teaches us that Adam said he had heard the voice. But what else is the voice but the Logos of God, who is also his Son? Not as the poets and mythographers speak of sons of gods begotten from intercourse, but as truth expounds, the Logos (Reason) that always exists (ἐνδιάθετος) in the heart of God. For before anything came into being He had Him as a counsellor, being his own mind (νοῦν) and thought. But when God wished to make those things which he determined on, He begot this uttered Logos (προφορικός), the first-born of all creation, not being thereby Himself emptied of reason, but having begotten reason and always conversing with his reason. Hence the holy writings teach us, and all the Spirit-bearing [inspired] men (πνευματοφόροι), one of whom, John, says, 'In the beginning was the Logos, and the Logos was with God;' showing that at first God was alone, and the Logos (Reason) was in Him. Then he says, 'The Logos was God: all things came into existence through Him, and apart from Him not one thing came into existence.' The Logos then being God and born (πεφυκώς, 'naturally arising from') of God, whenever the Father of the whole wishes, He sends Him to any place; and

---

j The word πρόσωπον is here used quite differently from the way in which it was afterwards employed in the doctrine of the Trinity: ἀναλαμβάνειν τὸ πρόσωπον is simply to act the part, the metaphor being taken from the theatre, as Humphry remarks in his note on this passage.

He, coming, is both heard and seen, being sent by Him, and is found in a place^k." The other passage runs thus: "God, having his own Logos (ἐνδιάθετον) placed in his own bowels, begot Him, *belching*^l Him forth along with his own wisdom before the whole. He had this Logos as a helper (ὑπουργόν) in those things which were created by Him, and He made all things by means of Him. He is called 'governing principle' (ἀρχή) because He rules, and is Lord of all things fashioned through Himself. He, then, being Spirit of God, and governing principle, and wisdom and power of the Highest, came down to the prophets, and through them spoke of the creation of the world and of all the other things. For the prophets were not when the world came into existence, but the wisdom of God which was in Him, and his holy word (Logos), which was always present with Him^m." Theophilus here and elsewhere calls the Logos the governing principle (ἀρχή) of Godⁿ. He attached this meaning to the ἀρχῇ translated in our version, 'In the beginning.' He calls Him also the commandment of God, and attributes to Him the lighting of the earth, and other separate parts of the creation^o. Though Theophilus does not speak of Christ, yet there is one passage in which he at first sight appears to refer to the historical Christ. He begins a reference to a saying of Christ thus: "The holy word (Logos) not only teaches us not to sin in act, but not even in thought^p." He then quotes Solomon, and then he quotes Matt. v. 28. But the words ὁ ἅγιος λόγος are better taken in the sense of the expression of the divine mind as given in the Scriptures, than as meaning the Logos.

The Spirit.—Theophilus allowed the doctrine of the Spirit to remain in his mind in a confused and unripe state. For if he had thought of the matter, how could he clearly distinguish between the mind of God, the reason of God, and

---

^k lib. ii. c. 22, p. 100 A–D.

^l The expression 'belching' or 'vomiting' refers to the first verse of Psalm xlv., xliv. in the Sept.

^m lib. ii. c. 10, p. 88 B; c. 13, p. 125 D.   ⁿ Ibid. i. c. 3, p. 71 A; ii. c. 13, p. 92 B.

^o lib. ii. c. 13, p. 92 D.   ^p Ibid. iii. c. 13, p. 125 D.

God's wisdom? What the mind does, the wisdom does. Accordingly we have seen that Theophilus called the Logos the Spirit of God, and wisdom, and that he described the Logos as uttering through the prophets the very words which he elsewhere ascribes to the spirit. Yet, as we have also seen, he gave personality to the spirit even in the very same passage [q]. He distinguishes the wisdom numerically from the Logos. His explanation of the spirit is also indefinite. He tells, in a passage already quoted, that the spirit is God's breath, God's respiration ($\dot{a}\nu a\pi\nu o\acute{\eta}$ [r]). God is said to give his "spirit which nourishes the earth." It is "God's breath ($\pi\nu o\acute{\eta}$) that gives life to all things." "If He were to keep his spirit (or breath) to Himself, all things would collapse." And man is said to breathe his spirit or breath ($\pi\nu\epsilon\hat{u}\mu a$ [s]). And he keeps up this idea in speaking of the spirit moving on the waters. "By the spirit," he says, "which is borne above the waters, he means that which God gave for animating creation as He gave life to man, mixing what is fine with what is fine; for the spirit is fine and the water is fine, that the spirit may nourish the water, and the water, penetrating everywhere along with the spirit, may nourish creation. For the spirit being one, and holding the place of light, was between the water and the heaven, in order that the darkness might not in any way communicate with the heaven, which was nearer God, before God said 'Let there be light [t].'" Theophilus means here to say that the spirit is to all creation what life (soul) is to man; that the external principle of this life of all things is water; but that this water was as it were dead until the spirit or breath of God moved on it, then the water became a living principle, and the two fine substances, or whatever else they might be called, being combined, are now the causes of all life in external nature [u]. The spirit is thus viewed as a pervasive

---

[q] lib. ii. c. 10, p. 88 C. quoted in p. 89. [r] Ibid. i. c. 3, p. 71 A.
[s] lib. i. c. 7, p. 74 A. [t] Ibid. ii. c. 13, p. 92 C.
[u] See Chrysost. Homil. in Gen. iii., quoted by Maranus, and given by Humphry and Otto.

influence. Theophilus speaks of the spirit as inclosing all. He says, "As the pomegranate, with the rind containing it, has within it many abodes and compartments which are separated by tissues, and has also many seeds dwelling in it, so the whole creation is contained by the spirit of God, and the spirit which contains is along with the whole creation contained by the hand of God [v]." Some have thought that Theophilus here refers to the Logos, but there is not the slightest proof of this in the works of Theophilus, and no good reason for it. Most commentators affirm that Theophilus does not speak of the Holy Spirit, but of the spirit of God, as if it were the spirit of the world. But then the question remains, Did Theophilus look on this spirit as personal or impersonal? And if personal, as he certainly seems to take it, then were there two spirits? It is most probable that Theophilus had not thought accurately enough on these points, that he would have identified the one spirit with the other, but that he would not have perceived the consequences which seem to us to follow from the identification. Theophilus, as we have seen already, calls the wisdom the offspring of God [x]. And he speaks of God "belching forth the Logos along with the wisdom." This might mean "by means of the wisdom;" but the words more naturally imply that the Logos and the wisdom came forth from God at the same time, before the creation of the world. Theophilus several times speaks of the Holy Spirit as speaking through the prophets. Thus, "We are taught all these facts by the Holy Spirit which spoke through Moses and the other prophets [y];" "We are taught by the Holy Spirit who spoke in the holy prophets, and announced all things before-hand [z]." He has the peculiar expression "the holy prophets who contained the Holy Spirit of God [a]." In almost all the passages where the spirit is spoken of as using the prophets, Theophilus calls him the Holy Spirit. In one passage Theophilus de-

[v] lib. i. c. 5, p. 72 C.   [x] Ibid. c. 3, p. 71 B.   [y] Ibid. ii. c. 30, p. 106 C.
[z] lib. ii. c. 33, p. 110 A.   [a] Ibid. iii. c. 17, p. 128 B.

scribes Moses as writing "by means of the Holy Spirit [b]." Theophilus speaks of the prophets as containing "the wisdom which is from God, through which wisdom they spoke [c]."

The passages in which Theophilus seems to speak impersonally of the Spirit are few, and most of these Theophilus himself would probably have regarded as personal. Thus, Theophilus not unfrequently describes the prophets as speaking with one and the same spirit [d], and in an hypothetical clause he uses the words, "they spoke by a divine and pure spirit [e]." The only other sentence in which one may doubt whether Theophilus spoke impersonally is in lib. ii. c. 38, p. 116 D, where he describes a man "seeking the wisdom of God," but in this case he is probably using wisdom in its common sense.

The passages adduced show sufficiently what relation Theophilus supposed to subsist between the Father of all, and the Logos, and Spirit. The Logos and Spirit are in the same relation to the Father as a man's reason and wisdom are to the man himself. They are completely under his control, do his behests, and their acts are entirely his acts. Of the relation of the Son to the Spirit nothing is said.

Angels, Devil, Demons.—Theophilus says nothing of angels, and little of the devil and demons. He had discussed the questions connected with the devil in another work. He mentions him in connexion with man's fall. He attributes to the serpent the attempt to introduce among men the worship of a multitude of gods [f]. He supposes the calling of Evoe or Evan in the worship of Bacchus to be an exclamation instituted by the serpent, because Eve was in the beginning deceived by the serpent and became the originator of sin. He speaks of him as "the evil-doing demon, who is also called Satan, who then spoke to her through the serpent, and who still works ($\dot{\epsilon}\nu\epsilon\rho\gamma\hat{\omega}\nu$) in those men who are inspired by him." "He is called demon and dragon

[b] lib. iii. c. 23, p. 133 B.   [c] Ibid. ii. c. 9, p. 88 A.
[d] lib. iii. c. 12, p. 125 A; Ibid. ii. c. 35, p. 111 C.
[e] lib. ii. c. 33, p. 109 D.   [f] Ibid. c. 28, p. 104 B.

because he ran away from God, for at first he was an angel[f]." Theophilus also attributes to his energy the murder of Abel by Cain[g].

With regard to demons, Theophilus remarks that the heathen poets were inspired by them; that even in his time these demons were exorcised in the name of the really true God, and the deceptive spirits themselves confessed that they were demons[h].

Man.—Theophilus thus describes the purpose for which man was created: "God, not needing anything Himself, and existing before the ages, wished to make man, that He [God] might become known to him. For him, therefore, God prepared the world[i]." He finds in the Mosaic account of man's creation proof of his dignity; "for when God says, 'Let us make man according to our image and likeness,' first of all He points out the dignity of man. For God having made all things by his Reason, and reckoning them all as byeworks, He reckons the making of man the only eternal work worthy of his hands[k]. Moreover, as if needing assistance, God is found saying, 'Let us make man after our image and likeness[l].' He also put all things under him[m]." Theophilus thus sets forth the prospects of man, if he had remained sinless. "God removed him from the earth of which he had been made into paradise, giving him the means of progress, so that increasing and having become perfect, and having, moreover, been declared god, he might ascend even into heaven possessed of eternity[n]." And all that he had to do was to work; that is, to keep the commandment of God[o]. The place of his abode was paradise. Theophilus regarded paradise as a place on earth. "That the paradise is earth, and was planted on earth, the Scripture says, Gen. ii. 8[p]." He differs here from many writers of his own time, who regarded

---

[f] lib. ii. c. 28, p. 104 D.
[g] Ibid. c. 29, p. 150 B.
[h] lib. ii. c. 8, p. 87 C D.
[i] Ibid. c. 10, p. 88 B.
[k] The reading ἀΐδιον has been changed into ἰδίων, 'the only work worthy of his own hands.'
[l] lib. ii. c. 18, p. 96 C D.
[m] lib. ii. c. 18, p. 96 D.
[n] Ibid. c. 24, p. 101 D.
[o] lib. ii. c. 24, p. 102 A.
[p] Ibid. p. 101 B.

paradise as between heaven and earth. He seems to notice this opinion, for he says, "Thus the district paradise was between earth and heaven, as far as beauty was concerned[q]." There is no reason to suppose that he regarded paradise as intermediate between heaven and earth in a local sense. It was merely as respects beauty.

Theophilus explains the ultimate destiny intended for man, which he here sets forth, by a parenthetical clause on the nature of man and his abode. He says, "Man was made in the middle, being neither entirely mortal nor entirely immortal, but capable of both. In like manner also the garden (paradise) in respect of beauty was made a mean between the world and heaven[r]."

Adam was created a child, and therefore could not properly receive knowledge. "But in age this Adam was still a babe (νήπιος), wherefore he was not yet able to contain the knowledge worthily[s]." Maranus supposes that Theophilus in calling Adam a babe alludes only to his innocence or his recent creation[t]. It is not likely that he would suppose Adam and Eve to be babes like other children, and therefore he must have supposed that their babyhood must have taken place in bodies larger than those of our babes. God therefore forbade him to eat of the tree of knowledge. There was nothing of a deadly nature in the tree, for knowledge is a blessing when rightly used. But children are nourished with milk, not with strong food. God wished simply to try Adam, and at the same time He was desirous that Adam should remain simple and innocent in his childhood for some time. But Adam disobeyed, and his disobedience caused him to be cast out of paradise. The tree of knowledge was not evil, but through disobedience man endured labour, pain, sorrow, and at last fell under death[u].

Theophilus expounds more fully the nature of man in lib. ii. c. 27. "Man," he says, "was by nature neither mortal nor immortal. For if He had made him immortal from the

[q] lib. ii. c. 24, p. 101 D. [r] Ibid. [s] Ibid. c. 25, p. 102 A.
[t] Pref. part ii. c. v. p. xxii. [u] lib. ii. c. 25.

beginning, He would have made him god. Again, if He had made him mortal, God would then appear to be the author of his death. He made him, then, neither immortal nor mortal, but, as mentioned above, capable of both, so that if he should incline to the things of immortality, keeping the commandment of God, he should receive as reward from Him immortality, and should become god; but if he should turn to the things of death, disobeying God, he should himself be the cause of death to himself. For God made man free and with power over himself."

We have already noticed the part which Theophilus assigns to Satan and Eve in the origination of sin. Theophilus nowhere connects the sin of Adam with any of his race. There is nothing directly contrary to the doctrine of original sin, and nothing in favour of it. He would probably have rejected it on account of the stress which he lays on the doctrine of free-will; but this is, of course, merely a matter of conjecture. All that he says about death, for instance, is that when Cain killed Abel "there was an entrance of death into this world to journey over the entire race of man up till this time[v]." He maintains, however, that all creation suffers by the fall of man. He speaks of the flesh-eating animals as transgressing the law of God, while other animals keep the law. He says that "all [animals] were created good, exceedingly good by God, but the sin connected with man has made them bad. For when man went astray they also went astray with him[w]." He compares their sin to the sin of servants who, when their master sins, sin along with him. And he adds: "But when man again shall return to a natural life, no longer doing what is evil, these also shall be restored to their original tameness[x]."

From the very first God designed that man should not remain in sin. "God did this as an act of great benevolence to man, that he should not always remain in sin, but in some way like banishing him, He cast him forth from paradise, that paying back the punishment for his sin within an appointed

---

[v] lib. ii. c. 29, p. 105 B.   [w] Ibid. c. 17, p. 96 B.   [x] Ibid.

time, and being chastised, he might afterwards be recalled." Theophilus finds a secret intimation of this in the circumstance that the placing of man in paradise is twice mentioned in Genesis[y], and he thinks that the second placing will be fulfilled after the resurrection and judgment. Even death itself will be an instrument in this restoration. "For as a vessel, when on being fashioned it has some flaw, is remoulded and remade, that it may become new and entire, in like manner is man affected by death. For somehow or other he is broken that he may rise in the resurrection whole; I mean spotless, and righteous, and immortal[a]."

The conditions of his gaining immortality are exactly the same as the original conditions on which he was made neither mortal nor immortal. "As man disobeying brought death upon himself, so obeying the will of God he who wishes can acquire for himself eternal life. For God has given us a law and holy commandments: every one who keeps these can be saved, and obtaining the resurrection, can inherit incorruption[b]." This arrangement is the result of God's free gift, "through his own philanthropy and mercy[c]." The meaning of the text here is doubtful. The words are, "That which man acquired for himself through carelessness and disobedience, this God now gives to him as a gift through his own philanthrophy and pity, when man obeys Him." This most probably means that God forgives man the sins which he committed, and does away with the effects of them. It might mean that God turns *death*, which man procured through his disobedience, into a blessing, so that he may attain incorruption.

Salvation, then, depends entirely on a man's conduct and the state of his heart towards God. Sometimes this state of heart is alone mentioned, and is called faith: "Then shalt thou see the immortal [God], being thyself immortal, if thou now put thy trust in Him[d]." And this faith and the fear

[y] lib. ii. c. 26, p. 103 A.
[a] lib. ii. c. 26, p. 103 B.
[c] lib. ii. c. 27, p. 103 D.
[z] Gen. ii. 8 and ii. 15.
[b] Ibid. c. 27, p. 103 D, p. 104 A.
[d] Ibid. i. c. 7, p. 74 B.

of God ought to take the lead in all things[e]. But more generally good deeds are spoken of either alone or combined with faith. Thus it is said that men become " pleasing to God through faith and righteousness, and well-doing [f]." And in a more exact description of the conditions of salvation it is said that God gave his law and sent his prophets to teach men that there is one God, that they are " to refrain from unlawful idolatry, adultery, and murder, fornication, theft, avarice, false swearing, wrath, and every incontinence and impurity, and not to do to others what they would not wish to be done to themselves; and thus," he adds, " he who acts righteously shall escape the eternal punishments, and be thought worthy of the eternal life from God[g]."

Theophilus says nothing of Christ's work in the salvation of men. But it is easy to perceive from what he has said of the conditions of salvation how he would be compelled to view it. It could be mainly, if not entirely, in exciting men to goodness, to a change of mind. Theophilus once asserts that God effects this change through the Reason (Logos) and the Wisdom. " This [ignorance of God] has happened to you on account of the blindness of your soul and the hardness of your heart. But if you wish, you can be cured. Give yourself up to the physician, and He will prick the eyes of your soul and heart. Who is the physician? It is God, who heals and makes alive through his Reason (Logos) and Wisdom[h]." And in this connexion it is important to note that Theophilus believed that man himself paid the penalty of his own sins[i].

Theophilus mentions several times the necessity of a change of mind (μετάνοια), and alludes expressly to the change of mind characteristic of Christianity. Speaking of the Jewish people, he says, that after they had broken the law, " God being good and merciful, did not wish to destroy them, but He, in addition to giving them the law, afterwards sent prophets from among their brethren to teach and remind them of the

[e] lib. i. c. 7, p. 74 B. [f] Ibid. ii. c. 38, p. 116 D. [g] Ibid. c. 34, p. 110 C.
[h] lib. i. c. 7, p. 74 A. [i] Ibid. ii. c. 26, p. 103 A.

requirements of the law, and to turn them to a change of mind, so that they should no longer sin[i]." Then he quotes several passages from the Old Testament in regard to change of mind, and at the conclusion states that "God wishes to turn the race of men from all their sins[k]." In giving the allegorical interpretation of the creation, he alludes to the Christian μετάνοια. He says, "Those things that were produced from the water were blessed by God, that this might be a proof that all men would receive change of mind and forgiveness of sins through water and the bath of a second birth, if they advanced to the truth, and were re-born, and received a blessing from God[l]." He finds symbols of those who do not change their minds but remain ignorant of God and impious, and given to earthly thoughts, in quadrupeds and wild beasts. "But those," he says, "who turn from their iniquities and live righteously, like birds fly up in soul, thinking of those things that are above and being well-pleasing to the will of God[m]."

Theophilus does not mention the Church or say anything of its constitution. He once, however, speaks of Churches. He compares them to islands with good harbours: "So," he says, "God has given to the world, tossed about on the waves and battered in the storms caused by sins, assemblies (συναγωγάς), I mean holy Churches, in which, as in the good harbours on the islands, are the teachings of the truth, to which those who wish to be saved flee, becoming lovers of the truth, and wishing to escape the wrath and judgment of God[n]." The teachings of error, that is, of the sects (αἱρέσεων), on the other hand, are like rocky islands on which ships are dashed to pieces. Theophilus alludes once to baptism in the extract made already[o]. It is stated there that all who come to the truth, and are re-born, and receive blessing from God, receive change of mind and forgiveness of sins through water and the bath of regeneration. There is not the

---

[i] lib. iii. c. 11, p. 124 A B.
[l] lib. ii. c. 16, p. 95 B.
[n] lib. ii. c. 14, pp. 93, 94.
[k] Ibid. c. 11, p. 124 D.
[m] Ibid. c. 17, p. 95 D, 96 A.
[o] Ibid. c. 16, p. 95 B.

slightest reason to suppose that Theophilus attributed any power to the water. In fact, his language proves the contrary; but he made acceptance of pardon simultaneous with the public confession of Christ. Some have supposed another allusion to baptism in lib. i. c. 12, p. 77 C, "We are anointed with the oil of God." Though we learn from Tertullian that oil was used in baptism, yet the context of this passage makes it likely that Theophilus did not use the words literally but metaphorically. He makes no allusion to the Thanksgiving, and the only remarks in regard to the Sabbath are, that what the Jews call Sabbath the Greeks call the Seventh, and this is its name among all nations, though the nations do not know why it is so called [p]. He makes no reference to its observance by either Jew or Christian.

Theophilus thus describes the general life of Christians: "Sound-mindedness is present with them, self-restraint is practised, marriage with one is preserved, chastity is kept, injustice is expelled, sin is rooted out, righteousness is habitually carried out, the law regulates their conduct, piety is a reality with them, God is acknowledged, truth rules, grace preserves, peace covers them, the holy word guides, wisdom teaches, life rules, God is king[q]." Theophilus mentions that Christians were forbidden to visit the gladiatorial combats, and that they believed it to be their duty to avoid all other public exhibitions (θεωρίας), "that our eyes and our ears may not be defiled, becoming partakers of the words sung there[r]." He also observes that they were commanded to obey powers and authorities, and to pray for them[s]. He recognises in the king a person "appointed by God to judge justly," and therefore he will honour with due honour, but will not worship him, for he is not God[t].

Future State.—The passages already adduced have given the main points of the doctrine of Theophilus with regard to a future state. He mentions "the resurrection and judg-

---

[p] lib. ii. c. 12, p. 91 D.
[r] lib. iii. c. 15, p. 126 D.
[t] lib. i. c. 11, p. 76 D.
[q] Ibid. iii. c. 15, p. 127 A.
[s] Ibid. c. 14, p. 126 C.

ment" together[u]. He alludes also to the "burning up of the world." Malachi the prophet foretold it[x], and the Greek poets agreed with the prophets in regard to it[y]. He demands belief in the resurrection, and confidence in God that He can raise the dead. "When it shall be," he says, "then wilt thou believe, willing or not willing; and thy belief will be reckoned as unbelief unless thou believe now." He points out the action of faith in earthly things—how the husbandman trusts the seed to the earth, the traveller trusts himself to the vessel and pilot, the pupil to his teacher, the sick man to the physician, and then he asks, "Dost thou not wish to trust thyself to God, who hast so many pledges from Him? first, because He made thee out of nothing." And after a little he asks, "Dost thou distrust the God who made thee that He can afterwards make thee[z]?" He regards various occurrences in nature as intimations by God of the resurrection,—the rising and ending of seasons, days and nights, the raising up of seeds and fruits, the production of large trees from small grains, often carried to great distances by birds, and springing up on rocks or tombs. "All these things," he says, "are wrought by the wisdom of God, so as to show through these things that God is able to make the universal resurrection of all men." And he finds a kind of resurrection taking place in man himself. For sometimes he sickens, wastes away, and then, through God's mercy, recovers his body and figure. It is true he does this by nourishment and juices turned into blood. "But this very thing is the work of God, who so fashioned man, and of no other[a]." He also finds in the moon "a proof of the resurrection which is to be," for "it pines away, and somehow dies, and then is re-born and increases[b]." He says in another passage[c], that in the variety, beauty, and multitude of seeds and plants, it is intended that there should be a sign of the future resurrection of all men.

[u] lib. ii. c. 26, p. 103 B.
[y] lib. ii. c. 37, p. 115 D.
[a] lib. i. c. 13, pp. 77 D, 78.
[c] lib. ii. c. 14, p. 93 C.
[x] Ibid. c. 38, p. 116 A.
[z] Ibid. i. c. 8, pp. 74, 75.
[b] Ibid. ii. c. 15, p. 94 C.

The principle of the judgment is thus stated: "He who gave the mouth to speak, and formed the ear for hearing, and made the eyes for seeing, will examine all things and judge justly, giving to each one his wages ($\mu\iota\sigma\theta\acute{o}\nu$), according to desert. To those that in patience seek incorruption through good works he will give eternal life, joy, peace, refreshment, and multitudes of blessings which neither eye hath seen nor ear heard, and which have not ascended into the heart of man. But to unbelievers and despisers, and those who disobey the truth and are obedient to injustice, when they have been filled with adulteries, fornications, man-pollutions, over-reachings, and the unlawful idolatries, there will be wrath and anger, tribulation and straits, and at last eternal fire will hold possession of such. Since then you have added, 'O friend, show me thy God;' this is my God, and I counsel you to fear and trust Him[d]." Theophilus here enumerates the rewards of the blessed. They are included in the word 'immortality,' freedom from corruption. And this freedom from death is to be conferred not only on the soul but also on the body. "For God raises up the flesh immortal along with the soul[e]." Some have taken the passage to mean that the body and the soul die together, and that both will be raised together. This possibly may have been the belief of Theophilus, but it is not likely; and the words we have adduced are better understood by laying the emphasis on the immortal. Make man holy and his soul becomes imperishable, incapable of death. But not only so, but God raises up his body immortal. The locality of man's future blessed abode is not discussed by Theophilus. One passage, however, leaves us to the inference that he regarded paradise as the region of the blessed. He says that in Genesis it is written as if man had been twice placed in paradise, that the first might be fulfilled when he was placed there, and that the second is to be fulfilled after the resurrection and judgment[f]. Theophilus thought that the doctrine of future punishments was stolen by

[d] lib. i. c. 14, p. 79 B C.   [e] Ibid. c. 7, p. 74 C.
[f] lib. ii. c. 26, p. 103 A.

the Greek poets from the Hebrew prophets, so that no one could have any excuse, or say, "We did not hear of it or know it[f]."

Scripture.—Theophilus gives no theory of inspiration. We have seen already that he speaks both of the Logos and the Spirit as inspiring. There is one passage which gives almost all the salient points of Theophilus's belief with regard to the action of the Spirit on men. It runs thus: "Men of God, carrying in them a holy spirit[g] and becoming prophets, being inspired and made wise by God Himself, became God-taught, and holy, and righteous. Wherefore they were also deemed worthy of being rewarded by becoming instruments of God (ὄργανα θεοῦ), and containing wisdom which is from Him, through which wisdom they spoke both with regard to the creation of the world and all other things. For they predicted also pestilences, famines, and wars. And there was not one or two, but many at various times and seasons among the Hebrews; and also among the Greeks there was the Sibyl; and all of them have spoken things friendly and harmonious with each other, both what took place before them and what took place in their own time, and what things are now fulfilling in our own day; wherefore we are persuaded also with regard to those things that are to happen, even as the first have been accomplished[h]."

The prominent points of this explanation deserve consideration.

It is to be observed that Theophilus states that God chose men on account of their holiness to be his instruments. Hence the Spirit is called the holy spirit which inspires them, and their writings are called "the holy writings," and are quoted with the words "the divine writing says," "the holy writing says," or simply "the writing says."

---

[f] lib. i. c. 14, p. 79 A; ii. cc. 36–38.

[g] The Greek is πνευματοφόροι ἁγίου πνεύματος; Wolf prefers πνευματόφοροι, 'borne along by the Spirit.'

[h] lib. ii. c. 9. pp. 87 D, 88 A.

It is also to be noticed that Theophilus divides the inspired into two classes—the prophets among the Hebrews, and the Sibyl among the Greeks. Under the Hebrew prophets Theophilus must have classed some at least of the New Testament writers. We have seen already that he reckons John among the πνευματοφόροι, the spirit-bearing [i]; the Gospels are reckoned alongside of the prophets [k]; a passage from Matthew is introduced with the words ὁ ἅγιος λόγος, "the holy word," and "the evangelical voice teaches [l];" and a passage from 1 Tim. [m] is introduced with the words, "the divine word orders us [n]."

The Sibyl was among the nations what the prophets were among the Jews, and Theophilus appeals to her as such [o], and couples her with "the other prophets," in contrast with the poets and philosophers [p].

The teaching of all the spirit-bearing was harmonious and true. "With regard to righteousness, which the law spoke of, the statements of the prophets and the gospels are found to agree, because all those bearing the spirit spoke by the one spirit of God [q]." They were able to describe the creation because the spirit was present at it, and the fulfilment of their prophecies is guarantee that "what is said through them in regard to the times and seasons before the flood is true [r]."

The subjects which the prophets discussed were "the things that took place before, how they took place; and present things, how they are taking place; and things to come, in what order they will be accomplished [s]." They also spoke of "righteousness, judgment, and punishment, and also with regard to providence [t]." Some of the other subjects which the prophets taught have already been referred to.

[i] lib. ii. c. 22, p. 100 C.
[l] lib. iii. c. 13, pp. 125 D, 126 A.
[n] lib. iii. c. 14, p. 126 C.
[p] lib. ii. c. 38, p. 116 A.
[r] lib. iii. c. 17, p. 128 C.
[t] lib. ii. c. 38, p. 116 A.
[k] Ibid. iii. c. 12, p. 125 A.
[m] c. ii. 2.
[o] Ibid. ii. c. 36, p. 112 A.
[q] Ibid. iii. c. 12, p. 125 A; iii. c. 17.
[s] Ibid. i. c. 14, p. 78 D.

Theophilus states that the prophets were "illiterate, and shepherds, and common persons u." He thus describes their influence on the world: "For as the sea, if it had not an influx and addition of rivers and fountains for its nourishment, would have been dried up long ago on account of its saltness, so the world, if it had not had the law of God and the prophets acting as streams and fountains of the sweetness, and tender mercy, and righteousness, and teaching of the holy commandments of God, would have failed long ago, on account of the wickedness and sin that abound in it x."

Theophilus names a considerable number of the prophets of the Old Testament. He shows himself anxious to prove that the books of Moses were older than any of the Greek books, and even than Zeus himself. He believed that the Greek poets stole many of their doctrines from these prophets. The books of the New Testament mentioned are "the Gospels," or, as it is called in one place, "the Gospel," the Gospel of John, and the first Epistle to Timothy. There are unquestionable references to several others of the letters of Paul. But these two instances are the only instances in which Theophilus intimates that he is quoting.

Of Theophilus's mode of interpretation almost nothing need be said. It was arbitrarily allegorical. Thus he sought in all the facts of the creation some symbol of great moral truths. Many instances have been given of this. Sometimes his explanations lead him into great absurdities, as when explaining the murder of Abel and the words of God, "The voice of thy brother's blood calls to me from the earth," &c., Gen. iv. 10-12, he remarks that the earth, struck with terror, afterwards did not take in the blood of man, nor indeed of any animal. This coagulation of the blood on the surface of the earth he thinks was caused by nothing else than man transgressing y.

---

u lib. ii. c. 35, p. 112 A. Ἰδιῶται: persons in a private station, and therefore not well acquainted with the world.

x lib. ii. c. 14. p. 93 C D.   y Ibid. ii. c. 29, p. 105 D.

Theophilus gives no hint to us of his interpretation of Judaism. He mentions that God was their lawgiver. He says, "Of this Divine law Moses, the servant of God, was the minister to the whole world, but most completely to the Hebrews who were also called Jews." He also notices that of "this law which is great and wonderful for all righteousness there are ten heads, which we have mentioned above." In the enumeration of the commandments, however, he does not divide them into separate commandments, he omits mention of the Sabbath and of taking God's name in vain, and he introduces several verses from Exodus xxiii.[z] In chapters 11 and 12 of Book iii. he shows that the gospels agreed with the law in all their requirements.

VI. LITERATURE.

Manuscripts.—There are three manuscripts of Theophilus to Autolycus. 1. Codex Venetus Græcus CCCCXCVI., preserved at Venice, the best of all, written in the eleventh century, according to Otto; 2. Codex Bodleianus Græc. Miscell. XXV., in the Bodleian Library, written about the middle of the fifteenth century; 3. Codex Parisinus DCCCLXXXVII., in the Royal Library in Paris, written in 1540, contains only the third book.

Editions.—The books of Theophilus to Autolycus were first printed in a collection of various pieces at Zurich, 1546, edited by Joannes Frisius, then in the Orthodoxographa of Joannes Heroldus, in Morell's edition of Justin, and in various of the great libraries. It was edited by Fell, Oxford, 1684, 12mo. A very good edition was brought out by Io. Christoph. Wolfius, at Hamburg, 1724, 8vo., which moreover contained many dissertations by various writers. Then came the edition of Maranus in 1742. In 1852 appeared an edition by William Gilson Humphry, S.T.B., Cambridge, 8vo. By far the best edition is that of Otto, Jenæ, 1861, 8vo., which gives

---

[z] lib. iii. c. 9; comp. iii. c. 11.

full information in regard to manuscripts, editions, and translations. There are two English translations, one by Joseph Betty, Oxford, 1722, 8vo., and another by the Rev. W. B. Flower, London, 1860, 8vo. Mr. Flower's translation is well executed, but it is marred by omissions and misprints.

CHAPTER VI.

ATHENAGORAS.

I. LIFE.

OUR information with regard to Athenagoras is derived from two sources; Philip Sidetes, and the inscription prefixed to the writings of Athenagoras in the manuscripts. The statements of Philip Sidetes are as follows: " Athenagoras was the first leader of the school at Alexandria, flourishing in the time of Adrian and Antoninus, to whom he also addressed his Apology for the Christians. He was a man who christianized in the cloak and was president of the academic school. He, before Celsus, having been eager to write against the Christians, studied the Divine Scriptures in order to contend more carefully, and was thus caught by the all-holy Spirit; so that, like the great Paul, he became a teacher instead of a persecutor of the faith which he persecuted. Philip says that Clemens the writer of the Stromata was his disciple, and Pantænus was the disciple of Clemens." This fragment was first published by Dodwell in an appendix to his Dissertations on Irenæus. Dodwell is inclined to place absolute confidence in the statements of Philip, though he thinks the words of Philip may have been slightly altered; for they are related by another, supposed by him to be Nicephorus Callistus. This person, whoever he was, tells us that Philip of Sida was a pupil of Rhodon, who was head of the Alexandrian school in the reign of Theodosius the Great. Philip of Sida Dodwell believes had thus access to the best sources of information. But it by no means follows that, because Philip knew the leader of the Alexandrian school, he was well acquainted with the history of the school, or could tell accurately who had been its leader three hundred years before his time. The only part of Philip's knowledge which we can test is what he states about Pantænus, and we know both from Clemens and Eusebius that he is entirely wrong. What others have said of Philip's character as a historian does not give us reason for confiding in his accuracy. He is mentioned both by Socrates and Photius. He wrote a vast number of books, but especially a history, which he did not call an ecclesiastical but a Christian history. Socrates accuses him of aiming at a grand style, introducing all kinds of things, philosophical, astronomical, arithmetical, musical, and thus rendering it useless to both learned and unlearned. He especially blames him because "he confounds the times of the history," mentioning the times of the emperor Theodosius, and going back to those of Athanasius the bishop[a]. The testimony of Photius is to the effect that the book was "disagreeable, more a show-off than of real use[b]." The narrative of such a writer, living as he did so long after Athenagoras, cannot be trusted. It is impossible to conceive that his words are pure fiction, but how many misapprehensions, mistakes, and exaggerations they contain no one can now decide[c].

The only other testimony is the inscription on the manuscripts. It runs thus: "The embassy (πρεσβεία) of Athenagoras the Athenian, a philosopher and a Christian, concerning Christians, to the emperors Marcus Aurelius Antoninus and Lucius Aurelius Commodus, Armeniaci, Sarmatici,

---

[a] Socr. Hist. Eccl. vii. 27.   [b] Cod. 35 (p. 7, a Bekker).

[c] See Cave, Lit. Hist. vol. ii. p. 34, and especially Clarisse, Commentatio Historico-Theologica de Athenagora, p. 10; who try to attach some authority to the statements by explaining how Photius committed the mistakes which we know he has committed.

and, what is greatest, philosophers." At what time this inscription was written and on what authority are matters entirely unknown. Internal evidence, as far as it goes, is entirely in harmony with these statements, and the counter-statements of Philip Sidetes, as we have seen already, are worthless. The statements themselves, however, are open to criticism. Lucius Aurelius Commodus may either be Lucius Verus, the colleague of Marcus Antoninus, or Commodus his son, who after the death of Verus was made partner in the government. The evidence in regard to this matter is not very strong and is sometimes conflicting, but unquestionably greater probability attaches to the opinion more commonly held by scholars, that it is Commodus the son that is mentioned[d]. We shall present the evidence.

Part of this evidence lies in the inscription itself, part in some passages of the Apology.

In the inscription there are three points that call for observation; the name, the appellations Armeniaci, Sarmatici, and the designation 'philosophers.'

The name Lucius Aurelius Commodus is appropriate only to the son of Marcus Aurelius, who succeeded him. Lucius Verus also bore the name of Commodus, but he laid it aside after he was admitted to a share of the government[e]. Lucius Verus is not styled Commodus in any of the inscriptions given in Orelli. The son of Marcus Aurelius was always styled Commodus.

The titles Armeniaci, Sarmatici, are full of difficulty. Marcus Aurelius did not conquer Sarmatia until after the death of Verus. On the other hand, the title of Armeniacus, victor of Armenia, is utterly inappropriate to Commodus, because Armenia had been conquered a considerable time before he had been admitted to a share in the government. The easiest way of getting rid of the difficulty is by supposing

---

[d] See Clarisse, p. 28; Otto, Athen. Opera Prolegg. p. 62; Mosheim, Dissert. de Vera Aetate Apologetici quem Athenagoras pro Christianis scripsit in his Dissertt. ad Hist. Eccl. pertinentes, vol. i. p. 272.

[e] Capitolinus, Ver. Vit. c. iv.

that Commodus the son is meant. If Verus were meant, then Sarmaticus must be a wrong reading, and every attempt that has been made at emendation has been wild. On the other hand, there are two methods of solving the difficulty if Commodus be the person addressed, either of which is not very objectionable. The first method, and that usually adopted, is to suppose that Athenagoras applied the term Armeniaci to both emperors, though it was appropriate only to one, because the father would have no objection to share his honours with the son. The other method, proposed by Tentzel and adopted by Mommsen, is to change Ἀρμενιακοῖς into Γερμανικοῖς, and this seems to me much to be preferred, though all the manuscripts are against it. There is something absurd in joining one of Marcus Aurelius's earliest titles with his latest; while it would be appropriate to join the two of the latest, victor of Germany and victor of Sarmatia; and the inscription would thus harmonize exactly with those that relate to Marcus Antoninus after the year 176f. Moreover, Commodus actually went with his father to the war in Germany, and had shared in the triumph over the Germans; and if the likelihood is that he is the person addressed, Athenagoras would not omit a title which Commodus would feel to be peculiarly honourable to him. Then the change of letters in the emendation is slight, and the mistake of the copyists is easily accounted for.

The last point in the inscription is the title of 'philosopher' given to Lucius Aurelius Commodus. Neither Lucius Verus nor Commodus have the slightest claim to such an appellation. Athenagoras, however, it is likely, would not have scrupled to give it either to the one or the other, from his desire to say the best of the emperors. If we were to make a choice as to whom the title would be more appropriate, we should prefer Commodus, for he had not as yet exhibited his contemptible weaknesses and his barbarous cruelty, while the voluptuousness of Lucius had become universally notorious.

f See Orelli, vol. ii. pp. 202-205; Inscriptions 861, 885, 887; and Clinton, Fasti Romani, vol. i. pp. 171 174.

The evidence in the Apology itself is derived principally from two passages. In speaking of God the Father and his Son the Logos, Athenagoras employs an analogy: "For as all things have been subjected to you, father and son, who have received the government from above ᵍ." The son here might mean Verus the son-in-law, but it far more naturally and probably means Commodus the real son. In fact, the analogy limps very considerably if the real son is not meant. Then in the concluding chapter ʰ occur the following words: "For who have a better right to obtain their requests than we who pray for your government, that ye may succeed to your throne, son following father, according to exact justice, and that your government may receive increase and addition, while all become subject to you?" There might here again be a possible reference to Verus, but there is an extreme improbability in the supposition. On the contrary, every expression favours the notion that these words contain an allusion to the rebellion of Avidius Cassius. The mention of the mode of succession is striking in itself. The emphasis laid on the justice of such a mode is also peculiar. And the strong assertion of the fidelity of the Christians would render it likely that there had been some attempt to undermine Aurelius, and snatch the throne from his heir. The exact time thus indicated is the end of the year 176, or in the year 177. Some other passages in the Apology give probability to this date: "Wherefore," he says, "admiring your mildness and gentleness, and your desire to be at peace with every one, and your kindness, all persons enjoy equal laws individually, the states share equal honour according to their worth, and the whole world through your intelligence enjoys deep peace ⁱ." In the reign of Aurelius the only period at which the world could be fairly said to be in the enjoyment of deep peace was from the end of 176 to the beginning of 178. The insurrection of Avidius Cassius had been crushed, the emperor had returned to Rome, and he and his son triumphed in

ᵍ Suppl. c. 18, p. 17 D.   ʰ c. 37, p. 39 D.
ⁱ c. 1, p. 2 B.

the end of 176. In 178 he was called away to the Marcomannic wars. Athenagoras elsewhere [k] speaks of the zeal of Christians in behalf of 'you and your house,' where the addition, 'your house,' is best explained by the supposition that the succession had lately been threatened by Avidius Cassius.

There are some other expressions and remarks in the Apology which have been supposed to help towards the fixing of the date; but in all cases but one the inference is unwarranted. Thus in an analogy Athenagoras speaks of those who flee for refuge to the palace [l]; and from this it is inferred that the emperor must have been at Rome. Then, again, conjectures are hazarded with regard to an Alexander mentioned by Athenagoras, and an inference is drawn from the conjecture with regard to the date of the Apology [m]. The only exceptional instance is a statement with regard to the slaves of Christians. He affirms that none of them was ever so brazen-faced as to accuse his master of the crimes which public rumour attributed to the Christians [n]. This statement we know to be not exactly true: for Justin Martyr [o] allows that tortures did sometimes wrest from the slaves of Christians accusations of abominable crimes against their masters. But it is easy to suppose that Athenagoras knew nothing of this. Towards the end of the year 177 the fearful persecution of the Churches in Vienne and Lyons broke out, and on that occasion slaves under the influence of tortures asserted that their Christian masters had committed the scandalous crimes commonly imputed to them. Now it is difficult to suppose that Athenagoras could have remained ignorant of this notorious fact, and consequently we are led to believe that the Apology was written sometime between the end of 176 and the end of 177. Moreover, if the Gallic persecution had taken place and time enough had elapsed for its becoming known, it is likely that Athenagoras would have made a distinct allusion to it. Still

[k] c. 3, p. 4 D.   [l] c. 16, p. 15 B.
[m] c. 26, p. 29 B. See Tillemont, Mémoires pour servir à l'Histoire de l'Églises, tom. ii. part ii. p. 557, and Mosh. Dissert. p. 289.
[n] c. 35, p. 38 B.   [o] Apol. ii. c. 12.

there is nothing like certainty in this argument. Minucius Felix, who probably wrote after Athenagoras, states that no one had been prevailed on to assert that they had seen the Christians commit the crimes of which they were accused [p].

There is still another point in the inscription which demands notice. The exact translation of πρεσβεία is 'embassy.' Now it has been matter of dispute whether Athenagoras really went on an embassy, or whether the word should not be translated simply 'apology,' or, as Otto renders it, *supplicatio* [q]. It seems to me very unlikely that the word πρεσβεία can be used here simply for an apology. There is no certainty in the matter; but the word seems to indicate that Athenagoras actually went as a deputation to the emperor and delivered in some shape or other the arguments which we now have in the Apology. We may well conceive that when the world was at peace, and all men but Christians were congratulating themselves on the blessings and privileges which they enjoyed in the reign of the beloved Marcus, Christians would deem it a favourable moment to present their case to the emperor. And he would be all the more ready to listen that he had now returned to Rome, that he had enjoyed along with his son unusual honours, and that all seemed to be thankful for his merciful deliverance from the treachery of Cassius. The laboured compliments in which the Apology abounds are also in harmony with the idea that Athenagoras had written at a season when the praises of the emperor were to be heard on every hand.

There is strong internal evidence that the inscription is the work of Athenagoras himself. Its simplicity is much in favour of its genuineness. It moreover contains one touch which is very characteristic. The work is styled πρεσβεία περὶ Χριστιανῶν, 'an embassy in regard to the Christians.' He does not style it an embassy in behalf of the Christians, but, like a philosopher, an embassy with regard to them [r];

---

[p] See Routh's note, Reliq. Sacr. vol. i. p. 338.
[q] Prolegomena, p. lxiv.
[r] See the abstract of the Treatise on the Resurrection.

not seeking to prejudice his reader one way or another until he should have the arguments laid fully before him.

The result of this investigation as far as Athenagoras is concerned is that he lived in the reign of Marcus Aurelius, and that he wrote his Apology towards the end of 176 or beginning of 177. Human curiosity has not been content with this meagre result, and endless conjectures have been hazarded with regard to him, such as that he is the same as Athenogenes. One of these conjectures, however, is not without interest in itself. Tillemont is inclined to think that Athenagoras was a Montanist. He bases this supposition on two passages; in one of which Athenagoras speaks of the prophetic state as a state of ecstasy [s], and in the other of which he speaks unfavourably of second marriages [t]. The refutation of this conjecture is that Athenagoras never once indicates his adhesion to the main proposition of Montanus, the authority of the Paraclete [u].

II. THE WORKS OF ATHENAGORAS.

The only works of Athenagoras which are extant are an Apology for the Christians, and a Treatise on the Resurrection. The Apology is mentioned, as we have seen, by Philip of Sida. A passage was also taken from it by Methodius, whose quotation is given in Epiphanius and in Photius [x]. In Epiphanius the extract is introduced by the words, καθάπερ ἐλέχθη, ὦ 'Αθηναγόρα; in Photius, καθάπερ καὶ 'Αθηναγόρᾳ ἐλέχθη. The similarity has led to the emendation of Epiphanius into καθάπερ τῷ 'Αθηναγόρᾳ, 'as was said by Athenagoras.' This is all the external testimony for the Apology. There is none for the Treatise on the Resurrection. Our whole information with regard to it is derived from the inscriptions in the MSS., which uniformly ascribe it to Athenagoras. Such a

---

[s] Apol. c. 9, p. 9 D.   [t] c. 33. p. 37 B.
[u] Maranus has devoted a whole chapter to the refutation of Tillemont's notion. Praef. Pars iii. c. cxiv. p. 114.
[x] Panar. lib. ii. tom. i. Haer. 64, c. 28 (21); Phot. Biblioth cod. 234.

lack of testimony leaves the authorship open to question. Yet every attempt to assign it and the Apology to another author, as to Justin [y], or to prove them the works of a later age [z], has been a failure. They are both in style, sentiment, and doctrine, the productions of the second century. There is nothing in them which can be adduced in any way irreconcileable with this supposition. And they are both remarkably alike in style and thought, so that no good arguments can be drawn from the one for regarding the other as not the work of the same author [a]. The date of the Apology has been discussed already: there is no clue to that of the Treatise on the Resurrection.

A work has appeared in modern times claiming to be the production of Athenagoras. Its title is, "Du vray et parfait Amour, escrit en Grec par Athenagoras Philosophe Athenien, contenant les amours honestes de Theogenes et de Charide, de Pherecides et de Melangenie,"—Paris, 1599, and 1612. The Greek original of this work never made its appearance. Modern critics have without exception refused to regard this work as the production of Athenagoras, and there is every reason to believe that there never existed a Greek original, but that the romance is the production of the professed translator, M. Fumee Domini de S. Genillac. A short account of this novel is given in Dunlop's History of Fiction [b].

III. THE CHARACTER OF ATHENAGORAS AND HIS WRITINGS.

The two works of Athenagoras are considerably superior to any others of the same age in literary merit. His style is good, and he treats his subject in such a way as to lay his arguments clearly and unmistakeably before his readers.

---

[y] See Le Moyne, Varia Sacra, tom. ii. p. 171. Le Moyne himself maintains that Athenagoras was the writer.

[z] Semler's Introduction to Baumgarten's Untersuchung Theologischer Streitigkeiten. Zweiter Band, p. 70 note.

[a] The absurd and trifling objections which have been made to the genuineness of one or other of these books are completely refuted in Clarisse. pp. 19-26.

[b] For further information see Clarisse, p. 61, and the references given there.

He deserves special praise for his practical clearness. He writes as a man who is determined that the real state of the case shall be exactly known. He introduces similes, he occasionally has an antithesis, he quotes poetry, but always he has his main object distinctly before his mind, and he neither makes a useless exhibition of his own power, nor distracts the reader by digressions. The Apology is the best defence of the Christians produced in that age. It is, as has been remarked of all the Apologies of this age, not a defence of Christianity, but of Christians. He takes up the main charge of atheism, and refutes it in a most masterly manner. He does not go out of his way to attack this person and that, as some of the others do; but treating the emperors with the highest courtesy and respect, and speaking well of the philosophers and poets, he adheres resolutely to his subject, and treats it in a calm and temperate tone. He could not, of course, help attacking heathenism, but his attack is not so vehement as was that of many heathen philosophers and littérateurs. And he oftener than once states that it was not his business to convict the idols, but that in showing that the accusations against the Christians were groundless, he wished to give the emperors his reasons for his new religion [c].

The Discourse on the Resurrection is a still more remarkable production. It is admirably written. The arguments are the result of great reflection. They are stated with thoroughly philosophical precision. And they were well adapted to gain favour with a philosophic audience. It is difficult indeed to conceive that its close reasoning could have been appreciated by an audience. That it was delivered, however, there can be no doubt. He states that his object was not to go into minute details, but " to show summarily to those who have come together what ought to be thought

[c] c. 18, p. 17 D. See also c. 20, p. 20 A, where he says, after describing the adulteries of the gods, " It was necessary to say this much." Otto quotes a passage from Pliny (note 21), in which that writer expresses his utter disbelief of these stories.

in regard to the resurrection, and to suit the arguments that lead to this to the capacity of those present [d]." He seems to have been in the habit of delivering discourses, for he says, "We sometimes place our remarks in defence of the truth before those in regard to the truth [e]." Of course this might refer to written works, but more probably the reference is to spoken discourses. We can scarcely believe that the mass of Christians would have been able to comprehend such arguments. Indeed, from Tertullian we know the contrary. And so we may suppose that Athenagoras gathered together a few philosophic friends, and laid his ideas before them. Some of the arguments which he has used will be found in many modern works, and some of the hints which he has given have been since worked out. On the other hand, his physiological arguments are for the most part based on mistaken notions. Altogether the treatise is a valuable and interesting one: and accordingly I have given a full report of it. In reading this abstract it must be remembered that justice is not done in it to Athenagoras. There is scarcely a superfluous word in the treatise itself, and therefore everything omitted tends to impair the effect. The only exception to this is where he expatiates on the order to be pursued in the arguments. He seems inclined to be too formal. But the fault is really no fault if we consider that the treatise was spoken. Nor is justice done to the language, which is beautiful in the original; and here and there we fall in with passages of considerable force. There is one of especial excellence, where he sums up the crimes and cruelties of tyrants [f].

It is noteworthy that Athenagoras does not appeal to Scripture in proof of the truth of the resurrection. The reason of this must have been that such an argument would have fallen in vain on the ears of his audience. But there runs through the whole of the treatise a consciousness of the truth of the doctrine, independent of the arguments adduced. The writer feels a certainty with regard to it which is not

[d] c. 23, p. 66 C. [e] c. 1, p. 41 B. [f] c. 19, p. 62 C D.

guaranteed by his reasoning. And this certainty is explained by the statement in the Apology, that theologic wisdom, [belief got through the prophets,] and worldly wisdom, [beliefs derived from mere human argument,] differ as much as truth from probability [g].

We turn now to these treatises that we may gather from them his relation to his times, to mythology, and philosophy.

Athenagoras throws some light on the persecutions of the Christians. He maintains that they took place "because, according to natural reason, vice is opposed to virtue, and things opposed to each other war against each other by a divine law[h]." He states that this habit of persecution had prevailed from the earliest times, "according to some divine law and reason that vice should war against virtue;" and he instances Pythagoras, Heraclitus, Democritus, and Socrates, as victims[i]. He gives us, however, no clear indication as to the law by which Christians were condemned. In fact, his words prove that they were condemned without being heard. The name 'Christian' was supposed to imply that the man was an atheist and a villain. He speaks of the accusations as a "common irrational opinion[k]," as the "common undiscriminating report[l]." In one passage he maintains that the persecutions took place contrary to laws. "This," he says, "is eating human flesh, when men in violation of the very laws which you and your ancestors have laid down in exact justice, should exercise violence, so that not even the rulers of the nations sent by you are sufficient for the trials of those who are not allowed when they are struck to refuse the blow, and must do nothing else than bless when they are evil spoken of[m]." In another passage, however, he intimates that there was a law against Christians. "What reason," he says, "is there why they [poets and philosophers] should be allowed to speak and write freely what they wish with regard to the divine being, but that a law should lie against us, who can demonstrate by signs and reasons of truth that which we think and have

[g] Apol. c. 24. p. 28. A.
[k] c. 11. p. 11 B.
[h] c. 3. p. 4 D.
[l] c. 2. p. 3 A.
[i] c. 31. p. 35 A.
[m] c. 34. p. 38 A.

rightly believed, namely, that there is one Godⁿ?" The expression (ἐφ' ἡμῖν κεῖσθαι νόμον) is indefinite, and we might guess either that Christians were condemned for atheism, or condemned for the expression of their atheism.

Whatever may have been the law, it is plain from the remarks of Athenagoras that he did not regard the emperors as parties to the persecution. In fact, he demands of them that they put an end by law to the persecution of Christians. "If the accusation," he says, "extends only to the name, it is your business, as the greatest man-loving and most wisdom-loving emperors, to put an end, by law, to the insults offered us, that as the whole world has shared in your benefits individually, and as states, so we may be grateful to you, glorying that we have ceased from being falsely accused [o]." He thinks that the emperors had not taken sufficient care of them. After mentioning that the whole world enjoyed deep peace, he says, "But we who are called Christians, since ye have not provided for us, but permit us, though doing no injury * * * to be tossed and driven about like booty, and persecuted, have dared to explain our position, * * * and beseech you to institute some investigations with regard to us, that we may at length be no longer slaughtered by vile informers [p]." So far were the emperors themselves from being active persecutors, that Athenagoras appeals to their procedure as proof of the innocence of Christians. "You yourselves," he says, "are witnesses that we commit none of these iniquities, since you order that no one give information against us" (κελεύοντες μὴ μηνύειν [q]). Indeed, Athenagoras seems to have appreciated the character of Marcus Aurelius, and he certainly lays himself open to the charge of flattery. He speaks of the emperors as surpassing all, as much in the extent and accuracy of their learning as in prudence and

[n] c. 7, p. 7 C.   [o] c. 2, p. 3 B.   [p] c. 1, p. 2 B C.
[q] c. 3, p. 4 D. Μηνύειν is an emendation for ὁμονοεῖν of the MSS., but it is so good that it has been received by Otto into the text. The fact is asserted also by Tertullian. See Otto's note.

power[r]; and as excelling all in piety to the real godhead[s]. He supposes, that being very fond of learning, they were not ignorant of the writings of Moses and Isaiah, Jeremiah and the other prophets[t]. He speaks of them as being intimately acquainted with the ancients in all things[u], and above all, as knowing their writings well[x]. He mentions oftener than once their attachment to philosophy[y].

In his treatment of mythology Athenagoras is uncommonly fair, and takes a view which might have well enough been taken by a philosophic heathen of deep moral feeling. He seizes upon the really weak points and exhibits them very much as a modern might do. It is in this department that his scholarship especially appears, and it is remarkable that his quotations are all made from writers well known to us, and that there are none from the middle or new comedy. He quotes largely from Homer, and Herodotus, and Plato. He has some of the Orphic fragments, and he quotes from Hesiod, Pindar, Æschylus, Sophocles, Euripides, Empedocles, Callimachus, and the Sibylline verses.

He traces mythology to low earthly views. "Turning up and down," he says, "round the forms of matter, they fall away from the God who is perceived by reason, and deify the elements[z] and their parts, sometimes calling them one name and sometimes another[a]." "Falling away," he says again, "from the greatness of God, and unable to penetrate above through reason (for they have no relationship that would draw them into the heavenly place), they have pined away round the forms of matter, and falling down [to earth] they deify the changes of the elements [stars][b]." He attributes the names of the gods to the creative genius of Orpheus[c], and proves from the statements of Herodotus, and

---

[r] c. 6, p. 6 C.   [s] c. 7, p. 8 B.   [t] c. 9. p. 9 D.
[u] c. 17, p. 16 B.   [x] c. 22, p. 24 A.   [y] c. 2, p. 3 D; c. 11, p. 11 C.
[z] στοιχεῖα generally means 'the stars,' which meaning is the one probably intended here.
[a] c. 22, p. 24 B.   [b] c. 22, p. 24 D.   [c] c. 18, p. 18 A; c. 32, p. 36 A.

the verses of the poets, that the names of the gods were originally the names of men [d]. He looks on the poets as the accredited historians of the deeds of the gods [e]. At the same time he maintains that some of them were thorough believers in the oneness of the deity, and he appeals to two verses of Sophocles, and to two passages of Euripides, one of which, in common with many other early Christian writers, he misinterprets.

Athenagoras's discussion of the mythology is remarkable for its completeness. He demolishes almost every defence of polytheism that could be made. He not merely shows the absurdity of worshipping idols, but he deals in a masterly way with those who said that it was not the idols but the gods that they worshipped [f]. He proves the radical weakness of polytheism from the variety of gods worshipped in different countries [g], and he endeavours to destroy the confidence of heathens in their mode of worship by showing that the idea of sacrifice is inconsistent with just notions of the divine character [h].

Athenagoras was well read in philosophy, and had a good philosophic mind. He gives, for instance, an admirable exposition of the Stoic doctrines [i]. He deserves especial praise for the fairness with which he treats philosophers. He asserts that most of them believed in the unity of God; mentioning by name Philolaus, Lysis, Opsimus, Plato, Aristotle, and the Stoics. He explains the success of their speculation on this point thus: "Poets and philosophers succeeded in this as in other things, by conjecture, being moved according to a close connexion with the breath which is from God (κατὰ συμπάθειαν τῆς παρὰ τοῦ θεοῦ πνοῆς), each by his own soul to seek if he can find and know the truth: but they have not been found capable of attaining to an accurate comprehension, since it was not from God that they deemed it right to learn with regard to God, but each one from himself j." He maintains that every true opinion is accompanied

---

[d] c. 29 & 30. [e] c. 30, p. 34 D. [f] c. 18, p. 17 C.
[g] c. 14. [h] c. 13. [i] c. 19, p. 19 A. [j] c. 7, p. 8 A.

by false ones. "Beside every opinion and argument which have a true foundation in existent things, there springs up something false: and it springs up not in consequence of any natural underlying principle or cause of a thing really existent, but it is worked out by those who have set a value on spurious seed for the conception of truth j." In one passage he attributes the deflection of Euripides and Aristotle from a steady belief in providence to the activity of the demons, who apparently disturb the order of the world, and act malignantly on men's minds.

Mosheim has asserted that Athenagoras was the first of the Christian writers who was an eclectic. This statement is incorrect: for it is now universally acknowledged that all philosophy at this period and for a considerable time before was eclectic. Athenagoras shows less of eclecticism than most. He is the only one of the Apologists whose philosophy is decidedly Platonic. His phraseology is Platonic. He continually contrasts γίγνομαι with εἶναι, 'becoming' with 'being,' νοητός with αἰσθητός, and he reasons Platonically [k]. His doctrine of the immortality and thinking powers of the soul is Platonic, and strikingly contrasts with that of Tatian. He hints the doctrine of reminiscence, and places the chief end of man in the contemplation of God or of real being. His notion of the Logos is also modified by his sympathy with the Platonic ideas. And his doctrine of general and particular providence finds a parallel in the Timæus. He also quotes most frequently from Plato, especially from the Timæus. All the quotations have reference to Plato's belief that God was one, uncreated, eternal mind, capable of being comprehended only by reason. He appeals to the famous passage of the Timæus, in which Plato says that it is impossible to make God known to all [l]. He adduces another famous passage from the same dialogue,—"God-sprung gods of whose works I am the fashioner and father [m],"—as proof that though Plato believed the sun, moon, and stars also to be gods, he

---

[j] De Resur. c. 1. p. 40 B; c. 11. p. 51 B.   [k] Apol. c. 8, p. 8 C. See note 5 in Otto   [l] Tim. p. 28 C; Apol. c. 6, p. 6 D.   [m] Tim. p. 41 A.

yet looked on them as created[n]. He asserts that Plato, feeling that the common people could not unlearn their stories about the gods, used language as if he believed these stories. In this way he explains Plato's statement with regard to his belief in the mythological traditions which occurs in Tim. p. 40 D E. He thinks it impossible that Plato could really have thought that an investigation into the nature of these lesser deities was beyond his power; but he supposes that Plato did not wish to confess that gods could not beget and be begotten[o]. Athenagoras finds in the use of the name of Zeus in the myth in the Phædrus[p], an accommodation to the popular mind, since Plato really meant the true God, as he speaks of Him as the Maker of the universe. He appeals to Plato as laying down a just mode of reasoning in regard to the nature of "that which becomes" and "that which is[q];" and he quotes Plato as maintaining that the world is capable of change and therefore capable of dissolution[r]. He adduces the famous passage from the second epistle to show how accurate Plato's notions in regard to God were; but does not make any remark on its bearing on the Trinity[s]. He asserts that the teachings of Plato and Pythagoras were not adverse to the doctrine of a resurrection[t]. The writings of Athenagoras show that he was not uninfluenced by other philosophies. He borrows a peculiar expression from Philo[u], and he agrees with the Peripatetics in regard to pleasures, that the right lies in the mean[x].

Athenagoras gives us little insight into his own philosophy. The principal beliefs of his own which he details relate to the constitution of man's nature. Being mixed up with theological questions, they are discussed in the chapters on his theology. He speaks of persons who are ignorant of natural and theologic truth, as if he distinguished the φυσικὸς λόγος from the

---

[n] Apol. c. 6, p. 7 A.
[o] c. 23, p. 26 A B.
[p] Phædr. p. 246 E; Apol. c. 23, p. 26 C.
[q] Tim. p. 27 D; Apol. c. 19, p. 18 D.
[r] Polit. p. 269 D; Apol. c. 16, p. 16 A.
[s] c. 23, p. 26 A.
[t] c. 36, p. 39 C.
[u] ἀγαλματοφορεῖν. De Resur. c. 12, p. 53 B.
[x] De Resur. c. 21, p. 64 B. See note 15 in Otto.

θεολογικὸς λόγος, contrary to the practice of the Stoics[y]. He may however, like them, have believed the theological to have been a part of the physical. In his Treatise on the Resurrection he frequently introduces a distinction between primary and secondary facts, but it will be seen from the instances[z] which he gives of these primary facts that they are quite different from those of the Scotch school. In one passage he makes an appeal to the common sense of men, but not in a strictly philosophical way. He says that "the common sense of all men (τῆς κοινῆς πάντων ἐννοίας) teaches us, and the objects that present themselves continually to the eye bear witness" to the fact that each thing has an end peculiar to itself[a].

Owing to a strict adherence to his subject Athenagoras does little or nothing directly for the defence of Christianity. He stakes the certainty of his belief (ὁ καθ' ἡμᾶς λόγος, as he calls it) on its being God-taught[b]. He appeals to the prophets as a sure source of knowledge, because they were inspired by God, and contrasts the certainty of their statements with the uncertainty of mere human opinions[c]; but he never proves that the prophets were inspired. He makes no allusion to miracles. His work, however, would probably be powerful in attracting intelligent minds to Christianity, for simply in the way of defence of Christians he gives a glowing account of their morality, and the power of their religion to influence the conduct. He appeals to the emperors as witnesses of the fact that those who promise to make their scholars happy through the solution of syllogisms, and instruction in affirmations, and axioms, subject, and predicate, and the like, do not attain such purity of soul as to love their enemies[d]; but "with us," he says, "you will find illiterate individuals, and handicraftsmen, and old women, who if they cannot in words present the advantage which proceeds from our doctrine, yet in deed exhibit the advantage which proceeds from their choice. For it is not words that they rehearse,

---

[y] c. 13, p. 13 A.
[a] De Resur. c. 24, p. 66 D.
[c] c. 7, p. 8 A : c. 9, p. 9 D.
[z] See abstract.
[b] Apol. c. 32, p. 36 C.
[d] c. 11, p. 11 C D : p. 12 A.

but good deeds that they show. Being struck, they strike not again; and plundered, they do not go to law. They give to those that ask, and love their neighbours as themselves[e]."

IV. ABSTRACT OF THE APOLOGY OF ATHENAGORAS.

To the emperors Marcus Aurelius Antoninus and Lucius Aurelius Commodus, Armeniaci, Sarmatici, and, what is greatest, philosophers.

Every nation throughout your dominions follows its own customs without hindrance. The inhabitant, for instance, of Ilium regards Hector as a god; the Lacedæmonian worships Agamemnon. Everywhere the people offer what sacrifices they like to whatever god they like. This you and your laws permit, since ye deem it impious that one should not believe in a god, but necessary that each should worship the gods of his choice, that men may be restrained from vice by fear of the gods. The whole world thus enjoys deep peace. On us Christians alone ye have not bestowed sufficient care, allowing us to be persecuted and plundered on no other pretence than that we bear the name of Christ. And it is not merely our goods that our enemies desire, but they wish to deprive us of life[f]. We make no objection to being punished, if we are found guilty. But if the only proof of the accusations hurled against us is our name, it is the duty of you philanthropic monarchs to repel the accusation by law. A name is neither good nor bad in itself, but becomes good or bad according to the deeds which lie under it. All others have a fair trial; we request the same privileges. We are accused of three crimes; atheism, Thyestean banquets, Œdipodean connexions. If these accusations are true, destroy us utterly; but if they are not true, grant us equal privileges with our enemies, and we shall conquer them[h]. I shall now refute the charge of atheism. The Athenians reasonably accused Diagoras, because besides revealing the mysteries he

[e] c. 11, p. 11 C D; p. 12 A. [f] c. 1.
[g] c. 2.   [h] c. 3.

tried to prove that there was no God at all. But we distinguish God from matter, saying that God is uncreated and that He made everything, and therefore we are falsely accused of atheism[h]. The poets and philosophers were not reckoned atheists, though they doubted the common notions of God, and said that He was one, and perceptible by mind alone. Euripides and Sophocles, for instance, declared his unity[j]. The philosophers also believed that there was but one God, and yet they were not treated as atheists. I cannot adduce the opinions of all, but I now appeal to those of Philolaus, Lysis and Opsimus, Plato, Aristotle, and the Stoics[k]. Poets and philosophers were allowed to state what they thought of the divine Being. Why should not the same privilege be granted to us, who can prove that God is one by the most certain arguments[l]? We reason the matter thus. If there were from the beginning two or more gods, they would occupy the same place or each one would be apart. But they could not occupy the same place. For uncreated beings are dissimilar, not being made after any type, and they are uncompounded. They cannot dwell apart: for there would be no place nor occupation for a second God[m]. If we had been content with such reasonings, our religion would have been human. But we base our faith on the prophets who were inspired by God. They frequently state the unity of God[n]. I have now sufficiently proved that we are not atheists, since we believe in one eternal God who made the world through his Logos. For we believe also in his Son, and in a Holy Spirit, and in a multitude of angels[o]. I am anxious that you should not be carried away by the prevalent prejudice against us, and therefore I wish to give an accurate account of ourselves. If you consider the precepts which we follow, you will see that we are not atheists. "Love your enemies," and suchlike, are our commands. We are not talkers, like the Sophists, but continually show good deeds[p]. If we did not

[h] c. 4. [i] c. 5. [k] c. 6. [l] c. 7. [m] c. 8.
[n] Exod. xx. 2, 3; Isaiah xliv. 6, xliii. 10, 11.—c. 9.
[o] c. 10. [p] c. 11.

believe that God presided over the world, how could we be thus pure in soul? We believe that we must render an account to God of the whole of this life, and we act accordingly. How then can we be regarded as impious[q]? Since many, however, accuse us because we do not sacrifice to the gods nor worship the same gods as the various states, I shall reply to them. God does not need sacrifice. He wishes rational service[r]. Those who accuse us of atheism because we do not worship the same gods as the states, do not agree themselves in regard to the gods. One state worships one god, another another; and thus all states would be impious, for they do not worship the same gods[s]. But suppose they did worship the same gods, why should we be branded as atheists because we can distinguish between God and matter while they cannot? When we praise any excellence in a vessel, it is the maker of the vessel whom we really praise. So God is the maker of the world; and it is absurd to worship forms of matter instead of Him[t]. The world indeed is beautiful; but we do not worship it, but its maker. So a subject does not neglect his emperor and bestow all his attention on the palace; but he admires the palace and honours the emperor. Plato bears witness to this; for he speaks of the heavens and the world as capable of change, and therefore they cannot be worshipped as gods[u]. The names of the gods also and their images are of recent origin. Herodotus says that Hesiod and Homer made the Greek theology and gave names to the gods. And the idols or statues of the gods are of so recent an origin that we can tell the names of every one of the makers[x]. Some reply to us that the images are not the gods, but are made only in honour of the gods. We shall therefore examine what is said of the gods themselves. Now it is agreed on by all in regard to each of them that he came into existence, Homer and Orpheus distinctly asserting their origin[y]. If they had an origin, then they are perishable. Both the Platonic school

---

[q] c. 12.   [r] c. 13.   [s] c. 14.   [t] c. 15.
[u] c. 16.   [x] c. 17.   [y] c. 18.

and the Stoics acknowledge this. Besides, nothing can take place without a cause, and the cause exists before the effect. Therefore there was an artist anterior to the water out of which the gods are said to have arisen[z]. Moreover, the shapes attributed to the gods and the stories that are related of them are highly dishonouring to the divine character, and indeed prove that they are not gods[a]. Even if poets were to affirm merely that the gods had flesh and fleshly desires, we should be bound to look on the opinion as nonsense. Suppose they were of flesh, yet they ought to be superior to anger and passion. Yet Homer represents Athena scowling at her father, Hera as not restraining her anger, Zeus as bewailing Sarpedon and unable to save him. Then Homer makes Aphrodite be wounded, and Ares mad and an adulterer; Aphrodite falls in love with Anchises, and Zeus is the victim of many loves[b]. But perhaps all this is mere poetic vagary and there is a natural explanation of the statements. But if Zeus be fire, and some other gods the other elements, then they are not gods. Or whatever other explanation be given, it reduces the gods to material things, and thus destroys their divinity. To the Stoics we submit this argument. If ye believe God to be uncreated, and eternal, and that the spirit of God which passes through matter receives names according to the differences in the matter, then we affirm that the forms of matter which constitute the bodies of the gods will be destroyed in the general conflagration. But who would believe that those whose bodies are destructible are gods[c]? But how, you may say, do some idols exhibit energies, if those in whose honour they are placed are not gods? We do not deny that wonderful works are sometimes done in the name of idols. But who are those who produce these results we know very well. In my attempt to show who they are, and that they are not gods, I shall appeal first to philosophers. Thales divides into God, demons, and heroes; Plato into the uncreated God, and into those produced by the uncreated one for the ornament of heaven, namely, the

[z] c. 19.   [a] c. 20.   [b] c. 21.   [c] c. 22.

planets and fixed stars, and into demons. Plato says that it is a task too great for him to describe the origin of the demons. He cannot mean that he really could not describe their origin. But since he believed that gods could not beget and be begotten, and since he had at the same time to deal with those who accepted the common traditions without question, he thus spoke, though he believed in one uncreated God[d]. I need not adduce any more testimonies. The poets and philosophers acknowledge one god; some of them thought of the common deities as if they were demons, some as if they were matter, and some as if they had been men. So we speak of God, yet at the same time believe that there are other powers concerned about matter, one of them directly opposing itself to the goodness of God, though he was created by God. The angels were to have special departments of the providence of God. Some of them neglected their duty, and from their intercourse with women were begotten the giants or demons[e]. The apparent disturbances which these evil angels and demons produce in the government of the world have led some men, such as Euripides and Aristotle, to doubt if there be a Providence at all. There is, however, nothing disorderly or neglected in the constitution of the world[f]. It is the demons that drag men to the idols; but the gods that please the multitude were originally men. The nature of the activity is proof that it is the demons who act, for they urge men to deeds which are contrary to nature, such as mutilation of the person. And that it is their activity is further proved by the circumstance that it displays itself even in the case of statues made in honour of persons alive or recently dead, as of Neryllinus, Alexander, and Proteus[g]. When a soul is tender and unacquainted with the truth, it is apt to form false notions; then the demons, who are concerned about matter, take advantage of these false notions, and make appearances flow into the souls as if from the idols. But when the soul has a rational motion either pointing out the future or healing

---

[d] c. 23.   [e] c. 24.   [f] c. 25.   [g] c. 26.

the present, the demons take the glory of this[h]. I shall say a few words with regard to the names. Herodotus and Alexander the son of Philip assert that the Egyptian priests told them that the gods were originally men. Herodotus, moreover, mentions their sufferings and their tombs[i]. The Greek poets assert of Heracles and Asklepios that they were subject to human passions and were men, but were afterwards made gods. There is no need to mention the like of Castor and Pollux, Ino and Melicertes[k]. The Sibyl asserts that most gods were originally rulers in earth, while some were made gods on account of their strength or their art. Antinous also was reckoned a god on account of the kindness which your ancestors showed to their subjects. The poets, the historians of the gods, mention their origin and their tombs. They were men therefore. I have thus shown then, as well as I could, though not so well as the matter might have been treated, that we are not atheists, for we regard as God the maker of the universe, and the Logos which proceeds from Him[l].

I shall now refute the other accusations which have been made against us. By a divine law wickedness is ever fighting against virtue. Thus Socrates was condemned to death, and thus are stories got up against us. But these stories will appear to any one incredible if he remembers that we regulate our lives according to God, and that we believe in a future life, in which the good will be eternally blessed[m]. It is not, however, wonderful that they should get up similar stories of us as those which they tell of their gods. We, however, are so far from committing the excesses of which we are accused that we are not permitted to lust after a woman in thought. Our law indeed compels us to keep the measure of righteousness. We therefore speak of the young as sons and daughters, we call others brothers and sisters, and we give to the aged the honour of fathers and mothers. Since we love them so much, we make it a matter of great care that their bodies

[h] c. 27. [i] c. 28. [k] c. 29.
[l] c. 30. [m] c. 31.

be kept uncorrupted[n]. We are so particular on this point that we either do not marry at all, or we marry for the sake of children, and only once in the course of our life[o]. And who are they who accuse us? Have they not wrought all iniquity themselves, and attributed like excesses to their gods? They really eat human flesh when they do violence to men who wish not only to be just but to be good and patient of evil[p]. No sensible man would accuse us of eating human flesh if he knew our character. Those who eat human flesh would first have to kill. No one has ever ventured to say that he has seen us kill anyone. On the contrary we refuse to visit the gladiatorial fights. We pronounce it wrong to procure abortion or to expose a child[q]. Who, moreover, who believes in a resurrection would convert himself into the tomb of those who are to rise again? As also we believe that we shall render to God an account of every deed, it is not reasonable that we should fall into the slightest sin. If any one deems the doctrine of a resurrection nonsense, we say to him that we injure no one by our belief in it; at the utmost we but deceive ourselves. It is beyond my purpose to show that even many of the philosophers believed in a resurrection[r]. We are very loyal to you, and therefore we expect that we shall obtain from you our request, as we have proved that the accusations are false, and that we are pious and gentle[s].

ABSTRACT OF THE TREATISE ON THE RESURRECTION OF THE DEAD.

Beside every truth there grows up a falsehood, which is the work of those who desire to corrupt the truth. This fact is proved by the great diversity of opinion which has prevailed among ancient and modern speculators. Hence in dealing with a subject there are two natural divisions, one in regard to (περί) the truth, and the other in defence of (ὑπέρ) the truth. That in defence of the truth is addressed to those

[n] c. 32. [o] c. 33. [p] c. 34.
[q] c. 35. [r] c. 36. [s] c. 37.

who disbelieve or doubt, and naturally follows that in regard to the truth, which suits those who are willing to receive the truth. But in many cases it is best first to refute objections before stating the positive reasons for our belief; a mode of procedure which we shall adopt in the present treatise[t]. Disbelief ought not to be unreasonable. Therefore those who doubt or deny a resurrection must either maintain that the creation of man took place without a cause (a position easily refuted), or, if they assign the creation to God, they must show that there is ground to deny a resurrection, in harmony with this fact. Now a resurrection can be denied, with this fact in view, only on two suppositions—either that God is unable to accomplish it, or that he cannot wish it. Incapability of accomplishment either arises from not knowing what is to be done, or from not having power at all or sufficient power to execute what is wished. But it is impossible for God to be ignorant of the nature of the body or the place to which the dissolved parts of it may go, because He was able to know them before they came into existence; and it is greater to know things uncreated than things created[u]. Then the act of creation is sufficient to prove God's power. For no greater power is required to bring the scattered parts of a body into one than originally to make it; whether we suppose that it was formed out of matter, or from the elements, or from seed[x]. Some indeed, admired for their wisdom, have given their assent to the doubts entertained among the many, which are based on the following circumstance. Many bodies, they say, are devoured by fishes or by wild beasts, and thus become united with their bodies. Some of these fishes and beasts are used to nourish men, and thus parts of the bodies of men pass through the animals into the bodies of other men. Moreover they appeal to cases where in the time of famine children have been eaten. Those parts which have successively been in different bodies, can in the resurrection only be in one, and therefore the other body cannot rise[y].

[t] c. 1.   [u] c. 2.   [x] c. 3.   [y] c. 4.

Now, in reply, I say, first, that these persons do not seem to me to know the power and wisdom of Him who fashioned and ordered this universe, and who has adapted a special kind of nourishment for each kind of animal. For it is only true congenial nouris[...] which enters into the composition of the parts. For [...] [el]ements are vomited or passed through; some of them w[ith]o[ut] the slightest change. Some undergo a change (πέψιν, cooking, digestion) in the stomach, and thereby lose their nutritive power. Some undergo a second change in the liver, and by this second change are converted into innutritive substance; and even after the nourishment has entered into the parts of the body, it may be rejected on account of some redundance which is wont to corrupt or turn to itself that which comes near it [z]. Only that which passes through the triple purification deserves the name of nourishment; for it, there is no doubt, really coalesces with the nourished body. But other substances are either destroyed, or, if their power is greater, are themselves destructive, and turn into corrupt humours. The proof of this is that pain and even death arise from such food. Hence it is plain that none of those things which are contrary to nature would ever be united to the body [a]. But suppose one were to grant that the nourishment coming from these things (we shall use the common mode of speech, and call it nourishment), even though it is unnatural, yet is separated and changes into one of the moist, or dry, or warm, or cold substances [b], yet no advantage will be gained from the concession; for none of these forms a real part of the body, for they do not remain always, and neither blood, phlegm, bile, nor breath (πνεῦμα) contribute anything to life. Then the nourished bodies will not require in the resurrection those things which they once needed. And, again, even if we suppose that the change advances even as far as flesh, there is no reason to suppose that this newly-made flesh will

---

[z] c. 5.   [a] c. 6.

[b] ἕν τι τῶν ὑγραινόντων ἢ ξηραινόντων: 'some one of those things which are moist or dry,' &c.

constitute a real and permanent part of the body, since the
flesh which receives it does not always retain what it receives,
and the flesh which is received is subject to many changes,
sometimes scattered by toils and cares, sometimes made to
pine away by disease. Especially subject to such changes
would be flesh nourished from uncongenial elements, being
sometimes swollen out, and sometimes rejecting everything in
every way and becoming less and less. I have thus shown
that bodies of men are not proper nourishment for men,
and then I have supposed that human flesh might become
nourishment, and on this supposition I have proved it to
be untrue that human bodies would ever form real parts
of bodies of the same nature[c]. But what need is there of
bodies which were never designed for nourishment? If any
one maintained that the human flesh was intended for food,
he would be compelled also to allow that murder was natural.
If human flesh then is unnatural nourishment, it could never
ultimately form a real part or portion of another human
body; and thus all the parts of the one body, whatever may
have become of them in this world, will be reunited in
harmony in the resurrection[d]. Since there are many other
topics in connexion with this subject, I have merely a remark
for those who take refuge in an analogy between the works of
men and those of God. A potter, they say, cannot renew
a vessel that has been broken or destroyed, so God cannot
raise, and cannot wish to raise, a body that has suffered
death. But such a comparison is insulting to God in the
highest degree; and it would have been much truer to have
maintained that what was impossible with man was possible
with God[e]. The other objection to the resurrection is based
on God's incapability of wishing it ($ἀβούλητον$). Now his
incapability of wishing it would arise from two causes; either
because a resurrection is unjust, or because it is unworthy of
Him. The injustice of the resurrection would relate either to
the person destined to rise, or to some other. But no spiritual

[c] c. 7.   [d] c. 8.   [e] c. 9.

nature (αἱ νοηταὶ φύσεις) would be injured, for the resurrection of man could form no impediment to their existence. Nor would irrational beings be injured, for they will not exist after the resurrection; and no injury can be done to what is not. But suppose they were to exist, they would be in a better, not in a worse state, after man's resurrection, being freed from every bondage. Besides, having no sense of justice they can have no sense of injustice. Nor is injustice done to the person about to rise, for he consists of soul and body. Now no injustice is done to the soul, for if no injustice is done to it while it dwells in a corruptible body, much less will there be injustice when it lives along with an incorruptible. Nor is injustice done to the body; for if no injustice is done while it is united corruptible with an incorruptible, much less will injustice be done when it shall be united incorruptible with incorruptible. Nor is it unworthy of God to raise the body; for if it was not unworthy of God to make a corruptible body, much less is it unworthy of Him to raise one which is incorruptible and free from suffering[f]. There is, moreover, a mutual connexion between God's capability of accomplishment with his capability of willing; for God can will anything that He can do, and can do what He can will.

We have already spoken of the arguments in defence of the truth, and those in regard to it. We now proceed to those in regard to the truth, and shall show that the doctrine of a resurrection is true from the cause according to which and on account of which the first man came into being, and those after him, though they came in a different way, and also from the common nature of all men as men, and from the judgment of men by their maker[g].

First, as to the reason of man's creation. Man might be made for no reason at all, or for the use of some one, or simply for life itself. But God, as being wise, makes nothing in vain. He did not make him for his own use, as He

[f] c. 10.   [g] c. 11.

is in need of nothing. He did not make him for the use of superior beings, as they are immortal, and do not require any contribution from men to their existence. He did not make him to serve the irrational beings, for irrational must ever be subject to the rational. Man therefore, according to the only reason that remains, must have been made for life, and this life accordingly is not one that is kindled for a while and then completely extinguished. But to those who bear his own image God has given an eternal permanence, that following his law they might live free from pain in the exercise of those virtues by which, while in corruptible bodies, they strengthened their life. Being made to live they can never cease to be, since they perform the only end of their existence by living, according to their nature; the soul remaining equably in the nature in which it was created, and the body being moved to its natural operations, and receiving the natural changes, the last of which is the resurrection[h]. Confident in these things we are content with the present life, notwithstanding its neediness and corruption, and we have an assured hope of a continuance of life in incorruption. For if the maker of this universe created man to partake of a wise life, and to continue in a contemplation of God's greatness, then the cause of his creation guarantees his continuance, and his continuance a resurrection[i].

We shall now prove a resurrection from the nature of man. But we may remark in passing that truth is demonstrated either by primary facts or by what follows from them. We ought to observe the natural order which there is in arguments. In the present case we naturally consider first the cause of the creation of man, that is, the intention which the Creator had in making man, and then to connect closely with this the nature of the men created, not as being second in order, but simply because it is impossible to discuss two subjects at once. After we have proved the resurrection from these two which are primary facts, we should then adduce the

[h] c. 12.   [i] c. 13.

arguments from providence, or, in other words, from a final judgment. Many lay the entire stress of the argument on this last point, thinking that the cause of a resurrection is the judgment. But they are unquestionably wrong: for in this case those who have done neither right nor wrong, namely young children, &c. who therefore do not require to be judged, would not rise again. But they do rise again, and are thus proofs that the resurrection takes place on account of the intention of the Creator and the nature of the created[k]. Man is composed of an immortal soul and a body suited to it at creation. God has assigned life not to the soul by itself, nor to the body by itself, but to men composed of these. The being is one who suffers alike the sufferings of the soul and the body, and does that which requires the services both of the senses and the reason, and the end[1] to all these must be one. But it can be one only if the being is the same in constitution. · And it is the same only if all its real parts are the same. But the parts will be properly united only if the parts that have been dissolved be again united in the composition of the being. Therefore the constitution of the same men proves a resurrection of the bodies that have become dead and been dissolved. Moreover, if reason has been given to men, not merely to distinguish existences, but also to observe the goodness and wisdom of God, then the rational judgment must exist as long as the things which it was to judge exist. But it cannot continue to exist unless the nature in which it is continues. Now it is man, not soul by itself, that received reason. Therefore man must continue for ever composed of both soul and body. But he cannot continue as man unless there be a resurrection. And if the nature of man does not continue, in vain has the soul been matched to the poverty of the body, and the body reined in by the soul. In vain is the practice of virtue, and the creation and nature of man is vanity. But vanity is not

---

[k] c. 14.

[1] The τέλος here seems to mean 'the ultimate and final state in which the being is to exist.'

known in God's works; and therefore the body will remain with the unending soul [m]. Let no one be surprised that we give the name of continuance to a life which is broken off by death and corruption. For the force of the words depends on the natures to which it is applied. In the case of those who are purely incorruptible the continuance is uninterrupted. But men were made with incorruptible souls but corruptible bodies, which however are to receive incorruption from a change; and therefore we expect the bodies as being corruptible to be dissolved, and at the same time we hope for a resurrection when they shall be changed into incorruptible. The same break of life we see in our daily life. For in sleep there is then a relaxation of the senses and natural powers, and yet we do not refuse to call it life. Why then should we despair of that life which follows the dissolution, even though it be interrupted for some time by a separation of the soul from the body [n]? The nature of man, then, has by the intention of the Creator to undergo a variety of changes. Who could foresee in the seed the powers which are ultimately developed? In childhood there is no appearance of those things which arise in the full-grown man, and so in the full-grown man there is nothing to intimate the decay of powers, nor in the decay of powers is there an indication of the dissolution of the body. Yet these things all follow by a natural sequence, and this sequence leads us to believe in a resurrection [o].

The arguments hitherto adduced are all of the same sort, for they are all based on the primary fact, the creation of man. We shall now discuss the arguments derived from the honour or the punishment due to each man according to a just judgment, and from the end of human life. First, then, of the argument from the judgment. As preliminary we remark that those who regard God as the maker of the universe must according to their principles believe that his care extends over all and each of his works. Now man, as

[m] c. 15. [n] c. 16. [o] c. 17.

needy, requires nourishment to sustain his life; as mortal, he requires succession to continue the race; and as rational, he requires justice on account of the law of nourishment and succession [p]. Now nourishment and succession have reference to man as composed of body and soul, and therefore man as composed of body and soul is responsible for the deeds. Moreover, it would be unfair to judge the soul alone or the body alone for the deeds in which both have taken an active part together. Now this judgment does not take place in this world. The bad sometimes continue to the end untried by evils, while the good are often afflicted and tormented. This judgment cannot take place immediately after death: for the parts of the body are then dissolved and scattered. There must, therefore, be a resurrection when this mortal, in the words of the apostle, shall put on immortality, and each shall receive the things which he has done in the body, whether they be good or bad [q].

To those who doubt a providence, we should have to discuss the previous question, whether God entirely overlooks the life of man or whether He superintends his own creatures. If there is no judgment, then men have no advantage over the brutes, virtue is nonsense, the threat of judgment utterly ridiculous, and the common law for all is, "Let us eat and drink, for to-morrow we die." The end of such a life is absolute insensibility. But if God does care for his creatures, then there must be a distinction between the good and the bad. We have shown that it does not take place in the present life. We can only draw attention to the additional circumstance that a mortal body could not bear the punishment due to some of those wretches who have slain many people, and plundered, and robbed, and tyrannized over nations. Nor after death can full justice be given [r]. For death is

---

[p] διὰ τὸ ἔννομον. Athenagoras seems to mean, as the scholiast remarks, that a certain kind of nourishment is right, and another kind wrong, as, for instance, eating of human flesh is forbidden. So the succession may be produced lawfully by marriage, unlawfully by unholy marriages or otherwise.

[q] c. 18.   [r] c. 19.

either an entire extinction of life, or the soul remains by itself indissoluble when the body is dissoluble. But if death be the extinction of life, then there is no judgment, a swarm of absurdities—and their head and fount, atheism—beset us on every hand. Again, if the soul remains alone incorruptible, then the judgment will not be just, for it was not the soul by itself that did the deeds to be judged, but man[s]. If, on the one hand, right deeds are honoured, the body will plainly receive injustice if it share with the soul the toil and get none of the reward. If, on the other, sins are punished, injustice is done to the soul if it alone pay the penalty of deeds done by both soul and body. The injustice is especially evident in the case of those sins which are occasioned entirely by the existence of the body, such as lasciviousness, violence, and avarice[t]. Even virtue and vice cannot be conceived in the case of the soul by itself. Virtues or vices are the virtues or vices of the man, not of the soul apart from the body. For how could there be manliness or endurance in the soul by itself, seeing that it can have no fear of dissolution? How could there be self-restraint, when there can be no desire for food, or sexual connexion, or the other pleasures and delights of this life? So with other virtues. Is it not absurd, then, that the punishment of vices which cannot take place if the soul be alone and by itself should be laid on the soul alone[u]? And it is most unreasonable of all to suppose that laws should be made for man, but that the consequences of obedience or disobedience should fall on the souls alone. Man, not his soul alone, receives the law; therefore man, not his soul alone, ought to receive the praise or the punishment. God did not tell the soul alone to refrain from adultery, murder, theft, robbery, and disgraceful conduct to parents. The command, "Honour thy father and mother," is not suitable to souls alone: for it is not soul-begetting souls that appropriate the names of father and mother, but men-begetting men. So also the vices of adultery, theft, and suchlike,

---

[s] c. 20.   [t] c. 21.   [u] c. 22.

are not possible if the soul be by itself alone. What I have now said will suffice. I have given the principal arguments. To those who wish to go more minutely into the matter I leave its more complete discussion[x].

The only part of our discussion that remains is the argument from the end or final cause (τέλος) of man. Each created thing must have a final cause peculiar to itself. Accordingly the final cause of man must be different from that of the irrational animals. For it cannot be mere painlessness—for then man would share this with inanimate things—nor even the pleasures of the body, which is the final cause peculiar to brutes[y]. Nor can it be blessedness of the soul apart from the body: for we are considering now the final cause not of one or other of the constituents of man, but of man himself composed both of soul and body. But if there is a final cause of man thus composed, and if that final cause cannot be found while men live in this world for many reasons previously mentioned, and if it cannot be found in the separation of the soul from the body, then the final cause of man must appear in some other constitution of the same being in the same way composed. Hence there must be a resurrection. For the same men cannot exist after this life, unless the same bodies be given to the same souls. In the resurrection, then, appears the final cause suitable to the nature of man. For one would not be wrong in stating as the final cause of a being endowed with thought and reason, an undistracted and uninterrupted spending of life in those things to which the natural reason is specially and primarily adapted, namely in the contemplation of Him who exists (τοῦ ὄντος) and unceasing delight in his decrees. The multitude of those who fail in reaching this final cause does not nullify the general design, since there is in each case a particular examination required as to the good or evil done.

[x] c. 23.   [y] c. 24.

V. THE THEOLOGY OF ATHENAGORAS.

God.—Athenagoras devotes a considerable portion of his defence of Christians to setting forth the truth that they believed in one God. "Our doctrine (λόγος) regards one God as the maker of this universe[y]." He attempts to prove the unity of God by a peculiar and unsatisfactory process of reasoning. We present it here as eminently characteristic of the speculations of the age; remarking only, that some parts of it are not very intelligible, and that the text has occasionally doubtful readings. "That, then, God the creator of this universe is one from the beginning, consider thus, that ye may have also the reasoning of our belief. If there were from the beginning two or more gods, then they would either be in one and the same place or each of them would be separately by himself. Now, then, they could not be in one and the same place; for if they are gods, they are not like, but they are unlike, because they are uncreated: for created things are like their models; but uncreated are unlike, since they have not come into existence from any thing [or any one], or after the manner of any thing [or any one]. But what if God be one [z], just as hand, and eye, and foot are parts in relation to one body, making up together one person out of them? Although Socrates, inasmuch as he is created and destructible, is compounded and divided into parts; yet God is uncreated and incapable of suffering and division (ἀπαθὴς καὶ ἀδιαίρετος), and is not therefore composed of parts. But if each of these gods is separately in his own place, since He who made the world is above the things which have come into being (τῶν γεγονότων, including *men*), and around the things which he made and put into order, where is the other god, or the rest of them? For if the world, having been

---

[y] c. 4, p. 5 C D.

[z] The supposed objection seems to be: Perhaps there are more gods than one, all together making one god.

made spherical, has been shut in by circles of heaven, and the maker of the world is above the things that have come into being, directing it [the world] by forethought for them, what can be the place of the other god, or the rest of the gods? For he is not in the world, since this belongs to the Creator, nor round about the world, for above it is the God the Creator of the world. But if he is neither in the world, nor round about the world, (for the entire space [τὸ πᾶν] round about the world is occupied by the Creator), where is he? Above the world and God? In another world, or round another world? But if he is in another world, or round another, then he is no longer round about us, for he does not rule the world; nor is he himself great in power, for he is in a circumscribed place. But if he is neither in another world, for all things have been filled by the Creator; nor round another world, for all things are occupied by the Creator; then he does not exist, since there is no place in which he is. Or what does he do, if while there is another to whom the world belongs, he is himself above the maker of the world, and not either in the world or around the world? But is there anything else where he may stand? Above him is God, and the things of God. And what place will there be if the maker has filled all that is above the world? Does he provide at all? But assuredly he has done nothing if he does not provide. If, then, he neither does anything, nor provides, and there exists no other place in which he is, this God who is maker of the world is the one and only God from the beginning [a]." It will be noticed that the argument here turns mainly on the belief that the notion of space is applicable to God—a belief which, as we have seen already, brought Justin Martyr into considerable difficulties. One of the propositions, that only created things can be like, is essentially Platonic. Athenagoras wisely remarks at the conclusion of this proof of the divine unity, that if Christians had been content with such arguments, one

[a] c. 8. pp. 8 C–9 C.

would suppose that their religion (τὸν καθ' ἡμᾶς λόγον) was human. It was the testimony of the prophets that rendered the doctrine of the divine unity a certainty, and Athenagoras proves it largely from the Old Testament [b].

Athenagoras asserts that God is unique in the most absolute sense. He denies even the possibility of a real antagonism to God Himself: for speaking of the devil, he says, "that if anything had opposed God it would cease to exist [c];" and he finds even in persecutions a divine law and reason [d]. He asserts "that the uncreated God alone is eternal" (ἀΐδιος [e]). In summing up his proofs that Christians were not atheists, he says, "It has been satisfactorily shown that we are not atheists, since we recognise God as one, the uncreated, and eternal, and invisible; free from all suffering, incomprehensible, and uncontainable (ἀχώρητος); comprehended only by mind and reason, surrounded with inexplicable light and beauty, and spirit and power, by whom the universe has been made through his Logos, and brought into order, and is now held together [f]." He furthermore describes the Divine Being "as incapable of death, of motion, or of alteration [g]," and as always harmonious with Himself [h].

The Divine Being is also in every respect perfect and needs nothing. "For God Himself is everything to Himself; light inaccessible, a perfect world, spirit, power, reason" (λόγος [i]). "There is no wrath, nor lust, nor appetite, nor child-making seed in God," he says, in discussing the mythology [j]: and therefore He does not need sacrifice, "being Himself the perfect fragrance, needing nothing either within or without Himself (ἀνενδεὴς καὶ ἀπροσδεής): but the greatest sacrifice to Him is if we know who stretched and rounded the heavens, and fixed the earth like a centre; who collected the water into seas, and separated the light from darkness; who adorned the sky with stars, and made the earth send forth every seed; who made the animals and fashioned man [k]."

[b] c. 9.   [c] c. 24, p. 27 A.   [d] c. 3, p. 4 D; c. 31, p. 35 A.
[e] c. 30, p. 34 C.   [f] c. 10, p. 10 B.   [g] c. 22, p. 23 D.
[h] c. 22, p. 23 A.   [i] c. 16, p. 15 C.   [j] c. 21, p. 20 C.   [k] c. 13, p. 13 B.

Athenagoras maintains the immateriality of God in the most positive language. "Is it not unreasonable," he says, "to accuse of impiety us who distinguish God from matter, and prove that matter is one thing and God another; and that the distance between them is great, for the Divine Being is uncreated and eternal, seen by mind and reason alone; but matter is created and destructible¹?" He says that Christians distinguish between the uncreated and the created, that which exists and that which does not exist ᵐ; that which is perceived by the mind and that which is perceived by the senses (τὸ νοητὸν καὶ τὸ αἰσθητόν ⁿ). We learn, both from the context and from other passages, that he regarded God as a νοητόν, for he again and again states that God is comprehended or seen only by mind and reason. He states, as we have seen already, that God is indivisible ᵒ and invisible ᵖ. And when he affirms that God is incomprehensible ᑫ, he probably means that God cannot be laid hold of by the physical touch ʳ. As we have seen, however, he believed that God filled the whole of space: but whether he felt any difficulty in reconciling this idea with God's immateriality, we cannot now know. He expresses none.

Athenagoras does not mention the omnipotence of God in express terms, but in a passage already quoted he speaks of Him as surrounded with indescribable power ˢ, and in his Treatise on the Resurrection, he asserts that God can do whatever He wishes ᵗ. Petavius imagined that Athenagoras also maintained that God wished whatever He could do: but, as we have noticed already, Athenagoras merely asserts that God *could* wish whatever He could do, and that the only reasons for his not being able to wish are that the thing was either unjust or unworthy of Him.

Athenagoras says little of the moral character of God. Several of the moral features of God have been noticed

---

¹ Apol. c. 4, p. 5 B. ᵐ A Platonic distinction, τὸ ὂν καὶ τὸ οὐκ ὄν.
ⁿ Apol. c. 15, p. 14 C. ᵒ Ibid. c. 8. ᵖ Ibid. c. 10. ᑫ Ibid.
ʳ Clarisse, p. 87. ˢ Apol. c. 10. ᵗ De Res. c. 11, p. 50 C.

already; such as his freedom from anger and desire. Athenagoras lays special stress on the goodness of God, just as Plato affirms the idea of goodness to be the highest. "The spirit concerned about matter," he says, "is opposed to the goodness of God (τῷ τοῦ θεοῦ ἀγαθῷ), which is an attribute of his and exists along with Him, as colour in a body, without which He does not exist, not as if it were a part of Him, but as being a necessary accompaniment, united and ingrained as yellow is in the fire, and blue in the ether[u]." In another passage he says that "God, being perfectly good, is eternally good-doing" (ἀγαθοποιός [x]). As a necessary consequence of his moral and rational nature, He requires that in worshipping Him we should "lift up holy hands," and bring to Him the "bloodless sacrifice and rational service[y]."

Many of the attributes of God make themselves apparent in creation and providence. Speaking of the antagonists of the resurrection he says, "Such seem to me to be ignorant of the power and wisdom of Him who fashioned and manages this universe[z]." And in his arguments he assumes that "vanity (τὸ μάταιον) has been driven away absolutely from all the works of God, and the gifts given by Him[a]." We have already translated several of the passages in which God is spoken of as the creator and fashioner of the world[b]. In none of these passages, however, is there a clear enunciation of the philosophical notion of a creation out of nothing. And the question has been considered a moot point whether Athenagoras believed in the eternity of matter or not. There are three passages which are appealed to as proof that he did regard matter as eternal. These three are as follows:—The Logos is described as "having come forth to be the idea and energy of all material things, which lay like a nature without quality, and like sluggish earth (ἀποίου φύσεως καὶ γῆς ἀχρείας [c]), the thicker parts being mingled with the lighter[d]."

[u] Apol. c. 24, p. 27 A.   [x] Ibid. c. 26, p. 29 D.   [y] Ibid. c. 13, p. 13 C D.
[z] Res. c. 5, p. 24 C: comp. ibid. c. 8, p. 48 C.
[a] Res. c. 15, p. 57 C; c. 12, p. 52 B.   [b] Apol. c. 4, p. 5 C; c. 13, p 13 B C.
[c] ἀχρείας is an emendation of Maranus for ὀχείας.   [d] Apol. c. 10, p. 10 D.

The second passage is: "But as clay by itself cannot become vessels without art, so the all-receiving (πανδεχής) matter did not receive separation, and shape, and order, without God the fashioner [e]." The third passage is as follows: "Matter requires an artist, and the artist requires matter; or how would the impressions arise apart from matter or the artist? Nor is it reasonable to believe that matter is older than God; for the creative cause (τὸ ποιητικὸν αἴτιον) must exist before the things that arise" (τῶν γινομένων [f].) In opposition to these passages it is urged that Athenagoras distinctly declares matter to be "created (γενητήν) and destructible," that he speaks of God as the Creator, as in the third passage quoted; and that he is in the habit of accommodating his expressions to the current modes of philosophical thought. A closer examination of his mode of thought will show that he could scarcely have formed a definite opinion on the subject. His views of the creation are mainly based on the Timaeus. He holds throughout the Platonic distinction between real being and mere becoming. That which really exists is ἀγένητον, incapable of becoming, remaining eternally the same. That which becomes or passes through a transitory stage of mere seeming does not exist. It is γενητόν, 'capable only of becoming.' But then the question occurs, What is this γενητόν before it comes into appearance? Plato replies that there is matter underneath it. Athenagoras calls it, in language very like that of the Timaeus, πανδεχὴς ὕλη, 'matter capable of all shapes and appearances.' Now this matter is ἄποιος. It has no qualities. It corresponds to the description of things in Genesis: "The earth was without form, and void." In philosophical language, matter is the incogitable. It is the negation of thought. And the work of the creator is to bring this incogitable into the cogitable. Matter thus becomes, or comes into appearance. The only thing, therefore, which the Creator could do, is to make it become; He could not create out of nothing: for it, even after its creation, is non-

[e] Apol. c. 15, p. 14 D.   [f] Ibid. c. 19, p. 19 B.

existent. This is its essential character. Nor can it be said that the matter out of which it arises is eternal, because no assertion can be made with regard to that which cannot be thought. Athenagoras goes as far as he can when he asserts that the creator must exist before the thing which becomes. He could not reasonably make any assertion with regard to that thing before it became; for then it could not be thought. The same fundamental doctrine as this appears in Plato, but with considerable modifications. The peculiarities of it arise from the circumstance that Plato identifies that which can be really known (νοητόν) with that which really exists.

In harmony with the spirit of the Timæus, Athenagoras dwells largely on the beauty and regularity of the world; and appeals to these in proof of the divine existence. "If," he says, "we were of the same mind as Diagoras, possessing as we do in the regularity, the universal harmony, the size, the colour, the shape, the disposition of the world, so many pledges that bind us to piety, reasonably should the prevalent opinion of our impiety and the cause of our persecution attach themselves to us [g]." In speaking of those who believe that the world is tossed about by an irrational chance, he says that they are of this opinion, "not knowing that none of those things which relate to the constitution of the world is irregular or neglected, but each of them has taken place through reason (λόγῳ), wherefore they never transgress the order appointed for them [h]."

Athenagoras again and again speaks of the providence of God. It is mentioned in the argument for the unity of God already quoted. He says that Christians regard "God the fashioner" as "holding together and superintending all things by knowledge (ἐπιστήμῃ) and art [i]." He affirms that "those who regard God as the creator of this universe, must assign the guardianship and providence of all the things that have arisen to his wisdom and righteousness, if they wish to abide by their own principles; and holding

[g] Apol. c. 4, p. 5 B C: see c. 16, p. 15 B C. [h] Ibid. c. 25, p. 29 A.
[i] Ibid. c. 13, p. 13 C.

these sentiments they must believe that not one of those things that are on the earth, or in heaven, is undirected or unprovided for; but they must know that the care of the creator extends to everything, invisible and visible alike, both small and great [k]."

God's providence is directed in a special manner to man. "We know," he says, "that God superintends our thoughts and our sayings by day and by night, and that He being entirely light, sees even the things which are in our heart [l]." This superintendence of God is a reason why Christians should feel certainty in their hope of a future and better life [m]; and why they should purify their souls since they know that they will have to render an account of their deeds to God [n]. While God has a general and universal superintendence of the whole, parts of it are assigned to angels [o]. The Logos and the Spirit have also their share in the maintenance of the world.

The Logos and the Spirit.—The doctrine of the Logos as presented by Athenagoras is the same substantially as that given by the other Apologists, but receives modifications from his Platonic philosophy. The Logos corresponds to the Platonic ideas, but is personal. Now the Logos must either be that which really exists, or that which comes into appearance. Athenagoras could not hold the latter alternative, and therefore he was compelled to bring before his mind the eternal existence of the Logos, and of the unity of Father and Son. In these two points Athenagoras is peculiar: he speaks of the Logos as a γέννημα when he goes forth to be the idea and energy of all material things; but the Logos was eternally in God, just as the Platonic ideas were eternally in the Divine mind before they mingled with matter and gave it intelligibility. So, again, as the Logos is in God, yet is *God's* reason, and therefore God Himself, in so far as one's reason is himself, God and the Logos are one. And in

---

[k] Res. c. 18, p. 60 B C.   [l] Apol. c. 31. p. 35 C.   [m] Ibid. c. 31, p. 35 C.
[n] Apol. c. 12, p. 12 A B.   [o] Ibid. c. 24. p. 27 C.

one passage quoted already, God is said "to be spirit and reason to Himself." We couple the doctrine of the Logos and the Spirit together, because the principal statements in regard to them both occur in the same passages. The reader will observe that in the passages adduced here, as in those from the other Apologists, the writer passes from the common use of the words λόγος, 'reason,' and πνεῦμα, 'spirit,' to the hypostatizing, without himself being apparently conscious of the transition.

There are three principal passages relating to the Logos and the Spirit, and their relation to the Father. The first is: "For we recognise also a Son of God. Let no one deem laughable the opinion that there is a Son to God. For we do not entertain sentiments with regard to God, even the Father, or with regard to the Son, like those feigned by the poets, who display the gods as no whit better than men. But the Son of God is the Logos (reason) of the Father in idea and energy; for according to Him and through Him all things were made [ἐγένετο], the Father and Son being one. But the Son being in the Father, and the Father in the Son, by the unity and power of spirit, the Son of God is the mind and reason (νοῦς καὶ λόγος) of the Father. Now if it should occur to you, on account of your exceedingly great intelligence, to inquire what is the meaning of the Son, I should say in few words that He is the first offspring to the Father, not as being created (οὐχ ὡς γενόμενον), (for from the beginning God, being eternal mind (νοῦς), had Himself in Himself the reason (λόγος), being eternally reasonable (λογικός),) but as having come forth to be the idea and energy of all material things which existed like a nature that has no quality, and useless earth, the thicker parts being mingled with the lighter. The prophetic spirit also agrees with what we now say, for he says, 'The Lord formed me the beginning of his ways to his works p.' And assuredly we affirm that that

---

p Prov. viii. 22. In our translation, "The Lord possessed me in the beginning of his way before his works of old."

very Holy Spirit which acts on (τὸ ἐνεργοῦν) those who speak prophetically, is an effluence of God (ἀπόρροιαν τοῦ θεοῦ), flowing from and being again carried back, as a ray of the sun. Who, then, would not feel doubt if he heard those called atheists who speak of God the Father, and God the Son, and a Holy Spirit, and exhibit their power in unity, and their difference in rank q?"

The second passage is as follows: "But men who have come to reckon life in this world as of very little value, who are sent on towards the future simply by their knowing God and the Logos which is from Him; by their knowing what is the unity of the Son in relation to the Father, what the communication (κοινωνία, 'sharing') of the Father in relation to the Son; what the Spirit; what the unity of all these, and the difference of them united, the Spirit, the Son, the Father r."

The third passage is to the following effect: "For as we affirm that there is a God and a Son, his Logos, and a Holy Spirit; the Father, Son, and Spirit being united in respect of power (κατὰ δύναμιν), because the Son is the mind, reason, wisdom of the Father, and the Spirit an effluence as light from fire s."

There is another passage referring only to the Logos: "As all things have been placed under you, father and son, who have received your kingdom from above * * * so all things have been subjected to one, namely, God, and the Logos which comes from Him, who is conceived by us as his Son inseparable" (ἐνὶ τῷ θεῷ καὶ τῷ παρ' αὐτοῦ λόγῳ υἱῷ νοουμένῳ ἀμερίστῳ t). A statement of a similar nature, though less distinct, is made in the assertion that Christians "reckon as God the creator of this universe, and the Logos which is from Him u."

The explanations of Athenagoras in regard to the Trinity are not very full or satisfactory. Some points are clear; many points he has left entirely untouched. He states again

---

q Apol. c. 10, pp. 10 B C D, 11 A.   r Ibid. c. 12, p. 12 C D.
s Apol. c. 24, p. 27 A..   t Ibid. c. 18, p. 17 D.   u Ibid. c. 30, p. 34 D.

and again the unity of Father, Son, and Holy Spirit. He calls the Son God, as well as the Father. But he does not give a clear explanation of how he maintained the unity of God with the divinity of the Son. The nearest approximation is when he states that the three were united or made one in respect of power. The power which all exercised was the same, because the Logos was the reason of God, and therefore his power was God's power; and the Spirit was an effluence from God, and therefore the power of the Spirit was also God's power. Athenagoras also intimates that the unity of Father and Son lay also in the unity and power of the Spirit. Some have attempted to translate the words πνεῦμα and δύναμις differently. They suppose that both words are expressions used to denote the divine existence. They translate the words τὴν ἐν τῇ ἑνώσει δύναμιν, 'their existence in unity;' and they translate ἑνότητι καὶ δυνάμει πνεύματος, 'in the unity and force of their divine existence.' But there are strong objections to this translation of δύναμις and πνεῦμα. There is no proof that δύναμις anywhere means simply existence apart from the force or activity usually implied in the word. When force is taken as an index of the being or nature, then δύναμις may be translated 'being;' but in neither of the passages in which δύναμις is used by Athenagoras can it have any such meaning. Besides, the idea of force is a less distinct idea than that of being, and would occur to the human mind before the more exact idea of essence or being: and therefore we should commit a great mistake if we were to take the more exact idea as equivalent o the more indefinite. Moreover, in the passage before us, we should have expected "unity in the power or being," and not "power in the unity." And in the other passage, where Father, Son, and Spirit are said to be united in respect of power, the reason assigned for this assertion, namely, that the Logos and the Spirit are God's reason and spirit, is not a satisfactory reason. We think, therefore, that in the passage before us, "power in unity" means, that owing to the connexion between God and his Son as his reason, and his

Spirit as his effluence, the power of God is at the command of the Son and the Spirit. The same objections lie against the translation of πνεῦμα, that it is more definite than the term itself. Athenagoras seems to mean in the expression quoted, that the Father and Son are one in that they possess one and the same spirit, and have the control over that spirit. We shall, it seems to me, best understand the whole doctrine if we throw ourselves into the position of Athenagoras. He looks on the Son of God as God's reason. He hypostatizes what we in our day should unquestionably make a faculty. Now the reason of God is eternally in Him, and therefore is eternal. What the reason of God advises to be done, God will do. Therefore the whole power of God is at the command of his Reason or Logos. God communicates his power to his Reason, and everything that is subject to the Father is subject to the Son. Father and Son in this point of view are inseparable. But the reason of God being God's possession, all the power which the Reason has is God's, and thus there is unity. But at the same time there must be a difference in rank, the Son and the Spirit being both under the control of the Father, and deriving their power from Him. The Reason went forth to be the idea and energy of all material things; that is, in our language, the order and harmony of creation are the results of God's thought. Athenagoras, however, has an especial reference to the ideas of Plato, and also to the doctrine of the intelligible or noetic world in the Timæus. The model of this world is in the Timæus the unseen, eternally-existent, ideal world, perceived only by the mind. According to Athenagoras the model or idea is the Logos. But not only is He the exemplar, but it is through his constant activity (ἐνέργεια) that the world is maintained in its state of intelligibility, that is, in our language, of order and harmony; just as Plato says that the creator produces in a created object the idea and force of the eternal exemplar[x]. The other passages in which Athena-

[x] Tim. p. 28 A.

goras refers to the Logos relate to his activity in creation. It is said oftener than once, that God made all things through the Logos which proceeds from Him [y]. "By whom" [God], he says in a passage already quoted, "the universe has been made through his Logos, and has been put in order, and is held together [z]."

There has been much useless discussion as to whether Athenagoras favoured Arianism, or Sabellianism, or some such later theory[a]. His position, as we have explained, belongs peculiarly to his age, but is modified by his Platonic reading. He differs from his contemporaries more in his silence than in his express statements. He does not say that the Father and Son were one, in that the Son's divinity was derived from the Father's. He seems to have avoided this mode of representation. But he unquestionably adopts this very mode when he speaks of the Spirit. The analogy by which he realizes the unity of Father and Spirit is a purely material one. Athenagoras also adopts the common expression γέννημα applied to the Son; but he makes no reference to the Son being begotten, and in using the word προέρχεσθαι seems to avoid the more common expression. His philosophy brought before him the necessity of the eternity of the Son [b].

Athenagoras does not once introduce the name of Jesus Christ into his works. We have, therefore, no means of knowing what connexion he thought subsisted between the Logos and the human Jesus. There may possibly be an allusion to his incarnation in the following passage, where he is discussing the earthly appearances of the Homeric gods: "Even if a god should take upon him flesh according to a divine economy, is he then a slave of lust [c]?" Athenagoras quotes the words of Christ several times. We shall notice the passages afterwards.

[y] Apol. c. 4, p. 5 C; c. 6, p. 7 A.   [z] Ibid. c. 10, p. 10 B.
[a] See Clarisse, pp. 94-100.
[b] See Dorner, Die Lehre von der Person Christi, vol. i. p. 440. His reason for this 'advance,' however, is utterly unsatisfactory.   [c] Apol. c. 21, p. 21 D.

The Spirit.—In Athenagoras the Spirit is nowhere called God. The words used to convey his notion of the Spirit are also purely material. He is "an effluence, flowing from and returning as a ray of the sun;" "as light from fire." There is no reason to doubt that Athenagoras looked on the Spirit as a being, not as a mere power, though the expressions which he uses are the very expressions which Justin condemns in his opposition to the emanation theory. Athenagoras, like the other Christians, had not had his attention called to the doctrine of the Spirit. In harmony at once with tradition and the idea involved in the Spirit as the Spirit of God, he does not call him God, and in harmony with the practice of the age he compares Him to material things without being conscious of the fatal mistake that lurks in the comparison.

He assigns to the Spirit the maintenance of the world. "All things are held together by the Spirit which is from Him [God][d]." In another passage he speaks of the world being guided by the Spirit of God as a chariot is guided by a charioteer[e]. Perhaps the phraseology here is modified by the train of thought in the context, where the correspondence of the idea of Zeus to that of the true God in the ancient poets is brought out. These passages show how indefinite Athenagoras's notions of the Spirit were: for the very same function of preserving the world is assigned to the Logos.

Athenagoras also attributes the inspiration of the prophets to the Spirit. The Spirit is consequently called the prophetic Spirit, as well as the divine Spirit and the Holy Spirit. The passages will be quoted afterwards.

Angels.—After appealing to the belief of Christians in Father, Son, and Holy Spirit as proof that they were not atheists, Athenagoras adds: "And not in these alone does the theological portion of our beliefs consist: but we also affirm that there is a multitude of angels and servants, whom God

the creator and fashioner of the world has distributed and
arranged by means of the Logos which is from Him, to be
occupied about the elements, and heavens, and the world,
and the things that are in it, and their regularity[f]." The
words 'and servants' are generally considered as explanatory of angels. The angels are the servants of God. The
clause at the commencement has been considered to imply
the worship of angels: but it really means no more than
that angels were supernatural beings. The τὸ θεολογικὸν
μέρος, the theologic side of Christianity, includes belief in all
those beings who are superior to man; and who are therefore
likely to inspire him with awe. In the Treatise on the Resurrection Athenagoras seems to designate the angels "natures perceptible by mind only" (νοηταὶ φύσεις[g]). He is
showing that no injury could be done to any one by a
resurrection, and affirms that none could be done to the
νοηταὶ φύσεις, and none to the irrational creation. He
styles the νοηταὶ φύσεις in another place[h] as those who are
"purely indestructible and immortal," and as "having been
from the beginning immortal, and abiding without end
solely by the will of Him that made them." It is needless to point out how entirely Platonic the classification
and language are. The influence of the Timæus is seen
also in the work which is assigned to them, the particular
care of certain parts of the universe. Athenagoras states
their work more precisely in a long passage in which he
mentions the fall of some of them, and the antagonism
especially of one to the goodness of God. We shall quote
the passage fully, and now merely draw attention to the
circumstance that Athenagoras claims prophetic authority
for his statements. "We have come to believe," he says,
"that there are also other powers engaged about matter
and acting by means of it: especially that there is one
opposed to God. We do not, indeed, affirm that there
really does exist anything in opposition to God, as discord

---

[f] Apol. c. 10, p. 11 A   [g] De Res. c. 10, p. 49 C.
[h] De Res. c. 16, p. 57 D.

opposes friendship, according to Empedocles, and night day according to the appearances in the sky, for if anything were really to stand up against God it would cease to exist, since its constitution would be dissolved by the power and strength of God ; but we say that the spirit which is engaged about matter is contrary to the goodness of God . . . . though he was made by God, as the other angels were made by Him, and entrusted with the management of matter and its forms. For this is the constitution of angels, that they should exercise providence for God over the things which He has brought into order, that God may have the universal and general providence of the whole, while angels are appointed over particular parts of it. Just, then, as in the case of men who have both virtue and vice in their own choice (since you would not honour the good nor punish the wicked, unless both vice and virtue were in their power, and some are found trustworthy in that which you entrust to them, and some unfaithful), so it is with angels. For some, with the freewill with which they were made by God, remained in charge of those things over which God had made and appointed them, while others acted insolently both in respect to the substance of their existence[1] and in respect to their rule; namely, he who was ruler of matter, and the forms that are in it, and the others who are engaged about this first firmament. Know that we say nothing for which we have not testimony, but that we are indicating that which has been proclaimed by the prophets. Those engaged about the first firmament fell into lust of virgins and were found incapable of resisting the charms of flesh, while the ruler of matter neglected his charge and became wicked in regard

---

[1] Τῇ τῆς οὐσίας ὑποστάσει καὶ τῇ ἀρχῇ. The interpretations of this clause are various. Otto translates τῇ τῆς οὐσίας ὑποστάσει, 'ob naturæ suæ conditionem,' and supposes that Athenagoras refers to their free-will. I suppose that by the substance of their existence is meant that which lay at the bottom of their genuine life. The love of women was totally in violation of this fundamental constitution ; thus they acted insolently in respect to it.

to the management of what had been entrusted to him. From those, then, who were enamoured of the virgins, those who are called giants were born[k]."

Of the wicked angels Athenagoras in the passage distinguishes three classes—first, the ruler of matter or the devil, a name which he does not employ; second, the evil angels who fell in love with women; and thirdly, the giants, their offspring.

In speaking of the devil Athenagoras calls him a spirit. He takes the utmost care to prevent his readers from supposing that the devil stood on an equality with God. There is no opposition of being to being. The devil was made by God, and could be destroyed by God. He is opposed only to the goodness of God. "The ruler of matter," he says in the following chapter[l], "manages and arranges things opposed to the goodness of God, as you may see from those very things which happen."

Of the angels and demons he says, that "having fallen from the heavens and being engaged about air and earth they are no longer able to penetrate into heavenly things, and the souls of the giants are the demons who wander about the world. The demons stir up movements like the constitutions which they received, while the angels cause movements like the lusts which they felt[m]." Through these movements which take place in men and men's affairs the devil, the wicked angels, and the demons cause people to renounce their belief in Providence. They, for instance, bring it about that men are sometimes prosperous contrary to justice. "But since," he says, in continuation of the subject, "the demonic movements and energies which proceed from the opposing spirit produce these disorderly impulses, moving men from within and from without, sometimes one way, sometimes another, individually and by nations, partially and generally, according to the proportion of their sympathy with matter and with divine things; on account of this some,

---

[k] Apol. c. 24, p. 27.   [l] Ibid. c. 25, p. 28 B.
[m] Apol. c. 25, p. 28 A B.

whose reputations are not mean, have thought that it is not by order that this universe exists together, but that it is driven about by an unreasoning chance[n]." These demons stand beside the blood of victims and lick them, and while the gods were originally men, the demons usurp their names, as may be inferred from the actions of the gods[o]. They attack tender souls who are easily deceived, and make them believe that appearances come from the idols, and that the intimations of futurity which lie hid in their own immortal souls are the results of idol worship[p].

It is noteworthy that Athenagoras connects his notions of the demons with the speculations of the Greek philosophers, and their division of the supernatural beings into "God, δαίμονες, and heroes." He attributes this division to Thales, but lays especial stress on Plato's teaching with regard to these δαίμονες[q].

Man.—The doctrine of Athenagoras with regard to man differs essentially from that of his contemporaries in respect to the soul. He regards the soul as purely spiritual, though its spirituality may be disturbed by its material tendencies. The πνεῦμα, or spirit of man, is not mentioned by Athenagoras. His whole teaching on this subject is Platonic. He states again and again that man was made by God, especially in treating of the purpose for which he was made and of his constitution. He asserts that "all men are of the same race (ὁμογενεῖς), as being sprung from the same commencement; for their commencement was the origination of the first human beings by fashioning" (ἐκ δημιουργίας[r]). He attributes the beauty of man to the creative power of God. Speaking of those who are guilty of licentiousness he says, with special reference to the body of man, " Dishonouring the beautiful creation of God. For beauty on earth is not self-made, but is sent forth by the hand and counsel of God[s]."

Man is composed of soul and body. He is neither soul

[n] Apol. c. 25, pp. 28 D, 29 A.
[p] Apol. c. 27, pp. 30 C D, 31 A.
[r] Res. c. 18. p. 59 D.

[o] Ibid. c. 26, p. 29 B C.
[q] Ibid. c. 23, p. 25 B C.
[s] Apol. c. 34, p. 37 C.

nor body, but both combined. This doctrine is a prominent feature in the Treatise on the Resurrection, as may be seen from the Abstract. The soul, indeed, is the principal and immortal part; yet the body is not to be despised. It was made to be corruptible in this life. But death is a *natural* termination to this its corruptible state, and it then passes into a state of incorruption. These various statements will be proved by extracts.

Athenagoras again and again states the constitution of man to be made up of soul and body. "He [i. e. man] is composed of soul and body[t]," he says, in showing that the resurrection can be no injustice to man; and then he proceeds to prove that no injury can be done to the immortal soul by being joined to an incorruptible body, if no injury was done it by being joined to a corruptible. "If," he says in another argument, "the entire nature of man generally has its constitution from an immortal soul and a body which was by creation united to it[u]." And in another passage where he contrasts the nature of those who were purely incorruptible with the inferior nature of man, he goes on, "the one class having been from the beginning immortal, and continuing so without end by the sole will of the Maker, while men have an unchangeable continuance in respect to their soul from their creation, but receive incorruption in respect to the body only by a process of change[x]."

The immortality of the soul is repeatedly affirmed. There is nothing definite in Athenagoras with regard to the origin of the soul. He in one place says that it is not souls that beget souls, but men that beget men[y]; and from this statement it has been inferred that he did not believe that the soul of man was fashioned from another soul. But the inference is unfair. In one passage he seems to mention the Platonic doctrine of Reminiscence. "The dispute," he says, "either turns on first principles, and then there is need only of recollection which stirs up the natural concept, or

---

[t] Res. c. 10, p. 50 A.
[x] Res. c. 16, pp. 57 D, 58 A.
[u] Ibid. c. 15, p. 56 B.
[y] Ibid. c. 23.

in those things that naturally follow the first principles[z]." The ὑπόμνησις here, however, cannot be identified with the Platonic ἀνάμνησις; for it might be reconciled with any philosophy of knowledge. The first or primary doctrines which he speaks of are those that directly concern nature, such as creation, while the φυσικὴ ἔννοια, or 'natural notion,' is the concept of such a natural primary dogma.

Death is the natural end to the body (τὸ τῇ φύσει προσῆκον τέλος[a]). The soul is then separated from the body, and the particles of the body scattered[b]. But this dissolution of the body no more impairs the continuity of man's existence than sleep destroys the continuity of his earthly life[c].

The soul of man belongs to those things which he calls νοητά, 'perceptible only by mind.' He has some remarks on the relation of the νοητά, 'intelligibles,' to the αἰσθητά, 'sensibles,' in the Apology[d]; but they are not easy to understand, and the text is doubtful. He tells the emperors that he does not think it prudent to dwell on certain topics, "speaking with regard to the intelligibles and sensibles, and their constitution, or proving that bodiless things are older than bodies (σωμάτων), and intelligibles take the precedence of sensibles, though we meet with the sensibles first in experience; for bodies are formed from bodiless things by an addition in their composition of intelligibles, and sensibles are formed from intelligibles." He here seems to state the Platonic doctrine that matter becomes cognizable only by a participation of an idea; that that which gives form and intelligibility to shapeless matter and makes it a body is a νοητόν or νοητά.

Athenagoras does not speak of any other part of man besides the soul and body. He says of his prospect of a future state, "We shall remain, not as flesh, even though we have it, but as a heavenly spirit[e]." And in another passage, which we shall afterwards quote more fully, he says

[z] Res. c. 14, p. 55 A.
[b] Res. c. 18, p. 61 B.
[d] Apol. c. 36, p. 39 B C.
[a] Ibid. c. 15, p. 56 C.
[c] Ibid. c. 17, p. 58 D.
[e] Ibid. c. 31, p. 35 D

that the soul by partaking of the material spirit is "no longer pure spirit [f]." He could not therefore have supposed the spirit to be different from the soul, but to be descriptive of the state of the soul.

One would have expected that Athenagoras would assign the reason and mental powers of man to the soul. This might be inferred from his dividing man into soul and body: for as they cannot belong to the body, they must belong to the soul. But strangely enough, he supposes that mind and reason belong to man, the compound of body and soul, and not to soul by itself. The notion of man as distinct from beasts is that of a being who is possessed of an immortal soul *and the power of rational judgment* [g]. Men are said "to act according to an implanted law and reason," and to "use an intelligent life and justice [h]." But this law and reason are implanted not in the soul by itself, but in man. "If," he says, "mind and reason ($\nu o \hat{u} s$ $\kappa a \grave{\iota}$ $\lambda \acute{o} \gamma o s$) have been given to man to distinguish intelligibles, not substances only, but also the goodness, and wisdom, and justice of the giver, then the judgment which was given for this purpose must remain as long as those things remain on account of which the rational judgment has been given ... Now, he who received mind and reason is man, not soul by itself [i]." We may easily suppose, however, that Athenagoras was pressed into this representation by his argument: for in the Apology he describes the soul as capable sometimes of seeing the truth, and even of giving hints of the future [k]. And in the Treatise on the Resurrection he assigns to the soul a power of judging.

Athenagoras in his discussion of the arguments for the Resurrection, separates widely the activity of the soul from that of the body. The body is said to desire earthly things; the soul to rule it. There are five important passages on this subject, two of which will be quoted when we treat of sin. The other three are—"If the nature of man does not continue, in vain has the soul been fitted to the need and

[f] Apol. c. 27, p. 30 C.   [g] Res. c. 24, p. 67 C.   [h] Ibid. c. 24. p. 67 B.
[i] Res. c. 15. p. 57 A.   [k] Apol. c. 27. p. 31 A.

affections (πάθεσιν) of the body, and in vain has the body been fettered in its efforts to obtain those things which it desires, yielding to the reins of the soul, and bridled by it; and vain is mind (ὁ νοῦς), and vain is prudence, and vain the observance of justice[l]," &c. The second passage runs thus: "The soul has by itself no feeling in regard to the offences which are committed in reference to bodily pleasures, or nourishment and care;" and "the body cannot judge by itself of law and right [m]." The third passage states distinctly the natural activity of the soul: "The soul's natural function is to govern the impulses of the body, and to judge and measure always by the proper criteria and measures that which happens" (τὸ προσπίπτον [n]).

Athenagoras speaks of the "pleasures of the soul[o]." He speaks also of the blessedness of the soul not existing apart from the body. "For there is not assuredly a blessedness of a soul that is separated from body [p]."

Athenagoras speaks much of the end for which man was made. "God did not make man in vain: for He is wise, and no work of wisdom is vain; nor on account of his own use, for He needs nothing [q]." He describes the purpose more exactly in these words: "Looking at the first and more general reason, we should say that God made man on account of Himself and the goodness and wisdom seen over all creation; but speaking in reference to the beings created, we should say that He made them on account of the life of the beings created [r]." Life then is the primary end; but this life must be a life in harmony with the nature of the being. "God," he says, "has allotted a perpetual continuance to those who bear his own image in themselves: that is, to those who carry along with them (συνεπιφερομένοις) mind, and are partakers of rational judgment; that knowing their Creator and His power and wisdom, and obeying His law

---

[l] Res. c. 15, p. 57 B C.   [m] Ibid. c. 18, p. 61 A.
[n] Res. c. 12, p. 53 D. Otto compares Cic. de Offic. i. c. 28.
[o] Apol. c. 33, p. 36 D.   [p] Res. c. 25, p. 67 C.
[q] Res. c. 12, p. 52 B.   [r] Ibid. c. 12. p. 53 A.

and justice, they may continue together free from toil in those things (τούτοις συνδιαιωνίζωσιν) by which they gave strength (ἐκράτυναν) to their previous life, although they were in corruptible and earthen bodies ᵗ." Otto translates ἐκράτυναν ζωήν, 'they endured the previous life.' But the idea seems to me to be that the knowledge of God is a knowledge which can be gained only while the person is obedient to God's law, is that which makes life a real living, and gives it consistency and strength. There is much dispute as to the idea to which τούτοις refers. Otto seems to me unquestionably right in applying it to the knowledge of God and obedience to his law. It is in this employment that men are to pass the ages of eternity (συνδιαιωνίζειν), just as now the only true life of man depends on his devoting himself to the knowledge of God. That Otto is right is proved by similar passages in which the end of man is stated. "If," he says, "the Fashioner of this universe made man that he might partake of an intelligent (ἔμφρονος) life, and, becoming an observer (θεωρόν) of his magnificence and his wisdom which appears in all things, he might remain together (συνδιαμένειν) in the perpetual contemplation (θεωρίᾳ) of these things, according to the design of the Creator and the nature which man has received, the cause of his creation guarantees his perpetual continuance ᵘ." And again, "No one would go wrong in saying that the end of an intelligent life and a rational judgment is an undistracted spending of the ages (ἀπερισπάστως συνδιαιωνίζειν) in those things for which natural reason is most especially and primarily adapted; that is, in the contemplation of Him who is (θεωρίᾳ τοῦ ὄντος), and in the unceasing enjoyment of his decrees ˣ."

Athenagoras acknowledges that the majority of men fail to reach the end suitable to men, in a passage immediately following the last quoted. But he gives no exposition of his doctrine of sin. There is no reason to believe that he knew anything of the doctrine of original sin. He certainly was ignorant of the doctrine of inherited condemnation. Arguing against the opinion that the only cause for a resurrection is the subsequent judgment, he says: "This is plainly proved to be false, from the circumstance that all human beings who die, rise again, but that all who rise again are not judged: for if the demand of justice for a judgment were the only cause of a resurrection, then, of course, those who have done neither evil nor good ought not to rise again; that is, those who are very young children: but since all are permitted to rise again, both other human beings and assuredly those who have died in their earliest years, these are proof that the resurrection does not take place primarily on account of judgment, but on account of the will of the Fashioner, and the nature of the fashioned y." It is scarcely possible to suppose that if Athenagoras had ever heard of the opinion that all human beings had shared in condemnation because they were in Adam, he would not have said something about it in the passage quoted.

Athenagoras says comparatively little of free-will in man, but, as we have seen already, he states the doctrine distinctly, and in the way and connexion in which his contemporaries insisted on it z.

He traces sin on the one hand to individual wilfulness, and on the other to the energy of the devil and demons. "Man," he says, "is, by the design of the Creator, in a state of order, both in respect to the nature given him at creation, which contains one common reason; and in respect to the disposition of his body, which does not transgress the law laid upon it; and also in respect to the end of life which remains equal and common: but in consequence of the reason which is peculiar to himself, and the energy of the dominant ruler [the Devil] and the attendant demons, one is driven and moved one way, and another another, though all of them have the same common reasoning powers a." Here it will be observed that Athenagoras distinctly frees God from any blame in man's sin. As far as

---

y Res. c. 14, p. 55 D.   z Apol. c. 24.   a Ibid. c. 25. p. 29 A B.

God's activity is concerned (κατὰ τὸν πεποιηκότα), man is himself a full illustration of the orderliness of the world. This order is seen in the nature which was given him when God created him (κατὰ γένεσιν): for this nature possesses the faculty of reasoning, which is one and the same in all. It appears also in the arrangement of man's body, so far as God's fashioning it is concerned (τῇ κατὰ τὴν πλάσιν διαθέσει), for it never violates the law which He has given to it. But then man chooses reasons for himself (κατὰ τὸν ἴδιον ἑαυτῷ λόγον). He abandons the universal reason and acts wilfully: and this wilfulness is fostered by the powers of evil. Harmony is destroyed, and man is so far an exception to the universal orderliness of the world. The context of the passage renders it indubitable that the drift of the passage [b] is as I have now given it.

The disturbing occasion in man himself is matter, or, in other words, the body. Athenagoras nowhere seems to imagine that evil was inherent in matter. On the contrary, he affirms repeatedly that the body is and will continue for ever to be an essential part of man. But the body is the occasion of most of the virtues and vices of man. He brings this out very fully in attempting to show that it is unfair to reward or punish souls alone for what was done by man, who is composed both of soul and body. "How is it not unjust," he says, "that the soul should be judged by itself for things for which according to its nature it cannot have a longing, nor motion, nor impulse—such as luxury, or violence, or avarice, or injustice, and the acts of injustice which are consequent on these? For if the most of such evils arise from men not controlling disturbing passions, and if they are disturbed by the need and wants of the body, and zeal about it, and care of it, (for on account of these things it is that there is possession (πᾶσα ἡ κτῆσις) at all [c], and that

---

[b] See the rest quoted above.

[c] The statement which Athenagoras makes here is that in consequence of the body arises the idea of property. But the first form of this idea is simple use, which ultimately becomes possession or property.

there is a use which is before this, that there is marriage also, and all the businesses of life in which, and in relation to which, is seen short-coming and the contrary,) where is justice?" &c.[d] Athenagoras goes on throughout the whole of this chapter and the next, exhibiting the virtues and vices which are rendered possible by the existence of the body.

It is also especially through matter that the devil and demons act on men. The devil himself is, as we have seen, the ruler of matter, and the demons move men according to the proportion of matter and the sympathy with divine things. The sympathy with divine things, the fellow-feeling (συμπάθεια) or kinship of the mind with heavenly and divine things, is that which preserves the true life in man. It is to this fellow-feeling, with the breath which is from God (κατὰ συμπάθειαν τῆς παρὰ τοῦ Θεοῦ πνοῆς), that Athenagoras attributes the impulse among the ancient poets and philosophers to seek the truth[e]. On the other hand, " the body draws the soul [in the case of sin] to fellow-feeling with and share in those deeds which it requires[f]." The demons were unable to mount up because they had not a fellow-feeling which would bring them into heaven (συμπάθειαν εἰς τὸν οὐράνιον τόπον), and therefore they pined after forms of matter[g].

The activity of the demons on the souls of men is thus described. He is accounting for idols, and their supposed activity. " First then the irrational and imaginative movements of the soul around opinions[h] produce different idols at different times. Some of these they take from matter, and some they fashion and beget for themselves. And this is the case with the soul most especially when it has partaken and become mixed up with the material spirit, not looking to heavenly things and their Creator, but downwards to earthly things,—in fact, entirely to the earth,—as being flesh and blood only, and no longer pure spirit. These irrational

---

[d] Res. c. 21, pp. 63 D, 64 B.
[f] Res. c. 21, p. 64 A.
[e] Apol. c. 7, p. 8 A.
[g] Apol. c. 22, p. 24 C.
[h] The whole expression here is Platonic; the movement of the soul and the δόξαι (or ' opinions') in contrast with ἐπιστήμη (or the ' knowledge ').

and imaginative movements of the soul give birth to idol-mad visions. But when a soul which is tender, easily led, ignorant of and unacquainted with strong beliefs, and which has not been accustomed to behold the truth (ἀθεώρητος τοῦ ἀληθοῦς), and to consider the Father and Maker of the Universe,—when such a soul gets stamped upon it false opinions with regard to itself, then the demons employed on matter, who are lickerish about the steams of the fat and the blood of victims and are in the habit of deceiving men, taking to their aid these false-opinioned movements of the soul of the many, make visions flow in upon them as if from the idols and images, by invading their minds, and the demons reap the glory of whatever rational movements the soul makes in harmony with its own nature as being immortal, either by way of predicting the future or healing the presentj."

Athenagoras says nothing about the scheme of salvation. He mentions salvation several times in treating of the discourse concerning the truth and the discourse in behalf of the truth. "The discourse concerning the truth, being necessary to all men for security and salvation, takes the first place in nature, in order, and in usefulness[k]." And then he states that it is first in usefulness, "because it is the cause of security and salvation to those who know[l]." He repeats the same idea in other words a few sentences farther on: "The one is necessary for all who believe and care about the truth and their own salvation[m]." It would not be safe to build much on these statements, because they are so indefinite; but we may believe that Athenagoras regarded the truth as the saving or preserving element of man's real life, and that it had this power only to those who really knew it, or, in other words, really believed it.

He says that Christians have a "hope of eternal life[n]." He dwells largely on their moral character, and the precepts which guided them. God is the rule of their life. "The

[j] Apol. c. 27, p. 30 C D. [k] Res. c. 11, p. 51 A. [l] Ibid.
[m] Res. c. 11, p. 51 B. [n] Apol. c. 33, p. 36 D.

unjudging slander of some does not darken our path onwards to rectitude of life; for we have a good character with God°." "Ye know," he says to the emperors, "that those whose life is regulated by God as the law (οἷς ὁ βίος ὡς πρὸς στάθμην τὸν θεὸν κανονίζεται) that each of us may be found guiltless and blameless before Him will not enter into the thought even of the smallest sin^p."

Athenagoras makes no mention of any of the peculiar institutions of Christians. He mentions the habit which prevailed among them of calling the young people sons and daughters. Those who were older they called brothers and sisters, and to those who were far advanced in years they gave the honour of fathers and mothers[q]. Some have supposed that he refuses to disclose the mysteries of the Christian religion. The supposition is utterly absurd. In speaking of the abominable practices of heathens, he exclaims, "O, why should I speak of things which ought not to be mentioned (τὰ ἀπόρρητα[r])?" There cannot be a doubt that Athenagoras is speaking of the abominable practices of heathens: the whole context proves this. The use of the word ἀπόρρητα in another passage of the same writer is in favour of it. And nothing could have led Rothe to imagine anything else but a pet theory.

Future State.—The principal statements with regard to a future state occur in the Treatise on the Resurrection, to the Abstract of which the reader is referred. Athenagoras did not believe that there is an intermediate state of sleep. The body is dissolved, but the immortal soul remains as active as ever[s]. He maintains also that it is the same bodies that will rise again. He affirms that it is absolutely necessary that the same men rise again, and he says that this cannot take place if the same bodies are not given to the same souls[t]. But then the bodies at the resurrection are to differ from the bodies on earth in this respect, that the former

---

° Apol. c. 31, p. 35 B.   p Ibid. p. 35 C.
q Apol. c. 32, p. 36 C.   r Ibid. c. 34, p. 37 C.
s Res. c. 16, p. 57 D.   t Ibid. c. 25, p. 67 D.

are to be indestructible, while the latter were destructible. Moreover, it is only the real essential components of the body that are again to come together[u]. Athenagoras seems to have supposed that there were some parts that really and properly belonged to the body, while others were accidental appendages. In the union of these real parts lay the identity of the body. He seems not to have been aware of the fact that all the particles of the body change within a certain period.

Athenagoras believed that animals would not rise again[x].

After the resurrection comes the judgment. As we have seen already, Athenagoras argues from the necessity of a judgment the necessity of a resurrection. He describes the judgment thus,—" The honour or justice [rewards or punishment] due to each man according to just judgment[y]." Again, he speaks of the proportion or reckoning ($\lambda \acute{o} \gamma o s$) of justice according to which God judges those men who have lived well or ill[z]. The fact of an expected judgment is appealed to as likely to have a strong moral influence on Christians. " Since we are persuaded," he says, " that we shall give an account of the whole of our present life to God, who has made us and the world, we choose this temperate, man-loving, and despised life, since we are of opinion that we shall suffer no such great evil here, even if some deprive us of life ($\psi v \chi \hat{\eta} s$), as the blessings which we shall receive there on account of a meek, man-loving, and temperate life, from the great Judge[a]." He describes more fully in another passage the life of the good hereafter, the blessedness of which he makes consist in freedom from change and passion, in the company of God. He mentions also that the wicked will be in fire. It runs thus: " We are persuaded that when we are removed from our life here we shall live another life, better than the life here, and heavenly, not earthly; inasmuch as we shall abide in the company of God, and in union with Him ($\mu \epsilon \tau \grave{a} \ \theta \epsilon o \hat{v} \ \kappa a \grave{i} \ \sigma \grave{v} \nu \ \theta \epsilon \hat{\varphi}$), free from

[u] Res. c. 7.
[x] Ibid. c. 10, p. 49 C; Apol. c. 31, p. 35 D.
[y] Res. c. 14, p. 55 C.
[z] Ibid. c. 18, p. 60 A.
[a] Apol. c. 12, p. 12 B.

change and passion[b] as respects our soul, not as flesh even though we have it, but as heavenly spirit; or that falling down along with the rest we shall live a worse life, and one passed in fire: for God did not fashion us as He did sheep or cattle, as a bye-work, and to perish and disappear. On this account it is not likely that we should wish to do evil, or deliver ourselves up to the great Judge to be punished[c]."

Athenagoras nowhere speaks of the Logos or Christ as judge.

The Scriptures.—Athenagoras, as we have seen, maintained that the truths believed by Christians were God-taught[d]. He appeals to the prophets as guarantees for his beliefs: and enunciates his theory of inspiration while making the appeal. "But," he says, "we have as witnesses of those opinions which we hold and have believed the prophets, who have spoken out by the Divine Spirit in them both with regard to God and things relating to God. You also, who surpass others in intelligence and in piety towards the really Divine Being, would yourselves affirm that it would be unreasonable for us to abandon our trust in the Spirit which proceeds from God, who has moved the mouths of the prophets as instruments, and give heed to human opinions[e]." In another passage he expresses the same ideas. "If, then, we were content with such notions, some one would think our teaching to be merely human. But since the voices of the prophets make our reasonings trustworthy, I think that you also, being very learned and very intelligent, have not been ignorant of the writings of Moses, or of those of Isaiah and Jeremiah and the other prophets, who being rapt away from the reasonings that were in themselves (κατ' ἔκστασιν τῶν ἐν αὐτοῖς λογισμῶν) when the Divine Spirit had moved them, uttered the things that were wrought in them, while the Spirit used them as a flute-player would blow into his flute[f]." Athenagoras announces in these passages most

---

[b] ἀπαθεῖς τὴν ψυχήν may mean 'with our souls incapable of suffering.'
[c] Apol. c. 31, p. 35 D.
[d] Ibid. c. 32, p. 36 C.
[e] Apol. c. 7, p. 8 A B.
[f] Ibid. c. 9, p. 9 D.

distinctly the theory of inspiration now designated the mechanical. He also expresses clearly the Montanistic idea of prophecy—that it took place while the prophet was transported beyond himself. But it would be unfair to Athenagoras to suppose that he imagined he was giving precise expression to any theory. He used the words evidently very much in the dark, and probably without the conception that inspiration admitted of theoretical explanations. His language would lead one to suppose that he believed every word in the Old Testament to be inspired. But if he did, it seems strange that he should have been so careless in quoting. In the very next sentence following the second passage which has been now translated, he professedly quotes from Exodus, yet the very form of the sentence is changed. And he never hesitates to change words whenever such a change suits his purpose [g].

Athenagoras makes no allusion to the inspiration of any of the New Testament writers. He does not mention one of them by name, and we cannot be sure that he quotes from any except Paul. All the passages taken from the Gospels are parts of our Lord's discourses, and may have come down to Athenagoras by tradition. He unquestionably quotes from the Epistle to the Romans; he quotes also from the First Epistle to the Corinthians, and on one occasion he introduces the quotation with the words "according to the apostle [h]." He quotes also from the First Epistle to Timothy, and probably from the Epistle to the Galatians. Some have found traces of passages from other Epistles.

In quoting the words of Christ, Athenagoras never mentions Christ by name: but simply uses the word $\phi\eta\sigma\iota$, 'he says.' He once departs from this usage in quoting a curious saying which is not found in any of our Gospels. The passage runs thus: "The Logos again saying to us, 'If any one kiss again for the reason that it has been pleasant

---

[g] On the passages quoted, see Lardner and Clarisse, p. 70.
[h] Res. c. 18, p. 61 C.

to him —ⁱ;' and the Logos then adds, 'Thus the kiss, or rather the salutation, is to be used with care, because it places us outside of eternal life if it be polluted but a little in thought ᵏ.'" The passage refers to the customary kiss in the congregation of Christians. It prohibits the repetition of the kiss from mere delight in it, as such a feeling is sinful. It may be very much questioned whether the τοῦ λόγου λέγοντος really refers to Christ. It is singular that the only departure from the common φησί should be in the case of a very questionable command. The suppositions in regard to the source from which the passage is taken are numerous, and all of them are purely conjectural ˡ.

Morality.—Attention has been already called to the high eulogium which Athenagoras has pronounced on the moral power of Christianity. There still remains the consideration of his opinions on some special points. First and most prominent of these are his decisions with regard to marriage. He quotes the assertion of Christ, that the looking on a woman to desire her is adultery; and states that to Christians "looking with pleasure is adultery" (τὸ ἰδεῖν ἡδέως μοιχεία ᵐ). He appeals, farther, to the unwritten statement generally attributed to Christ, quoted above. He then develops more fully his opinions on marriage. He maintains that a man ought to marry only once: that the only object of marriage is the production of children: and that any indulgence in sexual intercourse which has not this object distinctly as its aim is sin. His words are: "Having then a hope of eternal life, we despise the things that are in this life, even to the pleasures of soul: for each one reckons as his wife her whom he married according to the laws laid down by us, and he reckons her his wife only for the purpose of producing children. For as the husbandman laying down seed into the earth awaits the harvest, not throwing down additional seed, so the procreation of children is the measure of our

---

ⁱ The reader is to supply 'he sins.' ᵏ Apol. c. 32. p. 36 D.
ˡ See Otto's note on the passage for them.
ᵐ Apol. c. 32. p. 36 B.

desire ⁿ." It will be noticed here that Christians were not married according to Roman law, but according to laws laid down by themselves. They probably regarded marriage as a religious institution much more than a civil one; and as they could not be married according to the rites of pagan Rome, they instituted laws of their own.

Though Athenagoras does not say anything against marriage itself, he awards high praise to those who remained virgins. The passage above quoted runs on: " You would find many of those who are with us, both men and women, who have grown old in the unmarried state in the hope of being more in communion with God. If remaining in virginity and in the state of an eunuch recommends us more to God, and the advancing to thought and desire withdraws from God, much more do we refuse to do the deeds, the thoughts of which we shun °." Contrasting Christians with heathens, he calls them eunuchs and monogamists ᵖ.

Monogamy means, in the language of Athenagoras, marriage with one wife and no more during the course of a man's life. In the continuation of the passage already quoted he states this more fully and gives his reason: " For we do not indulge in the careful planning of speeches, but in the exhibition and teaching of deeds, either by remaining such as we have been born or by being content with one marriage: for a second marriage is a decent adultery ᵠ. ' For whosoever sends away his wife,' says He [Christ], ' and marries another, commits adultery;' not permitting to send away her whose virginity he has put an end to, nor to marry another. For he who deprives himself of his first wife, even though she be dead, is a concealed adul-

---

ⁿ Apol. c. 33, p. 36 D, 37 A.

° Apol. c. 33, p. 37 A. Athenagoras is rebutting the charge of licentiousness.

ᵖ Apol. c. 34, p. 37 D.

ᵠ Suicer supposes that Athenagoras means here that a man who marries a second wife after he has divorced his first is an adulterer, and continues an adulterer even if she should die. Sub. voc. διγαμία. But the whole context is against this explanation.

terer, transgressing the hand of God, (because in the beginning God made one man and one woman,) and dissolving the mingling of flesh with flesh which took place in their union for the communication of race[r]." The main argument here used is that husband and wife become one flesh. This is the arrangement of God. He who marries a second wife dissolves this union, and transgresses the ordinance of God. He deprives himself of his first and only real wife.

Many passages have been quoted already in which Athenagoras states that God will judge the thoughts of men. He states, moreover, that Christians literally followed the precepts given in the Sermon on the Mount. "For the loss which comes from our persecutors," he says, "has not reference to our money, nor the shame to our loss of character, nor the injury to anything of great importance: for we despise these things, even though they seem objects of interest to the many, for not only have we learned not to strike the man who strikes us, or to go to law with those who rob and plunder us, but to afford to the one set, even should they kick us on the head, the other side of the head to strike, and to the other set, should they take away a tunic, to give them also the cloak with it[s]." He expresses also the principle on which such conduct is based, though in different words from those of Christ. "For it is not sufficient to be just (for justice is a returning equal for equal), but our aim is to be good and patient in the endurance of evils[t]."

Christians were obedient to the emperors. They were "most piously and righteously disposed to the Divine Being, and your government[u]." At the same time they "gave up their lives unhesitatingly for the truth[x]." They refused to visit the gladiatorial shows, and they pronounced the procuring of abortions and the exposing of children to be sinful.

---

[r] Apol. c. 33, p. 37 B.
[s] Apol. c. 1, p. 2 C D; comp. ibid. c. 11, p. 12 A.
[t] Apol. c. 34, p. 38 A.   [u] Ibid. c. 1, p. 2 C.
[x] Apol. c. 3. p. 5 A.

Those who procured abortions or exposed their children were reckoned murderers [y].

Athenagoras made no opposition to the existence of slavery in the Church. He states distinctly that Christians had slaves: "There certainly are slaves belonging to us, to some more and to some fewer, whose notice it is impossible to elude; yet no one of these has even framed such lies against us [z]."

VI. LITERATURE.

The Legatio of Athenagoras is found in seventeen manuscripts. There are only three manuscripts, however, of an early date. The earliest and best is the Codex Parisinus CDLI, mentioned already. It contains scholia, which have for the first time appeared in Otto's edition. This MS. was written in 914. The second Codex is Codex Parisinus CLXXIV, also mentioned already, belonging to the tenth or eleventh century. And the third Codex is the Codex Argentoratensis, also mentioned before, belonging to the thirteenth century. Belonging to the fifteenth century there are the Codices Ottobonianus Græcus XCIV, and Ottobonianus Græcus CCLXXIV; in the Vatican at Rome, Codex Vaticanus Græcus MCCLXI; Codex Sirletianus, which should be in the Vatican, but has not been found there; Codex Lubanensis, in the Library of Lausanne (Lubani Lusatorum), and two Codices in the Bodleian Library at Oxford, Codex Bodleianus Græcus, Barocc. XCVIII; Codex Bodleianus Græcus, Barocc. CXLV. Belonging to the sixteenth century are the Codices, Codex Monacensis LXXXI, in the Royal Library of Munich; Codex Parisinus Supplem. Græc. CXLIII, in the Royal Library at Paris; Codex Bononiensis, mentioned before; Codex Claromontanus, mentioned before; Codex Ætonensis, in the Eton Library; and the Codex Angelicus, B. 1. 10, in the Library of S. Agostino, at Rome, which is a transcript of the Eton MS. by the same hand.

The three best manuscripts of the Legatio contain also the

[y] Apol. c. 35. p. 38 C D.   [z] Ibid. p. 38 B.

Treatise on the Resurrection. It is found also in Codex Parisinus CDL, in Codex Claromontanus LXXXIII, in Codex Claromontanus LXXXII, and in the Codex Ætonensis, all mentioned already. Besides these, Maranus used a manuscript called Codex Bigotianus, now lost. And Valla, who published a Latin translation of the Treatise on the Resurrection before the editio princeps of the Greek, must have used some manuscript, but which he used is now unknown. It is most likely however, as Otto conjectures, that he used one of two manuscripts very like each other which are now in the Florentine Library, called Codex Florentinus III. plut. IV.; and Codex Florentinus XXXII. plut. X. They both belong to the fifteenth century.

EDITIONS.

The Treatise of Athenagoras on the Resurrection appeared separately at first. The editio princeps was edited by Petrus Nannius, Lovanii and Parisiis, 1541, 4to. It subsequently appeared in the Mikropresbytikon, 1550; and in the Orthodoxographa of Heroldus, 1555. Both treatises issued from the press of Henricus Stephanus, under the care of Conrad Gesner, 1557, 8vo. Gesner's edition of both works was reprinted separately. And both works appeared in the collections of Lang, Morell, Fronto Ducæus, Maranus, Gallandi, and Oberthür.

Separate editions of the works of Athenagoras were prepared by Fell, Oxford, 1682, 12mo.; Rechenberg, Leipzig, 1685, 8vo.; and by Dechair, Oxford, 1706, 8vo. Dechair collated several manuscripts, and gave copious notes, his own and those of others, along with several dissertations. The Legatio was edited by M. Jo. Gottlieb Lindner, Longosalissæ, 1774, 8vo.; and by Dr. Ludwig Paul, Halis, 1856, 8vo. The best edition of Athenagoras is that of Otto, Jenæ, 1857. The text is based on the three best manuscripts already mentioned. The others have been either collated for the first time, or recollated for this edition. Prolegomena giving a full description of the manuscripts, editions, translations, and discussing the style and date, are prefixed; and useful notes and indices are given.

There is a translation of the Treatise on the Resurrection by Richard Porter, London, 1573, 8vo.; of his whole works by David Humphreys, London, 1714, 8vo. The translation of Humphreys is very unsatisfactory.

CHAPTER VII.

HERMIAS.

I.—LIFE AND WRITINGS.

NOTHING is known of Hermias. Maranus thinks that his work shows traces of an acquaintance with the writings of Justin Martyr and Tatian; and that therefore he is to be placed later than these writers. Worth imagines that the style of his wit marks him as belonging to a late age[a]. Lambecius and Tentzel, for reasons which Cave has shown to be unsatisfactory[b], have identified the Hermias whose work we discuss with Hermias Sozomenus the historian. In fact, all the guesses made with regard to this Hermias are baseless, and the fragment of his work gives no clear indication of any date or circumstance in his life.

The title of the fragment which bears the name of Hermias is Ἑρμείου φιλοσόφου διασυρμὸς τῶν ἔξω φιλοσόφων, or "A Satirizing of the Heathen Philosophers by the Philosopher Hermias." It has been placed alongside of the works of the Apologists because it is an attack on heathen philosophy. The writer begins with quoting the words of "the blessed apostle Paul;" "The wisdom of this world is foolishness with

---

[a] Worth's words mean exactly the opposite of this. His Latin is, "Ego certe plurimum vereor ut affectatæ istæ quibus scatet argutiæ sapiant recentius aliquod seculum." It is plain that Worth uses 'vereor ut' instead of 'vereor ne.' His Latin in other respects is liable to the reproach which Reiske has brought generally against English writers of Latin.

[b] Hist. Lit. tom. ii. p. 35.

God." Error commences with the apostasy of angels, who are the cause why philosophers do not agree. Hermias then goes on to prove that the opinions of the various philosophers are opposed to each other. He first takes up the nature of the soul, and shows how endless are their differences on that subject. Then he reviews their opinions on the origin of the world (περὶ τὰς ἀρχὰς τῆς φύσεως), and shows how utterly opposed are the opinions of philosophers on that point also. He concludes with the statement that he had related these things to exhibit the contradictoriness of the philosophic opinions, and the vanity and uselessness of philosophic pursuits, based as they are on no firm reason.

The following is a specimen of the work. He is speaking of the various opinions on the nature of the soul. "I confess I am vexed by the reflux of things. For now I am immortal, and I rejoice; but now again I become mortal, and I weep; but straightway I am dissolved into atoms: I become water, and I become air: I become fire: then after a little I am neither air nor fire: one makes me a wild beast, one makes me a fish. Again, then, I have dolphins for my brothers. But when I see myself, I fear my body, and I no longer know how to call it, whether man, or dog, or wolf, or bull, or bird, or serpent, or dragon, or chimæra. I am changed by the philosophers into all the wild beasts, into those that live on land and on water, into those that are winged, many-shaped, wild, tame, speechless, and gifted with speech, rational and irrational. I swim, fly, creep, run, sit; and there is Empedocles too, who makes me a bush."

II. LITERATURE.

I can nowhere get a satisfactory account of the MSS. of Hermias. Worth mentions three. One he thus describes, p. 213: "Codex MS. in Bibliotheca Cæsarea cujus meminit Lambecius, lib. vii. p. 54 Commentariorum in eandem."

The second belonged to Thomas Gale, who collated it with

the editions previously published, and gave the results to Worth, with notes.

He also mentions a Codex of Vossius.

A fourth was the manuscript from which Seiler made his edition. Dommerich says, "Adfuit olim in splendidissima Fuggeriana Bibliotheca Augustana." Dommerich knew of these four only.

Maranus used two Roman codices for his edition. Fabricius seems to mention two other codices. See his Bibliotheca Græca, vol. vii. p. 115, ed. Harless.

The first Greek-Latin edition of Hermias appeared at Basle, 1553, 8vo. The Latin translation was by Raphael Seiler. It appeared again in the collection of the early Greek Christian writings published at Zurich, 1560, and in the Auctarium of Fronto Ducæus, 1624. Worth added it to his Tatian, with his own notes and those of Gale. And it has appeared since in the collections of Maranus, Oberthür, and Gallandi. A separate edition was published at Basle with the notes of Hieron. Wolfius, 1580, 8vo., and another by Jo. Christoph. Dommerich, with the notes of Wolf, Gale, Worth, and his own, Halæ, 1764, 8vo.

CHAPTER VIII.

HEGESIPPUS.

1. LIFE.

OUR principal source of information in regard to Hegesippus is Eusebius. The historian derived all his knowledge of Hegesippus from his own work, and it is fortunate that he has given us the grounds he had for every statement which he has made. Eusebius believed him to be a Jew. In giving an account of his book he says: "And he writes many other things which we have already taken notice of in part in our History already, setting down the narratives, each at its proper time: and he also adduces some things from the Gospel according to the Hebrews and from the Syriac Gospel, and particularly from the Hebrew language, showing that he himself had believed from among the Hebrews, and moreover he records other things as if from unwritten Jewish tradition [a]." The fragments that remain also bear witness to his Jewish origin, both by their style and their subject. Hegesippus travelled to Corinth and Rome. "And the Church of the Corinthians," he says, "remained in sound doctrine (τῷ ὀρθῷ λόγῳ) up to the time of Primus, who had the oversight in Corinth; with whom I had converse on my voyage to Rome, and I remained with the Corinthians for several days, when we were refreshed by sound teaching (τῷ ὀρθῷ λόγῳ). And when I was in Rome I made

[a] Hist. Eccles. iv. 22.

a succession [b] up to Anicetus, whose deacon was Eleutherus. And Anicetus is succeeded by Soter, after whom is Eleutherus. And in every succession and in every city it is as the law and the prophets and the Lord proclaim [c]." It was probably on this passage that Eusebius based his statement that "Hegesippus relates that he came to Rome in the time of Anicetus, and remained there until the oversight of Eleutherus [d]." Jerome, according to his custom, translates Eusebius [e]. The words of Hegesippus do not say as much as Eusebius drew out of them; but they leave you with a considerable probability on the side of the inference of Eusebius. And it is indeed possible that there may have been circumstances related by Hegesippus which would confirm Eusebius in the inference made. The passage is at any rate sufficient to give us some idea of the date of Hegesippus, for he must have been in full vigour between the time of Anicetus and the time of Eleutherus, probably from 157–177. Eusebius in another passage states that Hegesippus "lived during the time of the first succession of the Apostles," (ἐπὶ τῆς πρώτης τῶν ἀποστόλων γενόμενος διαδοχῆς). And there is nothing improbable in this, for Polycarp also was a disciple of apostles and lived to the reign of Marcus Antoninus. Rufinus, however, either mistaking the Greek or reading διαδοχῇ, says that he lived immediately after the first succession of the apostles. Eusebius, moreover, adduces a passage from the writings of Hegesippus to show that his date was early. Speaking of those who set up idols Hegesippus said, "to whom they made cenotaphs and shrines as even up to the present time, to whom belongs also Antinous, the slave of Adrian Cæsar, in whose honour the Antinoan games are now celebrated, having been instituted in our day (ἐφ' ἡμῶν γενόμενος). For he

[b] The meaning of this passage, as Pearson showed, is that Hegesippus made a list of the overseers of the Roman Church. The word διαδοχή has been changed or a different meaning given to it, but Pearson's explanation is unquestionably the best. See Routh's notes in loc., vol. i. p. 268.

[c] Euseb. Hist. Eccl. iv. 22. [d] Ibid. 11.
[e] De Vir. Illust. c. 22.

called a city which he built by the name of Antinous, and instituted prophets for his worship[f]." The words ἐφ' ἡμῶν γενόμενος might indeed be applied to Antinous himself, 'Antinous who lived in our time,' but this is a matter of no consequence. For the passage, taken any way, established the fact that Hegesippus was alive in the time of Hadrian. Some, indeed, read γινόμενος, 'which take place in our day;' but the reading does not occur in the best manuscripts, and Eusebius could scarcely have quoted the passage for his purpose if such had been the reading in his copy of Hegesippus. The Alexandrian Chronicle[g] says that he suffered martyrdom in the reign of Commodus, about A.D. 180, but its statement cannot be depended on.

II. THE WRITINGS OF HEGESIPPUS.

There was only one work ascribed to Hegesippus in ancient times: and as it is of some importance to know the whole of the evidence in regard to this work and its character, we extract the various references to it in Eusebius. In mentioning the Christian opponents of heresy who flourished in the reign of Hadrian, Eusebius says, "Among these was known Hegesippus, many of whose statements we have already used, setting down some of those things that relate to the apostles as from his tradition. He certainly in five writings (ἐν πέντε συγγράμμασιν), recording the unerring tradition of the apostolic preaching in the simplest style, points out the time at which he was known, writing thus with regard to those who originally set up idols[h]." And then Eusebius quotes the passage already adduced in proof of his having lived in the time of Hadrian. In a subsequent chapter Eusebius discusses more fully the work of Hegesippus. "Among these," he says, in mentioning the writers that flourished in the time

---

[f] Euseb. Hist. Eccl. iv. 8.   [g] p. 262 ; p. 490 ed. Dindorf.
[h] Euseb. Hist. Eccl. iv. 8.

of Marcus Aurelius, "there flourished in the Church Hegesippus, whom we have known already, and Dionysius and Pinytus, Philip, Apollinaris, Melito, Musanus, Modestus, and Irenæus [i]. Their orthodoxy of sound faith derived from apostolic tradition has come down in writing even to us" (ὧν καὶ εἰς ἡμᾶς τῆς ἀποστολικῆς παραδόσεως ἡ τῆς ὑγιοῦς πίστεως ἔγγραφος κατῆλθεν ὀρθοδοξία [k]). "Hegesippus then in five books of Notes (ὑπομνήμασι) which have come down to us has left the fullest memorial of his own sentiments. In them he shows that he mingled with very many overseers, extending his journey even to Rome, and that he received the same teaching from all [l]." From these statements we gather that Hegesippus wrote five books, which he seems to have called ὑπομνήματα, "Notes or Memoranda." Eusebius gives this name to the work, as we have seen already; and once in quoting from it he mentions the fifth ὑπόμνημα (ἐν τῷ πέμπτῳ αὐτοῦ ὑπομνήματι). Stephanus Gobarus, likewise, in quoting from Hegesippus says: "Hegesippus, an ancient and apostolic man, says in the fifth book of his Notes" (ἐν τῷ πέμπτῳ τῶν ὑπομνημάτων [m]). The name suggests that the work was not a regular history, and the passage from the fifth book in Eusebius tends to show that he did not pursue the chronological order. It is not impossible, indeed, that he published some of the books before the others; and perhaps this was the reason why Eusebius placed him both among the writers of the time of Hadrian and among those of the reign of Marcus Aurelius. At least Eusebius believed that he was well known in the time of Hadrian: for there is no good reason for the opinion of Valesius that Eusebius as it were retracts his previous statements when he places him in the reign of Marcus Aurelius, for, as we have seen already, he expressly alludes to his previous notice of him. Jerome misrepresents the assertions of Eusebius in regard to the nature of the work. He says, "Hegesippus, who lived near the apostolic times,

---

[i] The passage is given elsewhere in full.
[l] Euseb. Hist. Eccl. iv. 22.
[k] Euseb. Hist. Eccl. iv. 21
[m] Phot. Bibl. Cod. 232.

weaving together all the histories of Ecclesiastical Acts from the death of the Lord even to his own age, and collecting from one quarter and another many things which tend to the profit of the reader, composed five books in simple language, so that he expressed the mode of speech of those whose lives he detailed[n]." There is no reason to suppose that Hegesippus had the slightest notion of what a history should be, or that he even had the wish to write a continuous narrative. He embodied in his work the narratives and facts which he had learned from tradition or in the course of his travels, without much order or polish.

The loss of this work creates a great gap in our knowledge of the early Church. Of all the early Christian writers Hegesippus is the only one in regard to whom there is good evidence that he was a Jew. The evidence, indeed, is not entirely satisfactory, for he might have known Hebrew and Syriac without having been born a Jew. Moreover, he might have been a Jew by nation and not one in religion. It is not impossible that he might have been born of Jewish parents who had become Christians before his birth, and that he might have learned the Jewish language and traditions at the very time that he was being trained in the Christian religion. Still the probability is that he was originally a Jew both by birth and religion, and that he passed from Judaism to Christianity. And at all events, he seems to have moved much in the circle of the Jerusalem Church, to have been well acquainted with apostolic traditions, and to have known a great deal in regard to the Jewish religionists at the time of the apostles. He of all others would have been peculiarly fitted to give us some idea of the relation of the Jewish-Christian Churches to the heathen-Christian.

Now in this respect it is important to observe that Hegesippus was perfectly satisfied with what he saw and heard

---

[n] De Vir. Illust. c. 22.

in the Western Churches. In a passage already quoted he states that the Corinthian Church held the truth, and that in every city the Church felt and thought as the law, the prophets, and the Lord proclaimed. Then it is also to be observed that Eusebius was perfectly satisfied with the orthodoxy of Hegesippus. The passages which we have already quoted, and which we gave in full expressly for this purpose, are decisive on this point. Eusebius could see no difference between the teaching of Hegesippus and that of Apollinaris, Melito, and Irenæus. Now if we can ascertain what was the teaching of Hegesippus, we know the doctrine prevalent over the whole Church; and if we trust Eusebius, we shall find the doctrine of Hegesippus in Melito, Apollinaris, and Irenæus. As he couples Hegesippus also with Justin, we shall find the essential ideas of his teaching in that writer. One would have thought that this would have been no difficult task, for the opinions of these writers are pretty well known, especially in the case of Irenæus, who several times gives us what he deems the essentials of his creed. Several writers however in former times, and some in the present day, argue in a different way, and come to a peculiar conclusion. Hegesippus they say was a Hebrew. Therefore he must have been a Hebrew Christian. But a Hebrew Christian is one who observes the law and looks upon Christ as a mere man. Therefore the whole Church was Unitarian in the days of Hegesippus. Now not to mention that this is a precarious way of ascertaining the truth, it is sufficient to notice that there is not the slightest proof that Hegesippus either kept the law or believed Christ to be a mere man. What Eusebius believed was that he had been born a Jew and had become a Christian; but whether he had become a Jewish Christian in the modern sense of the term, or whether he preferred Gentile liberty, is not stated. But whatever he was, this much is certain, that he had no objection to Gentile liberty. We know that he was at Rome at the very time that Anicetus, whose difference with Polycarp on the subject of the Passover has been noticed already, was overseer in the Roman Church, and he felt so much interest in this Roman Church that he drew up a succession of its overseers. Nay more, he seems, as far as we can guess, to have actually remained in Palestine after the Jews had been expelled, and to have been contented with Gentile Christianity in Ælia Capitolina. Of course this is only a supposition, but it has more likelihood than the other supposition that he retired from the Gentile Christians, which must be assumed as true on the hypothesis that he kept the Jewish law. On the whole, then, the evidence tends to prove that he was not even a Hebrew Christian in the sense of observing the law, and there is the most complete proof that he did not regard the observance of the law as essential to salvation. With the destruction of this premise the keystone of the two theories of the early Unitarians and of Baur is utterly destroyed. The Unitarians maintained that Hegesippus was an Ebionite or Nazarene, and that consequently the whole Church was in his day Ebionitic, though unfortunately the few Platonizing writers who formed a miserable exception to the mass have been the only writers that a subsequent corrupt age has preserved to us. Baur finds in Hegesippus a most determined antagonist of Paul, and his testimony is appealed to as proof that the Petrine faction had gained the predominance, not only in the Churches of the East but even in those of the West. Both theories run directly contrary to the repeated testimony of Eusebius and to all the information which we have in regard to the Western Churches. And they both fall to pieces, unless it be proved that Hegesippus insisted on the observance of the law as essential to salvation. The Unitarians and Baur have appealed to several passages in the fragments as supporting their conclusion. I shall notice their attempts at the proper place, but there is no need of arguing against them, for they are such glaring instances of arbitrary interpretation that an historical mind will at once reject them as utterly unwarranted. One of these passages has occurred already. It is said that Hegesippus used a gospel according to the Hebrews, and a Syriac (ἔκ τε τοῦ καθ'

Ἑβραίους εὐαγγελίου καὶ τοῦ Συριακοῦ). Lardner supposes that the text of Eusebius is here incorrect, and without proposing any emendation, believes the meaning of Eusebius to be that Hegesippus quoted from a gospel which was written in Syro-Chaldaic. He appeals especially to the description of the Gospel according to the Hebrews by Jerome. "In the Gospel according to the Hebrews," says Jerome, "which is written indeed in the Syriac and Chaldaic tongue [or Syro-Chaldaic tongue] but in Hebrew characters, is this history[o]." Perhaps this is exactly what Eusebius meant to say, though he has said it awkwardly. For Rufinus translates, "He discussed the gospel which is according to the Hebrews and Syrians." It is impossible to settle what this gospel was. It may have been the Hebrew of the Gospel of Matthew. It may have been an apocryphal gospel. But whatever it was, Eusebius says no more than that Hegesippus quoted from it; and he is no more to be set down as an Ebionite or observer of the law on that account than are Papias, Clemens, Origen, and Jerome, all of whom also quoted from the Gospel according to the Hebrews[p]. We have even somewhat of positive evidence that he did not appeal to an apocryphal gospel as authoritative. Eusebius states that he treated of apocryphal works. "And treating of works called apocryphal he relates that some of these had been forged in his own times by some heretics[q]." If Hegesippus had himself regarded an apocryphal gospel as genuine, Eusebius would not fail to tell us. Moreover, in the passage already quoted to the effect that in every city things were as the law, prophets, and the Lord proclaims, there is probably an allusion to our gospels. For the Lord in the passage can scarcely mean anything else than the Lord's sayings as recorded in the Gospels. Lardner supposes the whole of the New Testament to be meant; but

---

[o] Adv. Pelag. lib. iii. init. Lardner, Credib. part ii. c. 14.

[p] See Bull's Primitiva et Apostolica Traditio, c. 3. The chapter is a most complete refutation of the arguments of Zwicker and others based on Hegesippus.

[q] Euseb. Hist. Eccl. iv. 22.

there is no proof that the books of the New Testament had yet been collected into one, and the sayings of the Lord are in this age always quoted separately from other sayings or writings.

I now proceed to give an account of those fragments which have not yet been noticed. They almost all relate to the Church in Jerusalem, and give thus a glimpse into its history.

The first and most considerable of these relates to the death of the apostle James, the brother of our Lord. It is as follows: "The care of the Church was undertaken by James, the brother of the Lord, along with the apostles. He was named Just by all from the times of the Lord even to ours, since many bore the name of James. Now he was sacred from his mother's womb. He drank not wine nor strong drink, nor ate any living thing. A razor went not upon his head, he did not anoint himself with oil, and the bath he did not use. He alone was permitted to go into the holies. For he did not wear woollen garments, but linen. And he alone entered into the shrine (ναός), and was found lying on his knees and asking forgiveness for the people; so that his knees grew hard as a camel's, on account of his always bending on his knee in worshipping God and asking forgiveness for the people. On account then of his exceeding righteousness he was called Righteous and Oblias, that is, bulwark of the people and righteousness, as the prophets make manifest with regard to him. Some then of the seven sects that were in the people, which have been already described by me in my Recollections, asked him, 'What is the gate of Jesus[r]?' And he said that He was the Saviour. In consequence of this some of them believed that Jesus was the Christ. But the sects previously mentioned did not believe in a resurrection, or in one coming to give to every one

---

[r] The meaning of this question is matter of doubt. See Routh, Rel. Sacr., for the various opinions, vol. i. p. 215. The most probable is, "To what is it that Jesus is to lead us?" And James's answer is, therefore, "To salvation."

according to his works. But as many as believed, believed on account of James. When many then even of the rulers believed, there was disturbance among the Jews, Scribes, and Pharisees; for they said, 'All the people are like to expect Jesus as the Christ.' They said therefore, coming together to James, 'We exhort thee, restrain the people, since they are wandering over to Jesus, as if He were indeed the Christ. We exhort thee to persuade all, who come to keep the day of the passover, with regard to Jesus. For we all obey thee. For we and all the people bear witness to thee that thou art just, and respectest not the face of man. Persuade therefore the mob not to err with regard to Jesus. For all the people and we all obey thee. Stand therefore on the wing of the temple, that thou mayest be seen from above, and all the people may hear thy words well. For on account of the passover all the tribes have come together, with even the Gentiles.' Then the fore-mentioned Scribes and Pharisees placed James on the wing of the shrine, and called to him and said, 'Thou Just one, whom we all ought to obey, since the people is going astray after Jesus the crucified one, announce to us what is the door of Jesus.' And he answered with a loud voice, 'Why do you ask me with regard to Jesus the son of man? Yea, that person sits in heaven on the right hand of the great power, and is to come upon the clouds of heaven.' And many being fully assured and glorifying [God] at the testimony of James, and saying 'Hosanna to the son of David,' then again the same Scribes and Pharisees said to each other, 'We have done wrong affording such testimony to Jesus; but let us go up and cast him down, that being frightened they may not believe him.' And they cried, saying, 'O! O! even the Just has gone astray.' And they fulfilled the writing which was written in Isaiah, 'Let us take the righteous man, for he is useless to us; therefore shall they eat the fruits of their own works.' Going up, therefore, they cast the Just down, and said to each other, 'Let us stone James, the Just.' And they began to stone him, since he did not die when he was cast down.

But he, turning, bent his knees and said, 'I beseech thee, O Lord God the Father, forgive them; for they know not what they do.' And while they were thus stoning him, one of the priests, the sons of Rechab, the son of Rechabim, who were borne witness to by Jeremiah the prophet, cried, saying, 'Cease ye: what do ye? The Just prays for you.' And one of them, a fuller, taking the stick with which he pressed the robes, brought it down on the head of the Just. And thus he bore witness, and they buried him in the place beside the shrine, and his pillar yet remains beside the shrine. He has been a true witness to both Jews and Greeks that Jesus is the Christ. And straightway Vespasian besieges them[t]." In this narrative there are several points which will at once strike the reader as strange. It is certainly astonishing to find it asserted of an apostle that he never used the bath. The statement that his knees became as hard as a camel's has also been questioned. And the entire asceticism ascribed to James runs counter to all that we know of the lives of the other apostles. Yet there is nothing impossible in any one assertion. And there can scarcely be a doubt, that among the early Jewish Christians, who were far from being an intelligent class of men, there may have been many who, deeply and completely moved by faith in Christ, were yet so animated by the old Jewish spirit as to persist in practices which at the present day are supposed to be far from favourable to godliness. Scaliger[u] has attempted, moreover, to show that Hegesippus's statements are inconsistent with fact. He interprets James's entrance into the holies as an entrance into the holy of holies: and, accordingly, he maintains that James would not have been permitted to enter alone. He objects to the statement in regard to the nature of his dress. He denies the possibility of his standing on the wing of the temple. He asserts that the statements in regard to the observance of the Passover are incorrect. And he finds an unquestionable mistake in the statement that he

[t] Euseb. Hist. Eccl. ii. 23.
[u] In his Animadversiones on the Chronicon of Eusebius, p. 193.

never drank wine nor ate flesh; for that he must have done both in eating the passover with Christ. He has produced a few minor objections besides these. Subsequent writers, Petavius and Halloix especially, have defended Hegesippus, and clearly shown that some of the objections are obviated by a different interpretation, such as that against James's entrance into the holies; and that most of the objections were really unfounded, and the result of ignorance [x]. In recent times Stanley has maintained that the present narrative has not come down to us in its original state [y]; but he has not defined the extent or nature of the corruption of the text. He appeals to the probable omission of Hebrew words, an omission which would certainly prove that the text of Hegesippus is not in the most perfect state. Probably, in the time of Eusebius, the text was somewhat corrupt, as one might expect in the case of a writer who was seldom read, and whose Greek was confused at the best. But the omission of a few Hebrew words is no proof of intentional corruption of the facts. He, moreover, appeals to the differences in Epiphanius, Hær. lxxviii. 13; but Epiphanius does not quote the passage. He merely gives the characteristics of James's asceticism; and if we consider the nature of Epiphanius's mind, we should be rather surprised that he adheres so closely to the version in Eusebius. The whole narrative of Hegesippus is exactly the narrative which we should expect from a man who was fond of gathering up the stories of the past. It is, as Eusebius calls it, most minute (ἀκριβέστατα), it seizes special points, and yet at the same time it utterly fails to give a clear idea of the principal facts and a full view of the principal characters. Almost every statement is imperfect. There is something omitted which the writer has inartistically left to the reader to guess, and which we cannot now guess. There may be, moreover,

---

[x] See the notes in Routh.

[y] Sermons and Essays on the Apostolical Age, by Arthur Penrhyn Stanley, M. A., (second edition); "Essay on the Traditions of St. James the Just as Narrated by Hegesippus," pp. 325-341. It is well worth reading.

as there generally is in these gossipping narratives, slight inaccuracies. Nay, if we remember that a long interval intervened between the event related and the relation of it, and that this was probably the first time that it was so minutely related, we should not be surprised though there were serious mistakes. Any one who in the present day would write a narrative of the battle of Waterloo, trusting solely to his own traditionary knowledge of it, would probably commit many a serious blunder. Moreover, Hegesippus seems to have been but imperfectly acquainted with the Greek language; and probably had not had a first-rate education. So that even if he had been an eye-witness, he would have in some measure failed to seize the essential points, and to clothe in proper language the details which he deemed important. The narrative, therefore, cannot be relied on in all its minutiæ, but it is as true as most stories handed down in the same way. Josephus[z] in a sentence mentions the condemnation of James, and his words have been supposed to contradict Hegesippus. While Hegesippus makes the death of James the result of a secret conspiracy, Josephus says that he was publicly condemned; and while Hegesippus represents him as struck down by a piece of wood near the temple, Josephus says that he was delivered up to be stoned. The discrepancies, however, are not irreconcileable. Josephus expressly says that Ananus seized the interval between the death of Festus and the arrival of his successor Albinus to summon a court and condemn James and others. The affair, though formally regular, was hurried and urgent. And Josephus does not say that James was stoned, but that the sentence pronounced on him was that of stoning. Its execution may have been prevented by the violence of the mob or of an individual.

There are two questions that arise out of this narrative and the discussion of it. How far was the work of Hegesippus to be trusted? and what information do we gather from it in regard to his form of Christianity?

[z] Antiq. xx. 9. 1.

Both questions are easily answered. A book of Notes or Recollections, especially a gossipping book, is never to be trusted absolutely. There is, moreover, no reason to suppose that Hegesippus had a just appreciation of the nature of historical evidence. He wished to commit to writing the various scraps of information which he had gathered here and there; and doubtless he would not inquire very minutely into the truthfulness or accuracy of his authorities, and often his own memory might be at fault.

In regard to the second question not much can be said. It is plain that he believed that James regarded Christ as the Saviour of mankind. This is the only essential doctrine of Christianity in the fragment, and it is as positively stated as doctrine can be. We may confidently believe that Hegesippus held the same truth. But there is not the shadow of a proof that either James or Hegesippus regarded the law as binding. It is not even said that James observed the law. He went into the temple like other Christians of his own place and time. It is likely that he observed the law, as the early Jewish Christians did. But there is not a word to show that Hegesippus observed the law or regarded James as a model in his austerity. Hegesippus tells his tale without comment.

The next event in the history of the Jerusalem Church noticed in the fragments of Hegesippus is the appointment of a successor to James. "And after James the Just had borne witness, as our Lord did, for the same truth, again a son of his uncle, namely, Simeon the son of Clopas, is appointed overseer, whom all proposed as the second overseer, since he was the cousin of the Lord. On this account they called the Church virgin: for it had not yet been corrupted by vain teachings. But Thebuthis begins to corrupt it secretly because he was not made an overseer. After the seven sects he also was among the people. After them also were Simon, whence the Simonians; and Cleobius, whence the Cleobians; and Dositheus, whence the Dositheans; and Gorthæus, whence the Gortheans; and Masbotheus, whence the Masbotheans.

After these came the Menandrians, and Marcionists, and Carpocratians, and Valentinians, and Basilidians, and Saturnilians. They introduced each one his own opinion separately, and differently. After these came false Christs, false prophets, false apostles, who divided the unity of the Church with corrupt doctrines (λόγοις) against God and his Christ[a]." The text of this extract, like that of the preceding, is not preserved in the best state. No doubt this is owing in some measure to the original carelessness and awkwardness of the writer. I have given a translation somewhat different from that usually given. The statement in regard to Thebuthis is ἀπὸ τῶν ἑπτὰ αἱρέσεων καὶ αὐτὸς ἦν ἐν τῷ λαῷ· ἀφ' ὧν. This is the common text, though there are some variations. It has been taken to mean that Thebuthis belonged to the seven sects or derived his heresy from theirs. But this certainly is an extraordinary assertion. The seven sects were in many points opposed to each other, and therefore a man could belong only to one of these, or derive his doctrines from only some of them at the utmost. If we suppose that Hegesippus meant that Thebuthis belonged to one of the seven sects, the difficulty is not removed. The statement that "he was among the people" seems superfluous. Then the sentence quoted is succeeded by one commencing with another ἀπό, ἀφ' ὧν Σίμων, and Hegesippus is thus made to state that the five heresies subsequently mentioned flowed from the seven Jewish heresies. Then from these (ἀπὸ τούτων) are made to flow the principal Gnostic heresies: and from these (ἀπὸ τούτων) arose false prophets, false Christs, and false apostles. Such a genealogy of heresies is utterly inconceivable, and is, moreover, untrue. Indeed, Hegesippus himself states exactly the reverse. He asserts that they introduced each one his own opinion individually and differently (ἕκαστος ἰδίως καὶ ἑτέρως ἰδίαν δόξαν). By rendering the ἀπό 'after,' a sense in which it is used commonly enough, the statements become intelligible, true, and important. The mention of the oversight of

[a] Euseb. Hist. Eccl. iv. 22.

Simeon reminds Hegesippus that then Thebuthis began secretly to corrupt the Jerusalem Church. The mention of the secret corruption then leads him to notice that Thebuthis ultimately formed a sect, probably after the death of Simon, and gained favour with the masses. And then Hegesippus naturally describes the progress of heresy. He thus mentions, first, the heresies of Simon, Cleobius, Dositheus, Masbotheus, and Gorthæus, which seem to have been confined to Jerusalem, or, at the utmost, to Palestine. Hegesippus then advances to the more widely spread Gnostic sects; and alludes at last to the final phenomena of his days—the appearance of false prophets, and false Christs, and false apostles among the sects, and perhaps also among the Montanists.

The early Unitarian school and the Tübingen school appeal to this account of the heresies as proof that Hegesippus was an Ebionite. The reason, they say, why he does not mention the Ebionites is that he was one of them. It is far more likely, however, that Hegesippus made no mention of them for the very same reason that Irenæus and Hippolytus devoted only two or three sentences to them, namely, because they were a contemptible and insignificant sect. Contemptible in every sense of the term they were. If the Christian Church did at this time welcome all who trusted Christ, whatever other belief they had, if, as we know from Justin, they made no objection to those who observed the law or who looked on Christ as a man sprung from man, and could not agree to the opinion that He was God by nature, what reason was there why those who held these opinions should retire from the Church, except intolerable egotism, arrogance, and want of brotherly love? Baur seems to find also in the mention of the false apostles an allusion to the Apostle Paul—but it is questionable whether any but a member of the Tübingen school could appreciate such a remarkable discovery.

Hegesippus asserts that Thebuthis began to corrupt secretly the Church (ὑποφθείρειν). As the words stand, the reader is led to believe that this corruption began immediately on the appointment of Simeon to the oversight. From what Eusebius says elsewhere of Hegesippus's statements, we gather that the corruptions did not lift up their heads till about the death of Simeon. Eusebius extracts the account of the martyrdom of Simeon from Hegesippus, and then adds, "After these things the same author (Hegesippus) relating what happened in the time of the previously mentioned persons, adds that up to those times the Church remained a virgin pure and uncorrupted, for those who attempted at that time, if any such there were, to corrupt the sound rule of the saving proclamation were as yet skulking somewhere in obscure darkness." Hegesippus does not assert that there was no false teaching, but that this false teaching had not openly shown itself. It is probable, moreover, that the remarks of Hegesippus were confined to the Churches in Palestine, perhaps only to that in Jerusalem. The text of Eusebius proceeds as follows: "But when the holy chorus of apostles had in various ways ended their life, and that generation which had been privileged to hear with their own ears the divine ($\dot{\epsilon}\nu\theta\dot{\epsilon}ov$) wisdom had passed away, then did the uprising of godless error commence through the deceit of unsound teachers; who, since now no one of the apostles remained, henceforth with uncovered head attempted to preach up their falsely-named knowledge against the proclamation of the truth. These things said this person, somehow in this way, discussing these matters [a]." The last sentence is not in the best manuscripts, and Rufinus does not recognise it. Hence it is generally agreed upon that the previous sentence is the assertion of Eusebius alone, and had nothing in the work of Hegesippus corresponding to it. The style, moreover, is unquestionably that of Eusebius.

During the oversight of Simeon, in the Church of Jerusalem took place the interview between the relatives of Christ and the emperor Domitian. Hegesippus thus describes it: "There were yet surviving of the family of the Lord the grandsons of that Judas who was called the brother of the

[a] Euseb. Hist. Eccl. iii. 32.

Lord according to the flesh. Information was given against them as being of the race of David. Now an evocatus brought them before the emperor Domitian, who was as much afraid of the coming of Christ as was Herod. And he asked them if they had sprung from David. And they confessed. Then he asked them what possessions they had, and of how much money they were masters. And both of them said that they had only nine thousand denarii between them, and they said that they had this money not in silver but laid out on a piece of land of only thirty-nine acres, from which they had to pay their taxes and support themselves with their own hands. That then they showed him their hands, appealing in proof of their manual toil to the hardness of their body and the callous lumps which had been formed on their hands from their continual labour. That when asked with regard to Christ and his kingdom, what was its nature and when and where it would appear, they replied that it was not a worldly nor earthly kingdom, but a heavenly and angelic (οὐ κοσμικὴ μὲν οὐδ᾽ ἐπίγειος ἐπουράνιος δὲ καὶ ἀγγελική), destined to appear at the end of the age (αἰῶνος, 'world'), when coming in glory He would judge living and dead and give to every one according to his works. That Domitian did not pronounce any sentence of condemnation on them on account of these things, but despising them as men of low estate he let them go free, and put an end to the persecution against the Church by a decree; and that when set free they guided the Churches, for the double reason that they were at once witnesses (μάρτυρας) and that they were relatives of the Lord; and that after the establishment of peace they remained in life to the times of Trajan[b]." It will be noticed that we have the exact words of Hegesippus only to the commencement of the clause, "That then they showed him their hands." The sentences after this are unquestionably Eusebius's account of what Hegesippus said, and bear the plainest marks of his style. In a passage quoted by Routh from Eclogæ Ecclesiasticæ Historiæ, edited by Cramer, a writer affirms that Hegesippus adduced

---

[b] Euseb. Hist. Eccl. iii. 20.

the names of the grandsons, and that the one was called Zoker and the other James[c].

The last event in the history of the Jerusalem Church on which the fragments of Hegesippus throw light is the martyrdom of Simeon. The chapter of the Ecclesiastical History which Eusebius devotes to this subject deserves to be quoted entire. "After Nero and Domitian history says (λόγος κατέχει) that in the reign of him whose times we are now examining a persecution was raised up against us partially, and in cities, in consequence of the outbursts of the populace. In this persecution we have learned that Simeon the son of Cleopas, whom we have pointed out as having been appointed the second overseer of the Church in Jerusalem, ended his life by martyrdom. Of this that same Hegesippus is witness, several of whose statements we have already on former occasions adduced. Giving an account of some heretical persons, he adds that, as might have been expected, it was by these that Simeon was about this time accused, that he was tortured for very many days in many ways as being a Christian, that he astonished the judge himself and his attendants in the highest degree, and that his end was like the suffering of the Lord. But there is nothing like quoting the writer who relates these same transactions word for word somehow as follows: 'Some of these, to wit the heretics, accuse Simeon the son of Cleopas as being descended of David and a Christian, and thus he bears witness being 120 years old, when Trajan was emperor and Atticus consular deputy.' The same person says that it fell out that his accusers also were captured as being of the royal tribe of the Jews, for all those who were descended of that tribe were at that time sought out. By reckoning we can affirm that Simeon was one of the eye-witnesses and hearers of the Lord, basing our argument on the length of the time of his life, and on the circumstance that the writing of the Gospels makes mention of Mary the daughter of Cleopas, whose son our history has already shown Simeon to have been. The same writer asserts that others

[c] Routh, Rel. Sacr. vol. i. p. 284.

of the family of one of those commonly spoken of as the brothers of the Saviour, whose name was Judas, survived to the same reign after the testimony already narrated which they bore in regard to confidence in Christ before Domitian. He writes thus: 'They come then and guide every Church, as being witnesses, and as being relatives of the Lord. And after there had arisen deep peace in every Church, they remain until the times of the Emperor Trajan, until the time at which the forementioned Simeon, the son of Cleopas the uncle of the Lord, was falsely informed against by the sects, and was in like manner accused on account of the same belief (ἐπὶ τῷ αὐτῷ λόγῳ[d]) before Atticus the consular deputy. And being tortured for many days, he bore witness so that all were exceedingly astonished, even the deputy, at the way in which a man 120 years old bore the tortures: and he was ordered to be crucified[e].'"

Eusebius informs us that Hegesippus related that Cleopas, or Clopas as the name is often spelled, was the brother of Joseph[f].

Eusebius also quotes from Hegesippus a list of the seven heresies of the Jews which have been referred to oftener than once already. "The following were the different opinions in the circumcision among the sons of Israel, of those that were against the tribe of Judah and the Christ, namely, Essenes, Galileans, Hemerobaptistæ, Masbotheans, Samaritans, Sadducees, and Pharisees[g]." The meaning of the words "of those that were against the tribe of Judah and Christ" is somewhat doubtful. The most probable is that Hegesippus narrates all the sects of the Jews which had no connexion with Christianity, all those who had arrayed themselves against Christ, the special representative of the tribe of Judah. The mention of the Essenes is interesting. It is a complete historical refutation of De Quincey's theory that the Essenes were the early Christians, for one who no doubt

---

[d] It might be 'for the same reason,' but this translation does not harmonize so well with the context.
[f] Euseb. Hist. Eccl. iii. 11.
[e] Euseb. Hist. Eccl. iii. 32.
[g] Ibid. iv. 22.

knew the sect sets it down as opposed to Christianity. And it stands opposed to the theory of Baur that Hegesippus did not mention the Ebionites because he belonged to them: for Baur regards Ebionitism simply as a development of Essenism[h].

This is all the information which we get in regard to the Jerusalem Church from the fragments of Hegesippus. Eusebius seems to have prized the work very highly: and however defective its style, and however credulous the writer might have been, yet his work must have been one of great importance on account of the details which it gave of the Church of the apostles and first converts of Christianity.

The information which Hegesippus gave in regard to the Churches in Rome and Corinth has been quoted already, and indeed all the fragments which Eusebius has extracted have now been laid before the reader.

There is only one other fragment attributed to Hegesippus, that mentioned already as quoted by Stephanus Gobarus. The fragment is as follows: "'That the good things prepared for the righteous neither eye has seen, nor ear heard, nor have they entered into the heart of man.' Hegesippus, however, an ancient and apostolic man, in the fifth book of his Notes, I know not under what influence (οὐκ οἶδ' ὅ,τι καὶ παθών), says that these words have been said in vain, and that those who say these things give the lie to the divine writings and to the Lord saying 'Blessed are your eyes that see and your ears that hear[i],'" &c. Baur supposes that Hegesippus directed these words against 1 Cor. ii. 9, and he therefore discovers from this passage that he must be reckoned as one "of the most avowed opponents of the apostle Paul[j]." No theory could be based on a slighter foundation. For at the outset, it would be difficult to affirm that we have a genuine fragment of Hegesippus before us.

[h] See Dorner's Die Lehre von der Person Christi, vol. i. p. 222, note 65, which contains a very able and satisfactory refutation of Baur.

[i] Phot. Bibl. Cod. 232.

[j] "Wir ihn zu den erklärtesten Gegnern des Apostels rechnen müssen."— *Christenthum und die Ch. K.* p. 84.

And then if Stephanus Gobarus had read Hegesippus, he could scarcely have said "I know not under what influence," for he would have known that it had either been in opposition to the apostle Paul or in opposition to some heresy. Then, again, Hegesippus must certainly have been very senseless indeed if he opposed the statement of Paul that the blessings of the future state are inconceivably great by the words of our Lord, "Blessed are your eyes that see," &c. Then the words which are found in 1 Cor. ii. 9 are not Paul's own, but a quotation according to Origen from the Apocalypse of Elias, and Paul may have taken the ideas and most of the words from Isaiah lxiv. 3 [k]. So that there would be far more reason to imagine that Hegesippus opposed the Revelation of Elijah or the Prophecies of Isaiah than the Epistle of Paul. And, lastly, a satisfactory explanation can be given why Hegesippus placed the words of our Lord in opposition to the passage which occurs in the Apocalypse of Elijah and the Epistle to the Corinthians. Many of the Gnostics maintained that it was only the spiritual that comprehended Christianity, that only they could attain to the apprehension of the good. Some of them, as we learn from the recently discovered work of Hippolytus[l], used this passage continually as descriptive of the secret and mysterious doctrines of Christianity which only the qualified Gnostics could understand. There can scarcely be a doubt that Hegesippus directed his remarks against this application of the words: and the saying of our Lord which he quotes is a complete and satisfactory refutation of any esoteric Christianity unknown to the gospel writers, or unexpressed by them [m].

In 1740 Muratori published a very remarkable Latin fragment on the New Testament canon in the third volume of his Italian Antiquities. He conjectured that the fragment was

---

[k] I think it more likely that Paul quoted from some apocryphal work than from Isaiah, because in the Septuagint version of Isaiah there is not one word exactly the same as in Paul's quotation.

[l] Refut. Omnium Hær. v. 24, 26, 27; vi. 24. pp. 216, 222, 230. 262, Duncker and Schneidewin. [m] See Lechler, p. 463, note.

a translation from Greek, and that its author was Caius the Roman presbyter, who flourished in the beginning of the third century. That he was right in conjecturing the fragment to be a translation from the Greek has been generally acknowledged, but the evidence is not satisfactory. And there was no good reason for assigning it to Caius, the mere mention of the name of Miltiades being quite insufficient to establish the authorship. Moreover, if we are to trust the fragment itself, the writer according to the most probable interpretation of the passage must have lived before the time of Caius. The date indicated in the fragment, along with some other circumstances, led Bunsen to conjecture, that we have in the Muratorian fragment a portion of the "Notes" of Hegesippus. Before inquiring into the soundness of this conjecture we shall give an account of the contents of the fragment. The manuscript is an old one, the letters being uncial, probably a thousand years old, as Muratori conjectured in his day. It was discovered in a monastery at Bobbio, which was founded by Columban, an Irishman, in the beginning of the seventh century. The text is in a very corrupt state, and consequently it is sometimes impossible to get at the meaning.

The fragment is mutilated at the beginning, and opens with a sentence which probably referred to the second Gospel, but of which we can only guess the purport. "At which," it says, "he was present, and so he placed it." Then the fragment proceeds to describe the Gospel of Luke, but the sense has to be in many words guessed at. With various emendations it will read thus: "The third book of the Gospel according to Luke. Luke, that physician after the ascension of Christ, when Paul had taken him along with him as a companion of his travels, [or, when Paul had taken him as a follower since he was desirous of righteousness,] wrote it in his own name, as seemed good to him. He himself, however, had not seen the Lord in the flesh, and so he began to speak from the nativity of John, as far as he could ascertain the truth." The fragment next describes the Gospel of John. The greater portion of the text relating to this Gospel is at least intelligible and the information is interesting. "The fourth Gospel is that of John, one of the disciples. When his fellow-disciples and overseers urged him, he said, 'Fast ye together for me to-day for three days, and let us relate to each other what has been revealed to each.' The same night it was revealed to Andrew, one of the apostles, that, while all looked over, John should write out all things in his own name. And therefore, although various beginnings are presented by each book of the Gospels, this makes no difference as respects the faith of believers, since all things in all are declared by the one guiding Spirit concerning the nativity, concerning the passion, concerning the resurrection, concerning his intercourse with his disciples, and concerning his two advents." Here the text becomes confused: and all that we know is that the writer described the one advent as an advent of humiliation, and the second advent as yet future and destined to happen in regal power and splendour. The text then proceeds plainly enough: "What wonder is it, then, that John should adduce each thing so uniformly in his Epistles, saying in regard to himself, 'The things which we have seen with our eyes, and heard with our ears, and our hands have handled, these are the things which we have written.' For he professes himself not only a seer and hearer of the Lord, but a writer of all his wonderful works in order."

The next portion of the fragment describes the Acts of the Apostles. The text is corrupt, and there is no satisfactory explanation of the last clause. "Now the Acts of all the Apostles were written in one book. Luke embraced in his work to the best Theophilus only the things which were done in his own presence; and this is plainly proved by his omission of all mention of the death of Peter and of the setting out of Paul from the city to Spain;" or this last clause may be read, "and thus he avoids declaring plainly the passion of Peter though it was known to him, as also the setting out of Paul from the city to Spain."

The rest of the fragment is for the most part intelligible, though probably several sentences have been lost. It runs thus: "Then come the letters of Paul. The letters themselves declare to those who wish to know from what place or from what cause they were sent. First of all there was the letter to the Corinthians forbidding the schism of heresy, then that to the Galatians forbidding circumcision, and then he wrote more largely to the Romans, penetrating into the order of the Scriptures and showing that Christ is the foundation of them[n]. Concerning each of these we need not speak particularly, since the blessed apostle Paul himself, following the order of his predecessor John, does not write unless to seven Churches by name in the following order: first to the Corinthians, second to the Ephesians, third to the Philippians, fourth to the Colossians, fifth to the Galatians, sixth to the Thessalonians, seventh to the Romans. But to the Corinthians and Thessalonians, though for rebuke, he wrote twice. Yet it is known that there is only one Church scattered over the whole earth. And John also, although in the Apocalypse he writes to seven Churches, yet speaks to all. Moreover, one was dedicated to Philemon, and one to Titus, and two to Timothy, in consideration of his love and affection for them, yet also in honour of the Catholic Church and the order of the Church discipline. There is one also in circulation addressed to the Laodiceans, and one to the Alexandrians[o], forged in the name of Paul according to the heresy of Marcion, and many others which cannot be received by the Catholic Church. For it does not suit to mix vinegar with honey. The letter of Judas also, and the two letters of John above

---

[n] Or, as Volkmar more probably reads, supplying a word, "to the Romans, penetrating into the order of the Scriptures and showing that Christ is the foundation of them, to others he wrote more diffusely, concerning each of which."

[o] Credner tries to make three series of letters: one to the Laodiceans, one to the Alexandrians, and some forged in the name of Paul. He does violence to the text. He wishes to make the Epistle to the Alexandrians mean the Epistle to the Hebrews.

mentioned, are reckoned genuine in the Catholic Church. Also the Wisdom written by the friends of Solomon in his honour. We receive only the revelations of John and Peter, the latter of which some of our people do not wish to be read in the Church. Moreover, Hermas very lately in our times wrote the Pastor in the city of Rome, while his brother Pius sat as overseer in the chair of the Church of the city of Rome. And therefore it ought to be read (privately), but it ought not to be publicly read in the Church to the people, nor can he be placed among the prophets, as the number is complete, nor among the apostles to the end of time. Nor do we receive anything at all of Arsinous, or Valentinus, or Miltiades, who also wrote a new book of Psalms for Marcion, along with Basilides the Asiatic founder of the Cataphrygians [p]."

The arguments which Bunsen [q] adduces to prove that this fragment is part of the work of Hegesippus are the following.

The writer affirms that Hermas wrote the Pastor in his own times. Hegesippus, as we have seen, must have been alive in the time of the emperor Hadrian, and therefore he could well call the times of Pius (133–150) his own times. Hegesippus therefore *might* be the author.

Eusebius informs us that not only Hegesippus but Irenæus and the whole chorus of the ancients called the Proverbs of Solomon the "all-virtuous Wisdom," and that he also asserted that in his own times some of the apocryphal works had been forged by heretics. Bunsen thinks that this fragment contains the statements alluded to by Eusebius.

Then, Jerome says that ecclesiastical history relates that John, when he was compelled by his brethren to write, answered that he would do so if, fasting in common, all

---

[p] Volkmar reads, with better sense, "Nor do we receive anything at all of Arsinous or Valentinus. Moreover, the followers of Marcus wrote a new book of Psalms. We reject the Asiatic founder [Montanus] of the Cataphrygians, along with Basilides."

[q] Analecta Ante-Nicæna, vol. i. p. 126.

should pray to God; and that on the conclusion of the fast, being filled with revelation, he sent forth ('vomited forth,' *eructavisse*) that introduction which came from heaven, "In the beginning was the Word[r]." Jerome asserts also that John was the last of all that wrote a gospel, and that he wrote, at the request of the overseers, against Cerinthus[s]. Bunsen thinks that Jerome refers expressly to Hegesippus in the first passage. 'Ecclesiastica Historia' can mean only either the history of Hegesippus or the History of Eusebius. It is not the latter, and therefore it must be the former. And he thinks that in both passages Jerome derived the facts from Hegesippus.

The fragment is an interesting fragment; and it certainly would be a great gain to our knowledge of the history of the canon if satisfactory proof could be adduced that Hegesippus was the author. But Bunsen's arguments break down completely on close examination. We shall discuss each argument separately.

Bunsen states that he looks upon the mention of the date not as a proof of the authorship of Hegesippus, but simply as consistent with it. The passage itself, however, is open to serious question. Even if we were sure that Hegesippus was the author, we should have no satisfaction that the text is in anything like a sound state. On the contrary, there is every reason to believe that it is mutilated. It does not begin with the beginning; sentences also seem to have fallen out. There could have been no good reason for omitting to mention the first Epistle of Peter, as it was well known and universally received. And whatever the writer might have thought of the Epistle to the Hebrews, the Epistle of James, and the third Epistle of John, we should have expected some notice of them. If it is thus mutilated, why might it not also be interpolated? If, moreover, the translator was so ignorant of Latin, can we trust his translation? And what guarantee have we that he has not paraphrased and expanded the original?

The force of these remarks is peculiarly felt in dealing with

[r] Procem. Comm. in Matth. [s] De Vir. Illust. c. 9.

the paragraph which gives the date. The Pastor of Hermas was not well known to the Western Church, and it was not highly esteemed. It was regarded as inspired by the Eastern, and read in the Eastern Churches. We have seen, moreover, that it is extremely unlikely that Hermas was a real personage. It would be, therefore, far more probable that we have here an interpolation, or addition, by a member of the Roman or African Church, probably by the translator, made expressly for the purpose of serving as proof that the Pastor of Hermas was not inspired. The paragraph itself bears unquestionable marks of tampering. The expression " Bishop Pius sitting in the chair of the Church of the city of Rome" is without parallel in the genuine writings contemporaneous with those of Hegesippus.

Bunsen's first argument has really no force in it. In the very passage of Eusebius to which he refers it is plainly asserted that " not only Hegesippus, but Irenæus, and the whole chorus of the ancients, called the Proverbs of Solomon the 'All-virtuous Wisdom.'" So that nothing definite would be gained if the fragment did call the Proverbs of Solomon the 'All-virtuous Wisdom.' But the fragment does not call the Proverbs of Solomon the 'All-virtuous Wisdom.' It speaks merely of the 'Wisdom written by the friends of Solomon.' And since the writer reckons it among the books of the New Testament, the likelihood is that he did not mean by it the Proverbs of Solomon, but the work now classed with the apocryphal books of the Old Testament[t]. The second part of the assertion, that Hegesippus mentioned that apocryphal works were forged by heretics in his day, is also no proof. Many other writers must have made, and did make, the same statement. And this fragment does not make the precise statement, for it does not assert that in the time of the writer apocryphal works were composed.

In both passages of Jerome more is asserted than is to be found in the fragment. The fragment does not mention the

---

[t] See a very interesting and able article on this point by S. P. Tregelles. Journal of Classical and Sacred Philology. No. iv. March 1855.

first verse of John's Gospel, and says nothing of that Gospel having been written against Cerinthus and Ebionites. The mere phrase 'Ecclesiastica Historia' proves nothing. The work of Hegesippus was not an Ecclesiastical History. There is no proof, moreover, that Jerome knew anything more of Hegesippus than what he found in Eusebius. And the words 'Ecclesiastica Historia' may well mean 'Church History' in the indefinite way in which we may use the term.

There is good reason to believe that the fragment is of a date later than the time of Hegesippus, and that it is not earlier than the third century. If it had been a part of the work of Hegesippus, Eusebius would in all probability have quoted it. The information is so interesting, and the authority of Hegesippus was so great with Eusebius, that he would have hailed such early and sure light on a subject in which he was deeply interested. Moreover, there is no reason to believe that in the time of Hegesippus the books of the New Testament were collected in one volume, or were known to one man. Towards the time of his death, indeed, we have proof that there began a vigorous study of the New Testament writings, and therefore this argument does not go for very much. But if the fragment were the work of Hegesippus, it would be the first notice of the books of the New Testament; and certainly it would be very strange indeed that the first full notice of them had been neglected by all the ancients, and accidentally preserved to us in a Latin translation, which, if it ascribes it to any one, ascribes it to Chrysostom.

As we have said already, the reasons for regarding the fragment as a translation are not very satisfactory. In fact there is only one expression that positively points to Greek. It is "alia plura quæ in catholicam ecclesiam recepi non potest"—a neuter plural with a singular verb. If the ingenious conjecture of Tregelles could be substantiated in any way, the proof would be positive. "Some ancient writers," says Jerome, "affirm that it (the style of the Wisdom of Solomon) is that of Philo the Jew." Tregelles conjectures that either this statement was in the fragment, or was gathered from the fragment in a mistake by Jerome. He translates the Latin words "et Sapientia ab amicis Solomonis in honorem ipsius scripta"—καὶ ἡ Σοφία Σαλομῶνος ὑπὸ Φίλωνος εἰς τὴν τιμὴν αὐτοῦ γεγραμμένη. Or the text might have been ὑπὸ φίλων, and Jerome made a mistake.

It is far more likely that the fragment is not a translation, but an original composition by one belonging to the African Church. The Latin certainly seems to point to an African origin. The use of the words 'correptio,' 'intimo,' 'ordo scripturarum,' can best be paralleled from Tertullian[u]. The text has undergone corruption at the hands of the transcriber, and the use of 'secundo' for 'secundum' is a proof that the copyist lived at a time when the Latin language was breaking down into the Italian. There are, however, comparatively few of these peculiarities, and indeed the whole Latinity is not at all bad, except in the passages where editors have entirely failed to make out a complete text. We think, therefore, that Volkmar is wrong in supposing that we have in the fragment a specimen of the lingua volgata[x]. Volkmar maintains that the manuscript is so far from being corrupt that it is to be regarded as one of the most correct. On this supposition he traces the old Latin spelling through the mistakes of the Irish transcriber. He retains unknown words—such as 'duas,' used as a noun, and 'quia,' the nominative plural neuter of 'qui.' His attempt cannot be regarded as satisfactory. There are plain and evident corruptions in the manuscript. The carelessness of the transcriber is apparent in every line. And the exact use of the subjunctive is proof that it was originally composed by one who knew well the style of the best Latin writers.

[u] See Credner, Geschichte des Neutestamentlichen Kanon, von Carl August Credner, Herausgegeben von Dr. G. Volkmar, Berlin, 1860, p. 168.

[x] Hilgenfeld, in a recent work—Der Kanon und Die Kritik des N.T. &c. Halle, 1863—agrees with me in this opinion, but supposes the fragment to be a translation from Greek, and attempts to restore the Greek, p. 40.

It is impossible to assign an author to a fragment of which absolutely no mention is made in any ancient writer. We must content ourselves with an approximation to a date. Most have agreed to place it somewhere towards the end of the second or the beginning of the third century. The arguments for this are the use of such phrases as 'the Catholic Church,' 'ecclesiastical instruction or discipline' (ecclesiastica disciplina), which are unknown to any writer described in this volume; the emphasis laid on the number (seven) of the Churches which Paul and John addressed[y]; the strong assertion of the unity of the Church[z]; the omission of any notice of the letters of Peter and James, of the Epistle to the Hebrews and the third Epistle of John[a], if we could depend on the integrity of the fragment; the naming of the revelation of Peter[b], and at the same time the simplicity of the doctrine, for the teaching of the gospel is summed up in the birth, death, resurrection, and second coming of Christ[c]. The remark about Hermas is the reason for making the date of the fragment as early as the end of the second century. But if the words "nuperrime nostris temporibus," "very lately in our days," be taken to mean 'not in the days of the apostles, but within times which may properly be called our times when inspiration has ceased,' then there is no necessity for fixing an early date. And the words "sitting in the chair of the Church of the city of Rome" are not to be paralleled in Tertullian; but there are many such expressions in Cyprian. I should therefore be inclined to regard the fragment as having been written in Latin towards the end of the first half of the third century, probably in Africa. Volkmar supposes it to have proceeded from the Roman Church between A. D. 190 and 200, basing his assertions principally on the state-

---

[y] Cyprian, Test. adv. Jud. i. 20; Routh, Reliq. Sacr. vol. i. p. 416.

[z] passim in Cypr.   [a] See Routh's note, Reliq. Sacr. vol. i. p. 420.

[b] Routh, Reliq. Sacr. vol. i. p. 426.

[c] Most of these arguments have been well set forth by Stosch, whose opinions I know only from Routh, Reliq. Sacr. vol. i. p. 397.

ment in regard to Montanus. But that part of the text in which the assertion is made is corrupt, and becomes intelligible only through conjecture. And if it were certain that the text was as Credner and Volkmar suppose, the statement is quite insufficient to give a clue to the exact date. The adherence of Tertullian to Montanism, and the consequent spread of Montanism in Africa, which Credner assigns as reasons for the fragment being written before the time of Tertullian, may have been the very reasons why the Asiatic Montanus was mentioned at all.

It would be useless to discuss the various inferences which have been drawn in regard to the canon from this fragment. They will be found in Credner, Bunsen, and Westcott. If it be considered that the document is as yet an unauthenticated document, that its completeness is matter of question, that its date can be assigned only by internal evidence, and that not of the most satisfactory nature, perhaps the warm contentions which have arisen about this fragment as the first account of books received in the Catholic Church will cool down into a more scientific treatment of it.

Bunsen and Volkmar have both attempted to supply the portions of the fragment that have been lost—a useless piece of work.

It remains to mention a Latin history of the Jewish war which has been published under the name of Hegesippus. No one doubts that this is a compilation based on the Greek work of Josephus, and some of the manuscripts—the Ambrosian in Milan, and one in the Advocates' Library in Edinburgh—read Josephi or Joseppi instead of Egesippi. There are only two separate editions of this work—one by Cornelius Gualtherus Gaudavensis, Coloniæ, twice published, first in 1559 and then in 1575; and the other begun by Weber, and finished by Julius Cæsar, with the title, Hegesippus qui dicitur sive Egesippus De Bello Judaico ope codicis Cassellani Recognitus, Marburgi, 1864. It has been printed in several of the great libraries, as Weber mentions in his introductory note.

CHAPTER IX.

DIONYSIUS OF CORINTH.

I.—LIFE.

THE only information which we have with regard to this Dionysius is derived from Eusebius, and relates almost exclusively to his letters. In his History [a] Eusebius places Dionysius among the writers that flourished in the time of Marcus Aurelius. Jerome's version of the Chronicon sets Dionysius down in A.D. 171. Jerome himself, in his article on Dionysius in his De Viris Illustribus [b], says that he flourished under the Emperors Marcus Antoninus Verus and L. Aurelius Commodus. From the short notice which Eusebius gives us of his letters we gather that he was a man of kindly and peaceful disposition, of moderation in his dealings with his brethren, and of great earnestness in his zeal against heretics, yet always anxious to bring them back to the truth and the love of the brotherhood. He seems to have had no small degree of influence in the Church. His writings would have thrown great light on the inner life of the Christians in his time if they had been preserved.

II.—THE WRITINGS OF DIONYSIUS.

Eusebius thus introduces his notice of the writings of Dionysius: "And first we must speak of Dionysius, that he was entrusted with the seat of the oversight of the Church in Corinth, and how he gave a liberal share of his inspired

[a] Euseb. Hist. Eccl. iv. 21.   [b] c. 27.

industry (ἐνθέου φιλοπονίας) not only to those under him but to those in other districts, making himself most useful to all in the catholic Epistles which he wrote (ὑπετυποῦτο) to the Churches[b]." Eusebius probably calls the letters catholic because they were intended to be read to more Churches than one[c]. Eusebius then gives a list of the eight letters which he knew. There are no remains of these letters, except one or two quotations which Eusebius himself has made.

I. A letter to the Lacedæmonians. In this letter Dionysius instructed the Lacedæmonians in the truths of Christianity, and urged them to peace and unity.

II. A letter to the Athenians. In this Dionysius stirred up the Athenians to faith and a life according to the Gospel. He rebuked them for having almost departed from the truth since the time that their president Publius had died a martyr. But at the same time he mentioned his successor Quadratus as causing a revival of their faith through his zeal. He also affirmed that "Dionysius the Areopagite, who had been urged on to the faith by the Apostle Paul, as is recorded in the Acts, was first entrusted with the oversight of the Church in Athens[d]."

III. A letter to the Nicomedians. In this Dionysius defended the truths of Christianity against the attacks of Marcion.

IV. A letter to the Church in Gortyna and the other Churches in Crete, in which he praised Philip the overseer for the good deeds done by the Church under him, and warned him to be on his guard against the perversions of heretics.

V. A letter to the Church at Amastris and the Churches throughout Pontus. Dionysius mentioned in this that he wrote at the request of Bacchylides and Elpistus, he expounded some parts of Scripture, and gave many exhortations with regard to marriage and chastity. He urged them to give a hearty welcome to those who should return, whether from a

---

[b] Hist. Eccl. iv. 23. [c] See Routh, Reliq. Sacr. vol. i. p. 196.
[d] Eusebius appeals to Dionysius for this fact elsewhere in his History, vol. iii. p. 4.

course of evil conduct or heretical delusion. He made mention in the letter of Palmas the overseer of the Church in Amastris.

VI. A letter to the Gnossians. In this Dionysius exhorts Pinytus the overseer not to lay too heavy a burden on the brethren with regard to chastity, but rather to take into consideration the weakness of the many.

VII. A letter to the Romans; addressed, says Eusebius, to Soter the overseer; but the fragments show that it was really to the Roman Church. Eusebius has preserved four fragments of this letter. The first describes a custom of the Roman Church. "For this," says Dionysius, "has been your custom from the beginning, to do good to all the brethren in various ways, and to send resources to many Churches which are in every city, thus refreshing the poverty of the needy and granting subsidies to the brethren who are in the mines; through the resources which ye have sent from the beginning, ye Romans keep up the custom of the Romans handed down by the fathers, which your blessed overseer Soter has not only preserved but added to; sending a splendid gift to the saints, and exhorting with blessed words those brethren who go up to Rome, as an affectionate father his children [d]." The second fragment relates to the letter of Clemens Romanus, and has been quoted elsewhere[e]. The third fragment bears testimony to the interpolation of letters even in the lifetime of the author. "For," he says, "I wrote letters when the brethren requested me to write. And these letters the apostles of the devil have filled with tares, taking away some things and adding others. A woe lies on these. It is not wonderful then if some have dared to deal foully with the Lord's writings (τῶν κυριακῶν γραφῶν), when they have meddled with those which are not of such importance (ταῖς οὐ τοιαύταις) as these[f]." The fourth fragment asserts that "Peter and Paul, planting us in our city of Corinth, taught us in like manner, and teaching you in

[d] Euseb. Hist. Eccl. lib. iv. c. 23.   [e] vol. i. p. 100.
[f] Euseb. Hist. Eccl. iv. 23.

like manner in Italy, boldly bore witness at the same time^g," (about the same period, κατὰ τὸν αὐτὸν καιρόν). How far reliance may be placed on this statement is doubtful, as we have no means of ascertaining the critical character of Dionysius. If he means to say that Paul and Peter planted the Corinthian Church, we know he is wrong. But most probably he means that both of them laboured together there, and this surely is not improbable.

VIII. A letter to Chrysophora, a most faithful sister. Dionysius in this gave her rational nourishment (λογικῆς τροφῆς) suited to her.

The account of Eusebius throws no light on the doctrinal position of Dionysius. Eusebius describes one of his letters as ὀρθοδοξίας κατηχητική; and in another he says that he defends the rule of truth (τῷ τῆς ἀληθείας παρίσταται κανόνι). But he gives no indication of what this orthodoxy was. Dionysius evidently entered largely into the question of marriage, which then agitated the Christian world; and he also discussed the readmission of backsliders and heretics into the Church. He also devoted himself to the study of the Scriptures, giving expositions of them (γραφῶν θείων ἐξηγήσεις). Whether the 'divine writings' included the New Testament there is no means of determining. In one of the fragments preserved he mentions the 'Lord's writings' (τῶν κυριακῶν γραφῶν). It is not easy to settle what this term means, but most probably it refers to the Gospels as containing the sayings and doings of the Lord. It is not likely, as Lardner supposes [h], that such a term would be applied to the whole of the New Testament. It is in regard to the Gospels especially that heretics are elsewhere accused of falsification and corruption. There is no reference to the Bible in the words of Eusebius, "he defends the rule of the truth."

---

[g] Euseb. Hist. Eccl. ii. 25. The text here seems corrupt, and is at least difficult to understand. I have translated ὁμόσε with Pearson—*audacter*. Perhaps it is a corruption of ὑμᾶς. For a discussion of the passage, see Heinichen's note, and Westcott on the History of the Canon, p. 209.

[h] Credibility, part ii. c. 12.

The rule of truth is the fixed beliefs of the Church, which were uniformly handed down from one Church to another. We shall meet with it elsewhere. Dionysius also mentions the Lord's day as a holy day; and it is implied in his statement that Christians met and heard instructive works read to them.

Eusebius gives a list of the most prominent writers in the reign of Marcus Aurelius; and among them he mentions some in regard to whom little is known. These are Pinytus, Philippus, Musanus, and Modestus.

PINYTUS.

Pinytus is mentioned in the letter of Dionysius of Corinth to the Gnossians as overseer. He wrote a reply to Dionysius, asking him " to bestow on them stronger food, nourishing the people under him again with more advanced (τελειοτέροις) instruction, so that they might not by continually poring over milk-like words, insensibly grow old in a childish mode of life." These words would lead us to imagine that Pinytus was inclined to adhere to his strict notions with regard to chastity. Eusebius tells us, however, that he admired and welcomed the letter of Dionysius, and he says also that the letter of Pinytus was clear proof of the soundness of his faith, his interest in the people of his charge, his learning, and understanding in divine things[i]. Eusebius speaks of him also as overseer of those in Crete[k]; but the passage is probably corrupt. The words are, Πινυτός τε ἄλλος τῶν ἐπὶ Κρήτης ἐπίσκοπος. No satisfactory explanation of the ἄλλος has yet been proposed. Eusebius is the only author that mentions Pinytus. Jerome has, as usual, repeated Eusebius[l]. He adds, that he flourished under Marcus Antoninus Verus and Lucius Aurelius Commodus.

PHILIPPUS.

Philippus is also noticed by Dionysius of Corinth in his letter to the Church of Gortyna, as being overseer of the

---

[i] Euseb. Eccl. Hist. iv. 23.   [k] Ibid. iv. 21.   [l] De Vir. Illust. c. 28.

Church. He wrote a very excellent work against Marcion [m]. Jerome mentions him as living in the time of Marcus Antoninus Verus and Lucius Aurelius Commodus [n]. The statement of Joannes Trithemius [o], that he also wrote letters and various tractates which had not reached his time, makes it probable that works were forged in his name.

MODESTUS.

Modestus is placed beside Philippus both by Eusebius [p] and Jerome [q]. All that we are informed with regard to him is that he wrote the best exposition of the errors of Marcion. The work was extant in the time of Jerome. Jerome mentions also that other treatises were current under his name, but that they were rejected by the learned as spurious.

SOTER.

Dionysius mentions a letter written by the Church in Rome to the Church in Corinth,—" To-day we spent the Lord's holy day, in which we read your letter; which we shall always keep, reading it for our admonition, as the former, written to us through Clemens." As this letter was written in the time of Soter, Soter is set down as the author of it. It is most likely he was; but yet there is nothing known in regard to the matter, and the letter was a letter of the Roman Church to the Corinthian, not of an individual to individuals. Other writings have been attributed to Soter, but they are so universally recognised now as spurious that no notice need be taken of them here.

MUSANUS.

Nothing is known of Musanus except that he lived in the reign of Marcus Aurelius, and wrote a most convincing work

---

[m] Euseb. Hist. Eccl. iv. 25. [n] De Vir. Illust. c. 30.
[o] De Script. Eccles. c. 19. [p] Hist. Eccl. iv. 25.
[q] De Vir. Illust. c. 32.

addressed to some brethren who were inclined to follow the heresy of the Encratites, then just beginning to make its appearance[r]. Theodoret also mentions him among the opponents of the Severians[s].

[r] Euseb. Eccles. Hist. iv. 28. λόγος ἐπιστρεπτικώτατος, most calculated to make them turn back to the Church again.
[s] Fab. Hæret. lib. i. c. 20.

CHAPTER X.

MELITO.

1. LIFE.

MELITO was overseer of the Church in Sardis. We know nothing of his life, except that he went, as he tells us himself, to the East; even to the place where the scenes recorded in the Old Testament were transacted [t]. Polycrates of Ephesus speaks of Melito as a man "who had conducted all his affairs in a holy spirit [u]." As a mark of distinction he calls him Melito the eunuch. Why he should be singled out by this appellation has been matter of dispute. It may have been that he really had been a eunuch before his conversion to Christianity. Most modern writers, however, have been inclined to find some special praise in the expression; and as Origen was condemned for making himself a eunuch, and as there was actually an heretical sect who insisted on castration as necessary to admission into the kingdom of Christ [x], it has been supposed that Melito was not in reality a eunuch, but that the name implied merely an unusual degree of zeal in behalf of chastity. Rufinus in his translation of Eusebius seems also to have been of this opinion, for he paraphrases, "Melito, who was a eunuch on account of the kingdom of God, and who was filled with the Holy Spirit;" but his words are by no means precise. The opinion is nowhere set out in better language than in Cave—" Vitam duxit cœlibem et plane

[t] Euseb. Hist. Eccl. iv. 26. [u] Ibid. v. 24.
[x] See Woog. Dissert. i. c. 10.

cælestem ; unde Eunuchum eum vocat Polycrates Ephesius[y]." Yet it is scarcely possible to suppose that Melito should alone of all bachelors be singled out for the special epithet of eunuch : and as Polycrates does unquestionably appear to use it as an epithet of praise, it becomes likely that Polycrates looked on the literal act of castration as a deed of high merit; and such must also have been the prevailing sentiment both of the times of Melito and of Polycrates.

Jerome, at the close of his article on Melito[z], notices that Melito was praised by Tertullian. His words are, "Tertullian, praising his elegant and declamatory turn of mind in the seven books which he wrote against the Church in behalf of Montanus, says that he was reckoned a prophet by most of our people." Some of the best manuscripts read 'blaming' instead of 'praising;' but the context is against the reading. We do not know how far we can rely on the information here given; because the works of Tertullian referred to have perished. Some have based on the statement the inference that Melito was a Montanist; and the inference is supposed to be confirmed by the title of one of Melito's books, and by some of his opinions. The probability is that Melito had died before the heresy of Montanus came to occupy an independent position, but that he had, like Athenagoras, used language in regard to the prophets which was afterwards more in harmony with Montanist than with Catholic opinions. He lived in the reign of Marcus Antoninus, to whom he addressed his Apology for the Christians. As this Apology was written in A.D. 170, and as it was probably his last work, he is supposed to have died soon after. Nothing positive can be asserted in regard to this matter. It has been conjectured that he died a natural death; for Polycrates, who had an object in mentioning the merits of those whom he names, while asserting that he was buried at Sardis, says nothing of his having suffered martyrdom. "Why should I mention," he says, "Sagaris, overseer and martyr, who sleeps in Lao-

[y] vol. i. p. 43.   [z] De Vir. Illust. c. 24.

dicea, and Papirius the blessed, and Melito the eunuch, who conducted all things in a holy spirit, and who lies in Sardis, awaiting the oversight which is from heaven, in which he shall rise from the dead[a]?"

II. THE WRITINGS OF MELITO.

Melito wrote a great many treatises. Of most of these we know only the names, and of the others we have only a very few fragments. Even the list of his works, however, is interesting. The names of the books show us what subjects had begun to attract attention among Christians; and there is many a problem of early ecclesiastical history which would have been easily settled had we had all the works of Melito.

Our principal authority in regard to the works of Melito is Eusebius. Jerome has, as usual, simply translated his statements; and we have nothing more in the lists of Rufinus, Nicephorus, and Honorius Augustodunensis. We follow the list of Eusebius. "In the time of these," he says, "Melito and Apollinaris presented Apologies to the Roman emperor[b]." And then he adds, "Of these the subjoined writings have come to our knowledge. Of Melito,

I. The two books on the Passover." Eusebius, after giving the list, quotes the commencement of the work on the passover: "In the time of Servilius Paulus, pro-consul of Asia, at which time Sagaris bore his testimony, there was much discussion in Laodicea about the passover, which fell at the exact time in those days, and these books were written." Eusebius quotes this passage as an indication of the time at which the work was written. Unfortunately, no such name as Servilius Paulus is found in the historical records of this period; but a Servilius Paulus held the consulship in A.D. 166, and a Sergius Paulus was consul in A.D. 168. The likelihood is that it is one or other of these men that

---

[a] Euseb. Hist. Eccl. v. 24.
[b] Ibid. iv. 26. The passage is quoted in the account of Apollinaris.

is meant, and most probably the latter, as Rufinus actually reads Sergius instead of Servilius. The piece of information given in the extract is also of consequence, though unfortunately it is not enough to throw full light on a very important part of Church history. Melito asserts that there was much discussion (ζήτησις). This can mean only friendly investigation among the Christians—not controversy between Christians and heretics. The subject-matter of this inquiry was about the passover that "fell in those days at the exact time" (περὶ τοῦ πάσχα ἐμπεσόντος κατὰ καιρὸν ἐν ἐκείναις ταῖς ἡμέραις). The meaning of κατὰ καιρὸν it is not easy to determine. It is generally translated 'tempestive,' 'opportunely.' Hilgenfeld supposes the passage to mean that the passover took place according to the proper time in Melito's eyes, that is, on the fourteenth of the month Nisan[c]. But such a meaning is impossible; for what particular reason would there be for adding "in those days;" and there could have been no special reason for selecting the year of Sagaris's martyrdom for the inquiry. It seems to me that the writer means to say that in that particular year the passover happened to be on the very day on which Christ's crucifixion had taken place, and that consequently his resurrection was celebrated by the Asiatics on a Sunday, exactly as it was over the whole world. Hence arose the discussion as to the desirableness of continuing their old practice of following the Jewish fourteenth, or of regulating the paschal fast by the resurrection Sunday. There can be no doubt that Melito in this discussion stood up for the continuance of the old practice, and that he strictly observed the fourteenth day as the day of the passover[d]. Clemens Alexandrinus made mention of Melito in the treatise which he wrote on the passover; and Eusebius states that Clemens himself affirmed that he composed his work in consequence of that of Melito's. There is no reason, however, to suppose that Clemens wrote in opposition to Melito, even if we believe that Clemens wrote

[c] Paschastreit. p. 252. [d] Euseb. Hist. Eccl. v. 24.

on behalf of the Roman practice. For Irenaeus, who also approved of the Roman practice, set forth the grounds which Polycarp had for the observance of the fourteenth; and the traditions of such men as Polycarp and Melito might well be quoted to show how much need there was of friendly feeling, moderation, and Christian liberality on the part of the opponents of the fourteenth.

II. " Books on the proper Mode of Life and the Prophets" (καὶ τὰ περὶ πολιτείας καὶ προφητῶν). Jerome says "one book on the life of the prophets." Rufinus makes two books of them. The Syriac has "On Polity and the Prophets^e." Nothing is known of the work.

III. " A book on the Church " (ὁ περὶ ἐκκλησίας).

IV. " A book on the Lord's Day " (καὶ ὁ περὶ κυριακῆς λόγος). These two books—on the Church, and on the Lord's Day—were the first to treat of the subjects on which they were written. Unfortunately, not a single hint is given with regard to the nature of the works. We may guess that that on the Lord's Day had some connexion with the Paschal inquiry; but this is nothing but a guess in the dark.

V. " A book on the Nature of Man " (ἔτι δὲ ὁ περὶ φύσεως ἀνθρώπου). Jerome takes no notice of this work.

VI. " A book on Formation " (καὶ ὁ περὶ πλάσεως). This book evidently discussed the formation of man—this being the usual meaning of πλάσις—and may have been a continuation of that on the nature of man. Jerome calls it " librum de plasmate."

VII. " On the Obedience of the Senses to Faith " (καὶ ὁ περὶ ὑπακοῆς πίστεως αἰσθητηρίων). Jerome makes two works out of this one; one on the senses, and one on faith. Nicephorus and Rufinus do the same. The reading in Eusebius, however, gives good sense, and is more likely to have been changed than the easier reading of Nicephorus. The title means, as Valesius remarks, " the obedience of faith which is produced by the senses;" the obedience which we yield to those beliefs which depend upon the senses. The work was probably

^e Spicilegium Syriacum, p. 57.

written, as Valesius supposes, against heretics who affirmed that psychical souls could believe only their senses, while the spiritual attained a rational faith. Melito would strive to show, as Origen did after him, that no one can believe but through his senses. The whole subject would have a close connexion with the interpretation of Scripture, and with the nature of Christian faith [f].

VIII. "And in addition to these a book on Soul and Body, or of Mind" (καὶ πρὸς τούτοις ὁ περὶ ψυχῆς καὶ σώματος ἢ νοός). Two manuscripts omit 'or of Mind' (ἢ νοός), and substitute other words. So does Nicephorus. Jerome also says, "De Anima et Corpore, librum unum." Rufinus, on the other hand, has "De Anima et Corpore et Mente." There is no way of coming to a satisfactory conclusion on the matter.

IX. "A work on the Bath" (καὶ ὁ περὶ λουτροῦ). Jerome translates it "On Baptism." This is another very important work, which we may well regret.

X. "On Truth" (καὶ ὁ περὶ ἀληθείας).

XI. "And on the Creation and Generation of Christ" (καὶ περὶ κτίσεως καὶ γενέσεως Χριστοῦ). The word 'creation' was a stumbling-block to some transcribers and translators. Many have πίστεως. Jerome says simply "On the Generation of Christ." The ante-Nicene writers did not hesitate to apply the word κτίζω to Christ, especially as they believed the passage in Proverbs—"God created me the beginning of his ways"—had a special reference to Christ. But they used the word in a very wide sense, so as in no way to preclude them from believing in the eternal existence of the Son [g].

XII. "And his discourse on Prophecy" (καὶ ὁ λόγος αὐτοῦ περὶ προφητείας). Jerome translates "On his own Prophecy," but it is not likely that Melito would write a book on such a subject. Some have supposed that Melito's work was directed against Montanus, but if this had been the case Eusebius would have mentioned the circumstance and Tertullian would not have praised him. The subject of pro-

---

[f] See Valesius *in loc.*, and the passage of Origen referred to by him.
[g] See Valesius *in loc.*

phecy occupied much of the Christian mind at this period, and Melito would no doubt readily contribute his share to its discussion. His own claim to prophetic powers rests only on the unsatisfactory testimony which Jerome found in the books of Tertullian in defence of Montanus.

XIII. "And a work on Hospitality" (καὶ ὁ περὶ φιλοξενίας).

XIV. "And the Key" (καὶ ἡ κλείς). Nothing is known even of the nature of this work. Labbé, in his treatise "De Scriptoribus Ecclesiasticis [h]," mentions that there existed in the library of the Clairmont College, Paris (Collegii Claromont. Parisiis), a manuscript bearing the name of Melito, with the title of "The Key;" and a copy of this work is still extant in the Bodleian Library among Grabe's manuscripts. The Claromontan manuscript is said to be of the twelfth or thirteenth century; and its title, written in the the same hand as the rest of the work, runs thus : "Miletus Asianus Episcopus: hunc librum edidit quem et congruo nomine Clavem appellavit [i]." Woog, in his second Dissertation on Melito, gave the headings of the chapters [j], and an extract from the commencement as a specimen of the work, from which Keil justly inferred that the work is not of much worth [k].

XV. "And these on the Devil."

XVI. "And on the Revelation of John" (καὶ τὰ περὶ τοῦ διαβόλου καὶ τῆς ἀποκαλύψεως Ἰωάννου). Jerome separates these into two works: "one book on the Devil; one book on the Apocalypse of John;" and such seems to have been the intention of Eusebius. Both books would have been extremely interesting had they been extant. As far as we know, Melito was the first to write on the devil, and he was probably the first who systematically expounded the Revelation.

[h] tom. ii. p. 87.
[i] Gallandi Bibl. PP. tom. i. ; Prolegomena, c. 24, p. cxx.
[j] Paragraph 19.
[k] Fabricius Biblioth. Græc. vol. vii. p. 150, ed. Harless. See Routh, Reliq. Sacr. vol. i. p. 132. The fragment is given in Migne, vol. v. p. 1223. See also Piper, p. 63.

XVII. "And that on Corporeal God" (καὶ ὁ περὶ ἐνσωμάτου θεοῦ). Jerome copies the Greek in his translation (περὶ ἐνσωμάτου θεοῦ, librum unum), probably not wishing to translate it, or uncertain as to its meaning. Rufinus translates, "de Deo Corpore Induto;" and the Syriac, "On God who put on the Body:" both probably thinking of Christ. There can scarcely be a doubt that Valesius is right in thinking that Melito maintained in this book that God was corporeal. The passage which he quotes from Origen is satisfactory proof. Origen expressly states that Melito took the members of God mentioned in the Scriptures literally, and "left writings behind him with regard to God being corporeal" (ἐνσώματον [1]). The testimony of Origen is confirmed by that of Gennadius, also quoted by Valesius, who says [m], "Let us believe nothing corporeal in the Trinity, as Melito and Tertullian." Some, however, have maintained that Melito's work was on the Incarnation of Christ, and that it is the same as that of which Anastasius Sinaita spoke, with the title περὶ σαρκώσεως Χριστοῦ, "On the Incarnation of Christ." This opinion, it is affirmed, is also supported by the use of the word ἐνσωμάτωσις, applied to Christ in the Christian writers. In opposition to these statements it has to be remembered that we are not left in doubt with regard to Melito's sentiments on the corporeality of God; that the credit of a writer like Anastasius is very low, and besides, is not involved in the present case; and that, though the word ἐνσωμάτωσις is applied to Christ by Origen and subsequent writers, yet not even among them do we find the terms ἐνσώματος θεός applied to Christ. At least, the only instance which Suicer [n] adduces is this very title of Melito's book; and the other instance which we have seen in Origen is applicable only to God. There is another and stronger evidence to the difference between the two works.

---

[1] Origenis Opera, vol. viii. p. 49, Lommatzsch.

[m] De Dogmatibus Ecclesiasticis, c. iv. p. 337, of tom. i. of Oehler's Corpus Hæreseologicum.

[n] Thesaurus Ecclesiasticus, voc. ἐνσώματος.

Anastasius, in citing a passage from the treatise on the Incarnation of Christ, states that it was written against Marcion—a circumstance which Eusebius would probably have mentioned—and he cites expressly the third book. Now Eusebius in the case of all the other works is careful in stating how many books there are in each work, and he says expressly, "the work on Corporeal God."

XVIII. "Last of all, the book addressed to Antoninus" (ἐπὶ πᾶσι καὶ τὸ πρὸς Ἀντωνῖνον βιβλίδιον). The use of the term βιβλίδιον, as Valesius remarks, indicates that the work was a petition—a fact which we know also from one of the fragments of it. The phrase ἐπὶ πᾶσι has been taken by some to mean that the Apology was the last work which Melito wrote. The words admit of a different signification, but the probability is that Eusebius did mean to indicate the position of this work, in point of time, in regard to the others. In Jerome's version of the Eusebian Chronicle the Apology of Melito is placed under the tenth year of the reign of Marcus Aurelius—that is, A.D. 170. The Alexandrian Chronicle agrees with Jerome's version. The Armenian translation does not mention the work. One of the fragments contains proof to some extent that the Apology was written after A.D. 169, for Melito mentions the son of Marcus as likely to reign with him, while no notice is taken of Lucius Verus, who is, therefore, believed to have died before this time. Some have supposed that the fragment intimates that Commodus actually shared the government with his father at the time at which it was written, and hence they have assigned the arbitrary date of A.D. 175 or 176, or 177. But the words are, "The Roman power has increased, to which you have become the much prayed-for successor, and you will be with your son." They intimate distinctly only the anticipation that Commodus will share the government with his father, and they seem also to indicate that Marcus had then but just succeeded to the sole sovereignty. The word εὐκταῖος appears to me to indicate that many were anxious even before the death of

Lucius Verus, that Marcus should take the government into his own hands[n].

Eusebius has preserved three fragments of this Apology. They throw important light on the persecutions of the Christians in those times. They prove that they were usually local in their nature, and they show that the decrees of the emperors had comparatively little to do with them. The third fragment is interesting for another reason. It is an attempt to show that Christianity had been a blessing to the Roman empire. It maintains, like a modern writer[o], but with a different theory, that the Roman state had made great advances since the days of Augustus. And we also gather from it that Melito agreed with the other apologists in representing Christianity as something very old. The fragments are as follows: "For now the race of the pious is persecuted, an event that never took place before, being driven about over Asia by new decrees [probably of separate cities]. For shameless informers and men greedy of other people's goods, taking occasion by the injunctions (διαταγμάτων), publicly plunder, day and night, spoiling those who do no harm." And after other things, he says, "If this is done according to your order, be it so, it is well done: for a just sovereign will never decree unjustly; and we willingly take the reward of such a death. This only request we lay before you, that you yourself first learn to know thoroughly the perpetrators of this obstinacy[p], and then judge justly whether they are worthy of death and punishment, or of safety and quiet. But if it is not from you that this new counsel and decree comes—a decree which

---

[n] Piper (p. 103) adduces a special argument for A.D. 170. Two sons of Marcus Aurelius were alive on his accession to the sole sovereignty. But the expression τοῦ παιδός seems to intimate only one son. Annius Verus died in 170, and therefore the Apology could not have been written before that year. He notices, however, the circumstance that in all probability only one son would succeed the emperor, however many he may have had.

[o] Congreve, in his Lectures, noticed already.

[p] Τοὺς τῆς φιλονεικίας ἐργάτας. Valesius thinks Christians are meant by this expression, and he seems to be right. Nothing bad is therefore meant by it.

is becoming not even against a barbarous enemy,—much more do we entreat you not to overlook us in such a public plunder." To these again he adds, saying, "Our philosophy (ἡ καθ' ἡμᾶς φιλοσοφία) first flourished among barbarians. And then blooming among your nations, in the great reign of your ancestor Augustus, it proved a signal blessing to your kingdom. For since that time the Roman power has grown to something great and brilliant, to which you have become the much wished-for successor, and you will be with your son, if you keep the philosophy which has grown up with the kingdom, and which began with Augustus; which also your ancestors honoured in addition to the other modes of worship. And the greatest proof that our religion (τὸν καθ' ἡμᾶς λόγον) has flourished for good along with the empire which began well, is this, that no evil has occurred since the reign of Augustus, but on the contrary, all that is brilliant and glorious according to the prayer of all. Nero and Domitian alone of all, under the influence of designing men, have wished to accuse our religion. From them the habit of giving false information in regard to us has continued to propagate itself through irrational fashion. But your pious ancestors corrected their ignorance, frequently rebuking in rescripts many who had dared to get up some new outbreak against us, among whom appears your grandfather Hadrian, writing to many others, but especially to Fundanus, the proconsul of Asia: and your father, while you managed all things along with him, wrote to the cities not to indulge in outbreaks against us; addressing himself, among others, to the Larisseans, the Thessalonians, the Athenians, and to all Greeks. And we have strong confidence that you who have the same disposition as they with regard to us, and one much more philanthropic and philosophic, will do all that we ask of you."

There is no other fragment of Melito's Apology extant. The writer of the Alexandrine Chronicle quotes a passage from Melito which he apparently means to say he took from the Apology. It is unquestionably spurious, as we shall see immediately; but it is curious as one of those passages in which much has been made to depend upon a single word. It is as follows: "We are not worshippers of insensible stones, but we are worshippers of God alone, who is before all, and who is over all, even over Christ Himself, who is the Logos of God before the ages." Whiston frequently appeals to this passage in behalf of his Arian opinions. By a change of a letter, however—of ἐπί into ἔτι—the passage goes against him, and runs: "We are not worshippers of stones, but of God; and we are also worshippers of Christ," &c. And orthodox editors so translate it.

XIX. Eusebius knew another work of Melito's, which he mentions immediately after his quotations from the Apology. It was called Ἐκλογαί, or Selections, and was divided into six books. Eusebius quotes the Preface or Introductory Letter, in which Melito himself describes his book and gives the first list of the books of the Old Testament which occurs in a Christian writer. It runs thus: "Melito to his brother Onesimus, joy. Since you have frequently requested me in your zeal for the truth that extracts be made for you both from the Law and the Prophets with regard to our Saviour and our whole faith, and since you wished also to get an accurate knowledge of our books, how many they are, and what is their order, I have taken the trouble to do this, knowing your zeal with regard to the faith, and your desire to learn with regard to the truth; and especially that you prefer these things most of all from your desire which is towards God; striving as you are for eternal salvation. Going up then to the East and reaching even the place where they were preached and done, and learning accurately the books of the Old Testament, I have subjoined them and sent them to you; of which these are the names;—the books of Moses, five—Genesis, Exodus, Numbers, Leviticus, Deuteronomy: Joshua Nave, Judges, Ruth: four of 'Reigns'; two of Paralipomena (Chronicles); the Psalms of David; the Proverbs of Solomon, which is also called Wisdom; Ecclesiastes; the Song of Songs; Job; the Prophets Isaiah, Jeremiah, and the Twelve in one Book; Daniel, Ezekiel, Ezra. Of which I have made extracts, dividing them into six books." The omission of the book of Esther in this list has attracted attention. Some scholars assert it is not mentioned because it was still a moot point whether the book was canonical; while others maintain that both Esther and Nehemiah are included under the name of Ezra. The fragment seems to me to show that in the Christian Church even in Melito's times there must have prevailed considerable ignorance in regard to the Hebrew Scriptures. Of course large numbers of Christians would not be able to read. Many more could not probably afford to pay for copies of the Hebrew Scriptures even if they wished. Hence the advantage of such selections as those of Melito. But it is surprising that Onesimus should actually be in ignorance of the number of the books—should, in fact, merely have had a general idea of the collection, and that Melito should have gone up to the East to attain accurate knowledge on this point. The fragment does not say that Melito went to the East expressly with this object, but it seems to imply as much; and at any rate, great stress is laid on the circumstance that the knowledge was acquired in the place where the transactions occurred.

This is all the information which Eusebius gives us in regard to Melito. Besides the fragments given in Eusebius, there have come down to us two fragments from Anastasius Sinaita, four have been found in catenae, one occurs in the Chronicon Paschale, and Cureton has discovered in Syriac "An Oration to Antoninus Caesar," and five fragments. The fragments of Anastasius Sinaita are taken, one from the work already described on the Incarnation of Christ, and the other from a work styled Εἰς τὸ Πάθος, perhaps an address in commemoration of the Passion. The silence of Eusebius in regard to both these works is an argument against their genuineness; for he seems to have taken special care with the works of Melito, and it is very far from likely that books unknown to him would turn up for the first time only in the age of Anastasius. Anastasius, moreover, may have been misled by the name, and a work written by another Melito he may have taken for a production of the more famous one. Besides, the theological expressions in both extracts render them doubtful, to say the least.

Much need not be said of the fragments gathered from the Catenae. There is the greatest insecurity in any name found in them. We know that the names Melito and Meletius were confounded frequently, and we also know that there was a large number of writers in the Church bearing the name of Melito or Meletius[q]. The fragments in themselves are unobjectionable, with the exception of one (iv. in Routh), which says that "there are two things which afford forgiveness of sins—suffering for Christ [martyrdom], and baptism." Such an inordinate estimate of martyrdom is not found in any writer whose opinions are detailed in this volume, and is far more likely to be the statement of a later age.

"The Oration of Meliton the philosopher to Antoninus Cæsar" seems to us not the genuine work of our Melito. It is certainly not the Apology mentioned by Eusebius, for it does not contain the extract he has made, and it has no appearance of being a fragment, as Rénan supposed[r]. Cureton also, we think, is right in identifying it with the Apology mentioned in the Chronicon Paschale, in the year 164–65, and the fragment taken by Routh from the Chronicon finds a parallel in the Syriac work. But the whole style of the work is such as to lead one to believe that it was never presented to the emperor. The inscription affirms that Melito spoke the address before the emperor, and the concluding words contain a direct appeal to him: "But when thou, O Antonius (Antoninus) Cæsar, shalt learn these things, and thy children also with thee." Yet the greater part of the address cannot have been spoken, or even intended for Marcus Antoninus, or the writer must have been totally ignorant of his character. Thus, in the very first paragraph, the Stoic philosopher is warned thus: "But I say that this is not a

---

[q] See Woog, Dissert. i. par. 2.

[r] See Cureton, Spic. p. 7. Both Bunsen and Cureton are of opinion that it is not a fragment.

good excuse that a man be in error with the many, for if one only act foolishly, his folly is great; how much greater, then, must the folly be when the many are foolish together?" The same kind of remark is made in the next pages. Then, again, in page 43, line 15, he remarks, that those who despise the gods "diminish the revenue of Cæsar," not surely a very apologetic remark. Then, again, he remarks: " Perhaps one who is a sovereign may say, ' I am not able to conduct myself well because I am a sovereign. It behoveth me to do the will of the many.' He who should plead thus truly deserves to be laughed at [t]." Perhaps, also, we have in the following sentence an indication that the writer thought more of destroying idols than converting men to Christ: " For what advantage is greater than this, that a sovereign should deliver the people which is under his hand from error, and by this good deed obtain the favour of God [u]?" Supposing the work to be Melito's, and supposing that he did originally speak it, it is quite possible that he may have afterwards sat down to write it, and it is this written speech which we have. Granting this supposition to be tenable, yet we can scarcely account for the following appeal to his hearer or his readers without supposing that the writer entirely forgot his intention: " But touching Nebo, which is in Mabug, why should I write to you? for lo! all the priests which are in Mabug know that it is the image of Orpheus, a Thracian Magus [x]."

Besides, this Apology, if we are so to call it, does not contain one word in defence of Christianity. We may venture to affirm, with considerable certainty, that all the Apologies presented to Marcus Antoninus had for their object to avert the calamities and distresses that were crowding upon the persecuted followers of Christ. Not one word here, however, of Christians. The writer attempts to turn his readers

---

[s] p. 42, line 27. [t] p. 48, line 26. [u] p. 49, line 13.

[x] The Abbé Freppel has adduced some of these arguments to show that the authenticity of the Apology of Cureton is open to serious doubts. Les Apologistes, 2 Ser. p. 374.

or the emperor from worshipping idols to serving God. Putting together all these circumstances there seems to me a strong case for rejecting the work as Melito's. I lay no stress on Bunsen's argument, that it contains an allusion to the Second Epistle of Peter, or that it is confused. Most of the Apologies of the time are confused enough, and there are always two ways of accounting for an allusion, even were it proved that the Second Epistle of Peter was written later than the time of Melito. There is also nothing in the theology that is contrary to the theology of the time, and there is a good deal in harmony with it—such as its speculations on heathen mythology, and its reference to free-will.

The five Syriac fragments which Cureton has published cannot be regarded as genuine. One of them bears the inscription, "Of Meliton, bishop of the city of Attica," and another, "Of the holy Meliton, bishop of Ittica." Cureton thinks that the Syriac translator has inserted 'city' by mistake, and he hints[y] that these fragments were most probably the production of a Meletius or Melitius, bishop of Sebastopolis, in Pontus. But Socrates, who gives us the most ample notices of this Meletius, nowhere connects him with Attica. He was bishop of Sebastopolis, of Berœa, of Syria, and of Antioch [z]. Though the clue fails us here, yet there is considerable likelihood that the names were confounded; and at all events the reasons for rejecting these two fragments are strong. In the first place, the Syriac translator's note is of no authority, and at the best is puzzling. Then the fragments seem to be part of the spurious oration which Anastasius calls Εἰς τὸ Πάθος. For the extract which Anastasius makes occurs in both the Syriac fragments, with a slight difference. Anastasius's quotation runs thus, "God suffered under the Israelitish right hand." The Syriac fragments have it, "God put to death; the king of Israel slain by an Israelitish right hand[a]." The shorter fragment consists of only two other clauses.

---

[y] Cureton is exceedingly cautious, and scarcely as much as hints this. He leaves you to suppose that he wishes to hint it.

[z] See Socr. Hist. Eccl. lib. ii. c. 43, 44. [a] p. 55, line 18.

The larger fragment abounds in rhetorical periods. Thus: "This is He that was put to death. And where was He put to death? In the midst of Jerusalem. By whom? By Israel; because He healed their maimed, and cleansed their lepers, and gave light to their blind, and raised their dead. For this cause He died." Then we have shortly after an address to Israel: "For thou knewest not, O Israel, that this was the first-born of God who was begotten before the sun; who made the light to rise, who lighted up the day, who separated the darkness. . . . . Bitter were thy nails, and keen; bitter was thy tongue; bitter was Judas, to whom thou gavest hire; bitter," &c. Again: "The lights were hurried away, and the day became dark because they were slaying God, who was naked upon the tree." The whole style of this fragment is certainly not like anything we have of writings contemporary with Melito. There is nothing objectionable in the theology. The most marked phrases—the slaying of God—have been adduced, and it would be hazardous to affirm that Melito did not use such language.

One of the three remaining fragments is taken from a discourse "On the Cross." The work was unknown to Eusebius, and was probably written after his time. It speaks of Christ being invested with the Father, of not binding the singleness of his Godhead, of not changing the likeness of the Father. It must have been written considerably after the time when the idea of the two natures of Christ had become prevalent: for we have a studied contrast between Christ's activity as man and God at the same time.

The other two extracts are taken from works which purport to be—one on the "Soul and Body," the other on "Faith." Both works are mentioned by Eusebius, but both extracts seem spurious. The extract from the work on "Faith" concludes with calling Christ "the bridegroom of the Church, the charioteer of the cherubim, the captain of the angels, God who is of God, the Son who is of the Father, Jesus Christ, the king for ever and ever." The extract from "On the Soul and Body" contains nothing objectionable in it, and is not without beauty. Yet it is in bad company, it cannot be regarded as well authenticated, and its style is not unlike that of the other fragments. It describes the purpose of Christ's death thus: "For our Lord when He was born man, was condemned in order that He might show mercy; was bound in order that He might loose; was seized upon in order that He might let go; suffered in order that He might have compassion; died that He might save; was buried that He might raise up." There is a resemblance between this and one of the fragments from the Catenae[a], and one of the fragments attributed to Apollinaris. It is noteworthy that mention is made of the mother of Christ, either as Mary or as the Virgin, in each of the four larger fragments—a frequency of notice not usual in early writers.

There are two works bearing the name of Melito which are universally recognised as spurious. The one describes the death of the Virgin Mary, and the miraculous presence of the Apostles at that event, "De Transitu Virginis Mariæ;" and the other gives an account of some marvellous miracles of the Apostle John, "De Actibus Joannis Apostoli [b]."

We learn no more of the doctrines of Melito than what has been given in the fragments quoted, except in regard to one point. A writer, whose name was unknown to Eusebius, in opposing the heresy of Artemon, wrote: "Who is ignorant of the books of Irenæus, Melito, and the others proclaiming Christ God and man [c]?" In what way he spoke of Christ as God we do not know, but we may be tolerably confident that he never used the terms assigned to him in the work "On the Incarnation" already mentioned. There it is said, "The same, being both perfect God and man, gave assurance to us of his two existences (οὐσίας), his divinity through the miracles in the three years after his baptism, and his humanity in the thirty years (χρόνοις) which were before his baptism." The word χρόνος, used here as in modern Greek

[a] III. in Routh.
[b] See a full discussion of these works in Piper, p. 112 ff.
[c] Euseb. Hist. Eccl. v. 28.

for 'year,' is an indication of the lateness of the fragment. It is so used only in very late Greek [d]. And the application of the word οὐσία is still more decisive. It is here used as equivalent to what is now called "the two natures of Christ,"—a use of the word which was prevalent after the council of Nicæa [e].

[d] See Suicer *in voc.*; and especially Sophocles, Glossary *in voc.*
[e] Ibid.

CHAPTER XI.

APOLLINARIS.

I. LIFE.

THE only facts which we know with regard to Claudius Apollinaris are that he was an overseer of the Church in Hierapolis, a city of Phrygia, and that he lived in the reign of Marcus Aurelius. These facts are attested by Serapion[a] and Eusebius[b]. Eusebius sets him down as illustrious in the year 172, and the Chronicon Paschale in 170. He must have lived some years after, since he alluded to the miracle of the Thundering Legion which happened in A.D. 174. Nothing is known of his death.

II. THE WRITINGS OF APOLLINARIS.

Eusebius thus enumerates the writings of Apollinaris: "Of the many books of Apollinaris which are preserved among many, the following are those that have come to our hands: a Discourse to the forementioned emperor [Marcus Aurelius], and five writings addressed to the Greeks, and a first and second concerning truth, and a first and second addressed to the Jews, and those which he wrote after these against the heresy of the Phrygians which not long after was struck out into something new, but which at that time was as it were beginning to spring up, for Montanus was as yet but making

---

[a] Euseb. Hist. Eccl. v. 19. [b] Ibid. iv. 21, 26.

a commencement of his aberration along with his false prophetesses[c].

There are some points in this account which call for more minute examination. The first work mentioned is the Address to the Emperor. Eusebius mentions the same work elsewhere. "In the time of these," he says, "Melito overseer of the Church sojourning at Sardes, and Apollinaris overseer of that in Hierapolis, flourished exceedingly; who also addressed Apologies, each separately, for the faith to him who has been mentioned as Emperor of the Romans in those days[d] [Marcus Aurelius]." The Apology is mentioned also by Jerome[e]. Nothing remains of this Apology. Some have supposed that Eusebius makes reference to a passage in it, but there is nothing in Eusebius to indicate from what work of Apollinaris he gathered his information. The passage, however, is interesting in itself and deserves notice. It relates to the story current among the Christians, that the Roman army was saved from destruction by the prayers of the Christian soldiers, when Marcus Aurelius was hard pressed in a war with the Germans and Sarmatians. Eusebius asserts that the extraordinary event was recorded by heathen writers, though by them it was not attributed to the prayers of the Christians. He says also that Christian writers had handed down the event in a simple, guileless manner. "Among these latter would be," he continues, "Apollinaris, who said that from that time the legion that had produced the miracle through prayer had received from

---

[c] Αἱρέσεως μετ' οὐ πολὺν καινοτομηθείσης χρόνον. The exact meaning of these words has been matter of dispute. Καινοτομεῖν means 'to set up a new doctrine or doctrines,' and Heinichen translates here 'which rashly set forth new doctrines.' This unquestionably is the right translation, but as the setting up of new doctrines, as such, must have been contemporaneous with Montanus's departure from the Church, I think here both ideas are included in the word, so that Lange's translation also is right—'Quæ non multo post res novas in ecclesiam induxit.' The meaning is that at the time at which Apollinaris wrote Montanus was still in the Church, but that not long after he chose an independent and new sphere of action for himself. See Heinichen's note on the passage. Euseb. Hist. Eccl. iv. 27.

[d] Euseb. Hist. Eccl. iv. 26.   [e] De Vir. Illust. c. 26.

the Emperor a name akin to the deed, being called the Thundering Legion in the language of the Romans[f]." From this notice we can form no idea as to the exact words used by Apollinaris, nor the exact amount of information which he gave. The statement, however, even of the giving of a new name to the Meletine legion has been questioned. Dio Cassius[g] mentions a legion which he calls κεραυνοφόρος (thunderbolt-bearing), as existing in the time of Augustus, and stationed in his own day in Cappadocia; and Scaliger[h] quotes an inscription of the reign of Trajan, in which occur the words "Leg. Ful.," that is, Legio Fulminea, or Fulminatrix. The statement of Dion Cassius and the inscription have been set down as proving incontestably that Apollinaris must have been wrong: and the probability is that he was wrong, and that the name which he supposed to have been given by Marcus Aurelius, had been the name of the legion long before. The matter, however, is by no means absolutely certain. For Apollinaris asserts that the legion was called κεραυνοβόλος, 'thunderbolt-casting,' while Dion's legion bore the name of κεραυνοφόρος, and the unabridged inscription would be 'legio fulminea' more probably than 'legio fulminatrix.' If this be so, then it is possible that there was a legion which was called κεραυνοφόρος, from its bearing on its shields the sign of a thunderbolt; and Marcus Aurelius may have given to another legion the appellation of κεραυνοβόλος if he had supposed it in any way connected with a thunderstorm. We hear nothing of this Thundering Legion in contemporary heathen writers, but the name and the legion may both have soon vanished from history. No definite conclusion can be reached in regard to this matter, nor can we at all determine whether the testimony of Apollinaris was to the effect that there really had been an answer to the prayers of Christian soldiers.

The second work mentioned is five books (συγγράμματα) addressed to the Greeks, or, as Jerome translates, 'quinque adversum Gentes libri.' Nothing is known of this work.

[f] Euseb. Hist. Eccl. v. 5.   [g] lib. 55.   [h] Animadv. in Euseb. p. 223.

The third work is curiously described by Eusebius as a first and second book on truth. Why he did not say 'two books,' as Jerome says, is a problem. The problem is complicated by the notice of the next work: "A first and a second to the Jews." Jerome, who translates Eusebius, knows nothing of these first and second books to the Jews, and the clause is omitted in several manuscripts of Eusebius. The whole sentence of Eusebius might also be translated in a way considerably different from Jerome's notice. It might run thus: "A discourse addressed to the fore-mentioned king and to the Greeks: five writings; a first and a second concerning truth, a first and second to the Jews, and the work against the Montanists." According to this translation the Apology is addressed to the Emperor and Greeks. Then there are five writings: two on truth, two to the Jews, and one to the Montanists. Or it is possible to suppose the text of Eusebius corrupt, and to imagine that the words "two books addressed to the Jews" are the corruption of some other words describing the remaining three books of the συγγράμματα. This supposition is not without some likelihood, for Photius says, "There was read Apollinaris's work to the Greeks, both about piety and about truth [i]." His words have generally been translated, "There was read Apollinaris to the Greeks and on piety and on truth." Both translations are perfectly legitimate [j]. Photius, however, almost invariably devotes a separate paragraph to each work which he reads, and accordingly the first translation has this much in its favour. Perhaps, then, instead of the two books to the Jews, the history of Eusebius contained some words describing the third and fourth books, or the rest of the books as relating to piety. And then Eusebius's words would mean that Apollinaris wrote an Apology to the Emperor, five books addressed to the Greeks on truth and piety, and some writings on the

---

[i] Biblioth. cod. 14.
[j] Some lay stress on the repetition of the περί as in favour of separate books. Fabric. Delect. Argum. de Rel. Christiana, p. 160; Routh, Reliq. Sacr. vol. i. p. 171.

Montanist controversy. There is no mention anywhere else than in Photius of a work on piety.

The last work mentioned by Eusebius is the writings against Montanus. Eusebius describes Apollinaris as a "strong and irresistible weapon against the heresy named after the Phrygians [k]." His writings on this subject were warmly recommended by Serapion, overseer of the Church in Antiochia. "In order that you may see," he says, "that the activity of this false school of new prophecy has been abhorred by all the brotherhood in the world, I have sent to you the writings of Claudius Apollinaris the most blessed, who was an overseer in Hierapolis in Asia [l]." Commentators have been divided as to whether γράμματα should be translated 'letters' or 'writings.' The matter is not of much moment. 'Writings' is the most likely translation. If they were letters, they must have been writings; and the probability is that, even if Serapion here calls them writings, they were in the shape of letters.

Theodoret mentions that Apollinaris wrote against the Encratites (πρὸς τοὺς Σεουηριανοὺς 'Εγκρατίτας [m]), but whether he refers to a separate work or not cannot be determined. He praises him as not only well acquainted with divine things, but as having received culture from without [n], that is, in profane literature. Jerome seems to have had an equally high idea of his powers; for he reckons him among those who traced the poisons of the heretics to their sources in the schools of heathen philosophy [o].

The only other work that has been attributed to Apollinaris is one on the Passover. In the preface of the Alexandrian Chronicle occur the words, "Moreover, Apollinaris, the most holy bishop of Hierapolis of Asia, who lived near the apostolic times, in his work on the Passover taught similar things, saying as follows"—the writer then quotes the following two passages from the work: "There are some who through ignorance quarrel about these things, being affected in a way that

---

[k] Euseb. Hist. Eccl. v. 16. [l] Ibid. 19.
[m] Hæret. Fab. ii. 21.   [n] Ibid. iii. 2.   [o] Epist. ad Mag. 83.

should be pardoned; for ignorance ought not to be followed by accusation, but it stands in need of instruction. And they say that the Lord ate the sheep with his disciples on the fourteenth, and that He Himself suffered on the great day of unleavened bread; and they affirm (διηγοῦνται, 'relate,' perhaps 'explain') that Matthew says exactly as they have understood the matter to be; whence their understanding of it does not harmonize with the law, and the gospels, according to them, seem to differ." And again, the same person has written that in the same treatise " The fourteenth is the true passover of the Lord, the great Sacrifice, the Son of God, who was bound instead of the lamb; though He bound the strong, and who being Judge of living and dead was judged, and who was delivered into the hands of sinners that He might be crucified; who was exalted upon the horns of the unicorn; whose sacred side was pierced; who also poured out of his side two things that cleanse again, water and blood, discourse (λόγον) and spirit, and who was buried on the day of the passover, the stone being laid on his tomb ᵖ." Considerable stress has been laid on these two passages in recent discussions of the early Passover controversy, and a vast number of inferences have been made which are totally unwarranted. The passages, as they stand, throw no light on the nature of the controversy in which the writer of them took part. It may be doubted whether it was a practical controversy at all. It seems more of the nature of a discussion—it was a wrangling, at the bottom of which was ignorance, not difference of practice. And the writer simply undertakes to teach his readers the real state of the case. He may have observed the fourteenth of the month Nisan, or he may not. His language might furnish an argument either way. Christ was Himself the real passover—chose the day of the passover as the day of his sacrifice; and therefore Christians should always observe the Jewish passover-day as the day of Christ's suffering. The Jewish day

---

ᵖ Chron. Pasch. P. 6, Dind.

would henceforth be a Christian day. Or he might have reasoned—'Jesus Himself did not observe the real passover; the feast He held was on the preceding day. Therefore we are not bound to keep to the exact day of the Jewish festival, or, indeed, to observe it at all; but we may follow the inclination of the Church.' We do not know which way of reasoning the writer followed. Some have supposed that he followed the first, and accordingly they reckon Apollinaris among the observers of the fourteenth of Nisan. They suppose also that his antagonists were Ebionites. Others have supposed that he adopted the latter; and they place him among the upholders of the practice of the Roman Church. This latter supposition has the least to say for itself; for it not only works out the reasoning of the writer from statements which do not compel the particular mode of reasoning, but in consequence of this supposed reasoning it asserts an historical fact of which we know nothing elsewhere in contemporary writers. We do not know that in the time of Apollinaris the Roman method of celebrating Easter had at all come into vogue; and even if there were some slight grounds for supposing that it might have, yet there is no reason to suppose that the practice had found favour in Asia Minor. There was much discussion there about the exact time of Easter; but the nature of the discussion is unknown. Having thus disposed in a general way of the meaning of these two fragments, we may deal more concisely with the fictions which Hilgenfeld has based on them. He maintains that Apollinaris was the first representative known to us of the deutero-Johannean direction, the foundations of which are laid in the fourth Gospel, and which found a special obstacle in the Quartodeciman attachment to the time of the Jewish festival [q]. He supposes Apollinaris to be the great opponent of Melito. He supposes that in the words "Some who through ignorance wrangle about these things" Apollinaris had in view Melito and his party [r], and that he uses

---

[q] Paschastreit, p. 274. [r] Ibid. p. 256.

these mild terms because he had great respect for them; and he therefore believes that we have here a controversy between Jewish Christians and Catholic Christians. Now almost all these assertions are miserably defective in proof. The writer may have taken his notion of the day of Christ's suffering from John's Gospel: but that he placed a second Johannean tradition or gospel in opposition to a first, is utterly untrue. The writer states expressly that, as he believed, it was ignorance that led some to imagine there was difference between Matthew and John. The words καὶ στασιάζειν δοκεῖ κατ' αὐτοὺς τὰ εὐαγγέλια cannot mean anything else; and Hilgenfeld's attempt to make στασιάζειν to mean 'an inner want of unity' is not very successful. Then, again, it is scarcely possible to suppose that the writer would venture to call the Quartodeciman party 'some.' They must have formed an utterly overwhelming majority in Asia Minor. Nor is it likely that he would have the impudence to attribute the opinions of Melito and suchlike men to ignorance. Objections of a like nature might be taken to many other parts of Hilgenfeld's scheme. But there is one preliminary inquiry of an essential nature, which the critical school of Baur[s] and Hilgenfeld has not deemed necessary in this case. This inquiry is, Are the fragments genuine? The only testimony which we have to their genuineness is that of the writer of the Preface of the Chronicon Paschale: and his testimony is worth almost nothing. "The single testimony," Lardner modestly puts it, "of a writer of the seventh century can hardly afford full satisfaction on this point[t]." If the main suppositions of Hilgenfeld were true, there would be the strongest reasons for rejecting the testimony of the Chronicon Paschale. If Apollinaris were the first to defend the Catholic practice in regard to the passover, if he employed the learning which Theodoret says he had in convincing the vast majority around him who adhered to the practice of their forefathers,

---

[s] Baur is of the same opinion as Hilgenfeld: Das Christenthum, &c. p. 157.
[t] Credibility, part ii. c. 28, 11

how is it that nobody knows anything of him in this relation? How is it that he is ignored by writers on the passover? How is it that Eusebius and Jerome know nothing of his Treatise on the Passover? How is it that the Catholic Church so universally forgot their first great champion? Nay, Eusebius, as we have seen, places Melito and Apollinaris side by side in defence of the truth. How is this? "The peace-loving spirit of Eusebius," says Hilgenfeld, "disliked the controversy;" and so he places Melito and Apollinaris, the principal opponents, in a friendly way together. If this was the motive of Eusebius, it seems extraordinary that he should not have seen the work of Apollinaris on the passover— a work said to be on the Catholic side,—and that he should mention the work of Melito, on the Jewish-Christian side. The juxtaposition of the two writers is in fact, to a certain extent, proof that Eusebius knew of no quarrel between them, and consequently that he had never heard of Apollinaris's fame as the first champion of the deutero-Johannean tendency. The internal evidence, though necessarily slight, is also against the fragments. The persons attacked are persons who are ignorant, and who are not numerous. Such a state of matters is more likely to have been the case after the controversy had reached a certain amount of discussion, and light had been thrown on the subject in various directions. Certainly this was not the state of the case in Asia Minor in the time of Apollinaris. Then the writer seems to have had some plan of reconciling the statements of Matthew and John. But such a method would probably be devised only after the controversy had raged long, and the influence of tradition had died away considerably. Then the style of the second extract, and especially its antithetic turns, are more like the laboured discourses of the third century than the practical treatises of the second. The λόγος and the πνεῦμα are also questionable features. Altogether, the want of external evidence when it might have been expected, and the nature of the fragments themselves, decide rather against the genuineness of the fragments. Some have attributed them to Pierius of Alexandria, but there is no certainty in such conjectures [u].

Jerome attributes. chiliastic opinions to an Apollinaris, along with Papias and Irenæus; but, as Routh proves from Jerome himself, Apollinaris of Laodicea, a writer of the fourth century, is meant [x].

The only doctrinal point with which the name of Apollinaris is connected is Christ's possession of a soul, or $\psi v \chi \acute{\eta}$. Socrates, in his Ecclesiastical History[y], says, " Irenæus, and Clemens, and Apollinaris of Hierapolis, and Serapion, who was president of the Church in Antioch, declare in the works which they wrote, as a point settled among them, that He who became man was endowed with a soul" ($\emptyset \mu \psi v \chi o v\ \tau \grave{o} v\ \grave{\epsilon} v a v \theta \rho \omega \pi \acute{\eta} \sigma a v \tau a$). Of course this is Socrates' interpretation, and throws no light on the form of Apollinaris's opinion.

---

[u] See Tillemont, Mém. Eccl. tom. ii. part. iii. p. 91; Lardner, Credibility, part ii. vol. ii. c. 28, § 11; Routh, Reliq. Sacr. i. p. 167; Westcott, Hist. of Can. p. 248.

[x] Routh, Reliq. Sacr. i. p. 174; Hieron. de Vir. Illust. c. 18; Comm. in Ezech. lib. xi. cap. 36; Procem. lib. xviii. Comm. Esaiae.

[y] lib. iii. c. 7.

CHAPTER XII.

THE LETTER OF THE CHURCHES IN VIENNA AND LUGDUNUM.

1. THE AUTHORSHIP.

In the reign of Marcus Aurelius a violent persecution burst out in Gaul. Many Christians were thrown into prison, and at last some were beheaded, thrown to the wild beasts, or they perished through suffocation. While in prison the martyrs wrote letters on various subjects to different men and Churches. Eusebius has preserved a fragment of one of these letters, and he has told us the subject of others. We extract all that Eusebius says in regard to this matter[a]. " As now for the first time Montanus and Alcibiades and Theodotus were acquiring the reputation of being prophets among many in Phrygia (for the performance of very many miracles of the Divine grace even at that time throughout different Churches induced many to believe that these men also had the gift of prophecy), and as a difference existed in regard to these men now mentioned, again[b] the brethren in Gaul subjoin their own judgment with regard to them at once pious and most orthodox, publishing also divers letters of the martyrs who had been perfected amongst them, which they wrote while yet in chains [in prison] to the brethren in Asia and Phrygia,

---

[a] Hist. Eccl. v. 3, 4.
[b] The "again" refers to the circumstance that Eusebius has already quoted several portions of the "Letter of the Brethren in Gaul."

and not only so but also to Eleutherus, who was at that time bishop of the Romans, sending as it were an embassy for the sake of the peace of the Church. The same martyrs also recommended Irenæus, at that time an elder of the Church (παροικίας) in Lugdunum, to the person already mentioned as bishop at Rome, bearing the most ample testimony to the man's character, as the subjoined words show:—' We pray that you may have joy in God in all things and always, Father Eleutherus. We have urged our brother and partner Irenæus to carry this letter to you, and we exhort you to consider him as commended to you, for he is zealous for the covenant of Christ. For if we knew that righteousness procures position for any one, we should recommend him especially as an elder of the Church, which he indeed is.'"

The date of these letters depends on the date which we assign to the persecution in Gaul. Eusebius in his Chronicle sets the persecution down in the seventh year of Marcus Aurelius, i.e. A.D. 167. But in his History he says expressly that it took place in "the seventeenth year of the Emperor Antoninus Verus," i.e. of Marcus Aurelius. It is natural to suppose either that the statement in the Chronicon does not really disagree with the statement in the History, or that the statement in the History is the mature and deliberate conviction of Eusebius after he had examined the whole matter, and therefore a correction of the statement in the Chronicon. The letter recommending Irenæus, however, was at one time matter of keen discussion between Episcopalians and Presbyterians; and one of the ablest defenders of Presbytery found it suitable to his object to adopt the earlier date. The letter recommending Irenæus, argued Blondellus[c], was really written in A.D. 177. It certainly calls him an elder or presbyter. But the persecution took place in 167. Therefore in that year Pothinus, bishop of the Church in Lyons, must have perished; and therefore in that year Irenæus must have succeeded to his place, as Eusebius tells us he did.

[c] Apologia pro Sententia Hieronymi de Episcopis et Presbyteris (1646), sect. ii. 8.

Irenæus was bishop, therefore, when he went to Rome, but he is called elder in the letter. Therefore elder and bishop are applied to the same man and mean the same office.

The only arguments having the semblance of weight which Blondellus adduces for adhering to the Chronicon are a statement of Orosius, confirmed, as he thinks, by Sulpicius Severus and some of the chroniclers, and the circumstance that Eusebius relates the miracle of the "Thundering Legion" after the persecution.

The passage of Orosius[d] states that severe persecutions of the Christians in Asia and Gaul arose by command of Marcus Antoninus in the days of the Parthian war; and then that these were followed by the plague. But we have here either a very indefinite date, or an inaccurate one: for the Parthian war was over before A.D. 167. But even if the opinion of Orosius was opposed to that of Eusebius it would not count for much.

In regard to the other matter, Eusebius does indeed place his account of the "Thundering Legion" after the narrative of the persecution; but, as Pearson noticed, he nowhere states that the miracle took place after it, but, on the contrary, his words imply that he had broken the order of his narrative in introducing it.

Pearson replied to Blondellus in a satisfactory manner[e]. He suggested that probably Eusebius in his Chronicon did not intend to assert that the persecution in Gaul took place in the seventh year of Marcus Aurelius. In that year he mentions the martyrdom of Polycarp. This reminds him of persecutions in general. He then adds: "Fourth Persecution. Very many were slain gloriously in Gaul on account of the name of Christ;" and after this he takes no further notice of persecutions in this reign. Pearson's explanation finds corroboration in the manner in which the Armenian version is printed, if the printed text corresponds to the manuscript. For general events are separated from those

[d] lib. vii. c 15.
[e] In his Vindiciæ Ignatianæ, Pars Posterior, c. xiii. p. 159.

which belong to special years, and this fourth persecution is one of the general paragraphs.

About ten years after the appearance of the Vindiciæ Ignatianæ, Henry Dodwell published his Dissertationes Cyprianicæ [f]. In his dissertation De Paucitate Martyrum [g] he revived the opinion of Blondellus, and tried to establish it by new arguments. He allows that the appeal to Orosius is unsatisfactory, and he entirely destroys the argument of Blondellus for Presbytery by maintaining that Eleutherus was bishop of the Romans at the time of the persecution, and that Irenæus went to him in the seventh year of Marcus Aurelius, recommended by the martyrs. His new arguments are derived from the letter addressed by the Christians in Gaul to the Christians in Asia and Phrygia, describing the persecution. The arguments are principally two. The first relates to the fair or festival ($\pi\alpha\nu\acute{\eta}\gamma\upsilon\rho\iota\varsigma$) which is mentioned in the letter. This festival Dodwell supposed must be the games appointed by Augustus in his own honour. Suetonius [h] gives as the date of their institution the consulship of Julius Antonius and Fabius Africanus, that is, in the year of Rome 744, according to the Varronian computation. But it is probable, Dodwell says, that the games were celebrated every fifth year. Therefore the games cannot have been celebrated in A.D. 177, for this is not a year on which the games would fall, but they were celebrated in the year 820 of the city of Rome, that is, A.D. 167, and therefore this is the date of the persecution in Gaul.

The second argument is based on the circumstance that the letter mentions only one Cæsar. Commodus shared the empire with Marcus Aurelius in A.D. 177, and therefore the persecution must have taken place in A.D. 167.

Dodwell added a few other considerations to support his opinion.

His arguments were opposed by Pagi, who entered into a correspondence with a friend of Dodwell's, Lloyd, by

---

[f] The octavo edition is dated 1684, but the preface is dated 1682.
[g] Dissert. xi. sect. xxxvi. [h] Claudius, c. ii.

Tillemont in his Notes, Sur les Martyrs de Lion[i]; by Ruinart in his Acta Martyrum, both in his Preface and in his introductory remarks on the Letter of the Churches in Vienna and Lugdunum; and by Mosheim in his Observationes Sacræ[j].

Pagi[k], in his critical remarks on Baronius, replies to the first argument of Dodwell that it is a mere assumption that the games were celebrated every fifth year. It is more likely that they were celebrated every year. And he also adduces instances in which games were celebrated earlier and later than at the usual intervals. He appeals especially to one case in which the games took place in Lugdunum[l] in a year that would not be the proper year according to Dodwell's calculation. Mosheim went further than Pagi. He draws attention to the circumstance that the letter itself furnishes no warrant for the identification of the festival with the festival of Augustus. The festival alluded to may have been the festival at the altar of Augustus, but that it really was is pure conjecture. It may have had something to do with the celebration of the triumphs of Marcus Aurelius. Or they may have been games instituted by Sextus Ligurius Galeria Marinus. We have to add to this remark of Mosheim, that such is the want of precision displayed by the writers of the letter that it is nowhere expressly stated that the persecutions took place in Lugdunum. The letter does not say so, though it may be inferred. Eusebius does not say so. Nor is mention made of the exact locality in Sulpicius Severus, or in Orosius, or in the Chronicon Paschale, or in Syncellus. The local chroniclers seem to have settled the matter, though it is not unlikely that the letter itself may have mentioned Lugdunum as the scene of the tortures of the Christians.

The reply to the second argument of Dodwell is easily

---

[i] Tome Troisième, Première Partie, p. 398.

[j] p. 174 (Amsterdam, 1721).

[k] Annus 179. A reprint of the work of Baronius, with Pagi's critical remarks, edited by Augustinus Theiner, is now appearing at Bar-le-Duc.

[l] Suet. Calig. c. xx.

given. If the expression "Cæsar" prevents us from assigning the persecution to the year A.D. 177, it as certainly prevents us from assigning it to the year A.D. 167; for in that year Marcus Aurelius and Lucius Verus were joint emperors. But the truth is, that the word proves nothing at all but the carelessness of the writers. They very likely did not know from whom the order issued, but it came in the emperor's name, and they speak of him simply as Cæsar.

Few after these discussions adopted the opinion of Dodwell[m]; and so conclusive did the arguments on the other side seem to Lardner[n] that he refused to discuss the matter. "Nor do I expect," he says, "that any learned man who has a concern for his reputation as a critic, should attempt a direct confutation of this opinion."

The persecution, then, took place in A.D. 177. Eusebius mentions two things confirmatory of this date. He states that Eleutherus in this year succeeded Soter in the bishopric of the Roman Church. All who have discussed the dates of the Roman bishops, except Dodwell and Pearson, agree that Eleutherus was appointed after A.D. 167.

Eusebius mentions also that the martyrs discussed in their letter the case of the Montanists. In his Chronicon Eusebius places the rise of Montanism in the eleventh year of the reign of Marcus Aurelius, according to Jerome's version, or the twelfth year, according to the Armenian version. The persecution must have taken place after this event.

Blondellus imagined that the letters were not written by the martyrs, but by the brethren in Gaul; and Salmasius supposes that as bishops were generally selected for martyrdom, it was bishops who composed the letters[o]. But there is no evidence to contradict the direct assertion of Eusebius that they were written by the martyrs. And we know from the letter of the Churches descriptive of the persecution that

---

[m] Clericus [1743] adopted it in his History. Ad annum 167, p. 710.
[n] Cred. part ii. c. xvi.
[o] Walonis Messalini, De Episcopis et Presbyteris (1641), p. 271.

bishops were not the only victims of heathen fury, but deacons also, and unofficial Christians, and women and boys.

The discussion of the fragment of a letter relating to Irenæus we must defer till we arrive at the history of Irenæus. We notice here merely that our translation differs somewhat from the common translation.

In regard to the letters on Montanism, all that we really know is that the object which the martyrs had before them was the peace of the Church.

The sufferings which the Christians endured in Gaul are described in a letter addressed by the Churches in Vienna and Lugdunum to the brethren in Asia and Phrygia. The whole of this letter Eusebius gave in his collection of Martyria now lost. In his History he extracted only those portions which seemed to him appropriate to the work: and it is these extracts alone that we possess. The whole letter may have been extant in the time of Gregory of Tours, and even of later chroniclers, for they give a complete list of the sufferers[p]. But they make no additions to our real information, and some of their statements flatly contradict the accounts given in the letter.

We have now to discuss the authorship, date, and genuineness of this letter. Strangely enough, while much attention has been given to the date of the persecution, little notice has been taken of the literary questions connected with this interesting document. Indeed, the extracts which Eusebius gives have almost universally been considered to be genuine, and scholars have generally imagined that, if they settle the date of the persecution, they settle the date of the letter. One solitary voice has been lifted up to assert that the whole letter is a forgery, and that the entire story of the persecution of the Christians of Gaul in the reign of Marcus Aurelius is a fabrication of a date later than the Decian persecution. The

---

[p] Ado and Usuardus. They include Zacharias in the list, not perceiving that it is Zacharias father of John the Baptist to whom allusion is made in the letter.

anonymous work which tried to prove these assertions was styled Raisons qui invalident l'Authenticité de la Lettre des Eglises de Vienne et de Lyon. 1761^q. The author seems to have gone most minutely into the discussion of the letter, and though his arguments have convinced nobody, yet some of them are based on portions which at first awaken suspicion, but which when fully considered only confirm the truthfulness of the narrative.

The parts which awaken suspicion are those that speak of apparent miracles, and those which relate apparent improbabilities.

There are two passages that seem to assert that miracles took place. The first states that the body of Sanctus recovered in the second torture its erect position and its former shape. But before this can be proved to be a miracle, it must be shown that such an occurrence is naturally impossible. This has not been done. The style of the letter, moreover, is somewhat inflated. The writer is apt to exaggerate. And we may have here merely a rather rhetorical account of what really took place. The body of Sanctus had recovered its energy during the relaxation from torture, and in the midst of the second agonies it seemed to be stronger than it was before. Instances of similar occurrences are adduced by Florius[r].

Objection is also taken to the passage in which a revelation is said to have been made to Attalus. But the answer is at hand. The writer does not say in what way the revelation was given. It is possible that he may have meant nothing *supernatural*. But even if he did, all we gather from this is that the Churches in Vienna and Lugdunum believed in the reality of supernatural revelations in their own day. The fact which is attested is that Alcibiades was persuaded by Attalus to give up an ascetic mode of life. The Christians of Vienna

[q] I know this work only from Lumper's notice of it. He has also adduced the arguments of Zola and Florius against it: but his mode of quoting is such that I do not know what he has taken from Zola and what he has taken from Florius. Lumper, pars x. p. 541.

[r] Lumper, pars x. p. 558.

and Lugdunum thought that Attalus was led by revelation to appeal to Alcibiades. They may have been right or wrong in this opinion, but the opinion does not diminish the trustworthiness of the narrative.

Then there are some apparent improbabilities in the narrative. It is asserted, for instance, that on account of the joy which beamed in the countenance of the confessors some thought that they were really anointed with perfumes. Now this may be an exaggeration. But if we remember how closely in the ancient mind gladness and perfumes were associated, perhaps we may not be astonished that some imagined that the Christians had really perfumed themselves.

There is at first sight a difficulty with regard to the person under whose presidency the persecutions took place. He is simply called ἡγεμών. Vienna was the mother city of Lugdunum, but the two towns belonged to different provinces, and were under different rulers. If this were the case, then the Christians of Vienna, it is supposed, would not be punished by the governor of Gallia Lugdunensis, but of Gallia Narbonensis. Many answers can be given to this[s]. The Christians of Vienna may have flocked to Lugdunum to help their suffering brethren, as Lucian describes them doing in his life of Peregrinus, and may have then been apprehended. The persecution was at first a popular outbreak, and it is not likely that governors of provinces would be jealous in keeping within their jurisdiction in such a case. There are instances, moreover, of governors overstepping the limits of their jurisdiction, and they were allowed to do so by law in certain cases. But, moreover, there is a probability, as Valesius shows, that at this time the province of Lugdunum was under the control, not of a proconsul or procurator, but of a Legatus Caesaris. The mention of a chiliarch and of soldiers leads to this inference. And if this were the case, then his powers would extend to Vienna[t].

---

[s] The following are given by Florius, in Lumper.

[t] Valesius thinks it probable that Severus, who afterwards became emperor,

The history of Attalus seems to be in some of its details improbable. The mob swelled with furious indignation at the sight of Attalus, but the governor, learning that he was a Roman, sent him to prison with the rest to await the decision of the Cæsar. The Cæsar's decree comes. It is that those who confess should be punished, that those who deny should be set free. The words expressive of the first part of the decree are peculiar. They are, ἐπιστείλαντος γὰρ τοῦ Καίσαρος τοὺς μὲν ἀποτυμπανισθῆναι. Hesychius has τυμπανίζεται· πλήσσεται, ἐκδέρεται, ἰσχυρῶς τύπτεται. Suidas gives τυμπανίζεται· ξύλῳ πλήσσεται, ἐκδέρεται καὶ κρέμαται. He also gives ἀποτυμπάνισον· ἀνηλεῶς τι φόνευσον, but this reading is the result of emendations, for there is something wrong in the text. Gataker has gone minutely into the various meanings of this word, and has adduced many passages in which it is used[u]. Some of the ancients, as Chrysostom, state that ἀποτυμπανισμός meant decapitation; but the usage of the word shows that it was applicable to any kind of death that was accompanied by torture. The main idea of it seems to be the infliction of severe torture, especially by striking. The severity would generally be so great as to end in producing death; but this is not necessarily implied in the word. We agree with Tillemont and others, in opposition to Valesius, that Rufinus has given the right meaning in his translation, 'that those who persisted should be punished:' " ut persistentes quidem punirentur." The object of the Cæsar's decree was to apply torture to those who refused to deny Christ, in the hope of compelling them to submit to his power. Valesius takes the word to mean ' to kill,' but he adopts this meaning to suit the statement made in regard to the conduct of the governor. The governor, after receiving the rescript, beheaded those who were Roman citizens, and sent the rest to the wild beasts. But we may well doubt

---

was at this time the emperor's legate in Lugdunum. See Lardner's Works, vol. vii.; Testimonies of Ancient Heathens, c. xv. s. ii. p. 157 note.

[u] See Suicer in voc.

whether the governor carried out the instructions of the emperor. The emperor allows him to apply torture to the Christians, if they persisted in their religion. The governor takes his own way in carrying out this general command, and beheads Roman citizens, while he exposes the others to the wild beasts. But Attalus was not in the number of those who were thus killed. And in the end he was not beheaded, but was put to death, most likely by being stabbed in the throat, as those exposed to wild beasts usually were. Now this is an apparent improbability, but it is not in reality unlikely. The statement which says that the governor cut off the heads of those who had the citizenship of Rome does not mean that he actually cut off their heads, but that he sentenced them to decapitation. Attalus among the rest would receive this sentence; but the governor, to gratify the people, as is expressly said, exposed him to the wild beasts. The proceeding was a violation of the usual method, and Rufinus in his translation makes it a violation of Caesar's command.

There is nothing, then, in the Epistle to prevent us from believing that the extracts which Eusebius has made were really written by the person who composed the letter for the Churches of Vienna and Lugdunum.

There is one passage in Eusebius which settles the date of the letter. It has been quoted already. Eusebius informs us that the brethren in Gaul noticed in the letter the spread of Montanism. They gave their own opinion with regard to it, which Eusebius characterizes as pious ($εὐλαβῆ$, possibly 'cautious') and most orthodox, and they appealed to the letters of the martyrs in regard to the same matter. The letter must, therefore, have been written shortly after the persecution, while the treatment of Montanism was yet undecided among the Churches of Asia and Italy.

There is nothing in the letter which is opposed to this early date; and there are some things which harmonize with it.

Thus, the letter speaks in a remarkable manner of the approaching appearance of the Devil. The persecutions of the Christians were a prelude to his coming, which is to be without restraint. Similar expectations are to be found in some contemporary authors, but the expectation soon vanished from the Church. This expectation of his coming was joined with a belief in his speedy and entire condemnation. Reference seems to be made to this in the statement that Blandina was reserved for another contest, that she might make the condemnation of the crooked serpent unquestionable, though it may also refer to her own complete triumph over him.

Then, again, the story of Alcibiades is one that could scarcely have been invented after the Decian persecution. Up till this time abstinence from the common articles of food savoured of the Encratites or some of the heretical Gnostics, and therefore it was prudent in Alcibiades to give up his austerity that he might lend no countenance to any heresy. But a hundred years after many of the foremost men of the Church had become imbued with ascetic sentiments, and the conduct of Alcibiades in abstaining from all food but bread and water would have been regarded as proof of superior sanctity.

We may also remark that, though the writer indulges in exaggerations, and, if we may so speak, has pitched his whole narrative in a high key, yet we find none of the absurd stories or statements which disfigure most of the Martyria. It stands out in marked contrast with the Martyrium of Polycarp. Compare, for instance, the treatment of the relics of the saints in each narrative. The writer of this letter simply says that they were swept into the Rhone. One would have thought that such a distinct assertion would have prevented relic-worship in Lugdunum; but relic-worshippers are superior to history. Gregory of Tours supplements the narrative given here in the following manner:—" While the Christians were filled with the greatest sorrow, as if the blessed remains had perished, by night the martyrs appeared to faithful men in that place in which they had been thrown into the fire, standing entire and uninjured, and turning to the men they said, 'Let our remains be collected from this place, because no one of us has perished.' When these men brought back this news to the rest of the Christians, they thanked God and were strengthened in the faith, and collecting the sacred ashes, they built a basilica of wonderful size to their honour (peace being afterwards restored to the Churches). Now that place in which they suffered is called Athanaco[x]."

Œcumenius[y] mentions Irenæus as the composer of the letter, but he evidently does so on mere conjecture. Many modern scholars have been of the same opinion, but there is no evidence to determine the matter; and the circumstance that no one before Œcumenius speaks of Irenæus as the author renders it likely that there was no tradition to that effect.

The style of the letter, as has been remarked already, is loose. It abounds in antitheses and strong expressions. It also mixes up incongruous figures. Its statements are not, therefore, to be looked on as cold historical accuracies[z]. But we differ entirely from Clericus in thinking that this is a disadvantage. We should infinitely prefer a writer who was filled with the greatness and glory of such a mighty struggle and conquest as is here portrayed, even though he does not mention the name of the governor who condemned the Christians, though he is careless in giving particulars of persons and dates, and though he does not hold his pen firmly in his hand, to a writer who had no sympathy with such marvellous courage and heroic endurance and faith.

II. LITERATURE.

The letter is printed in all the editions of Eusebius's Ecclesiastical History, as it forms an integral portion of that work. It is also printed separately in Olshausen's Historiæ Ecclesiasticæ Veteris Monumenta Præcipua, Berolini, 1820;

[x] I have translated from Lumper, who extracts the passage from Gregory.
[y] Quoted in Routh, vol. i. p. 336.
[z] See Kestner, De Eusebii Auctoritate et Fide Diplomatica, p. 34, note 68.

in Routh's Reliquiæ Sacræ, vol. i. p. 295, with ample and valuable notes, and in Migne's Patrologiæ Cursus, series Græca, vol. v.

It was translated by Lardner in the fifteenth chapter of his Heathen Testimonies (Collected Works, vol. vii. p. 156), and by Lord Hailes (David Dalrymple) in his Account of the Martyrs at Smyrna and Lyons in the Second Century, with Explanatory Notes: Edinburgh, 1776. I have made free use of this translation in the one I have given. It is also translated in all the translations of Eusebius.

III. TRANSLATION OF THE LETTER.

It began thus:—"The servants of Christ who sojourn in Vienna and Lugdunum of Gaul to the brethren throughout Asia and Phrygia, who have the same faith and hope of redemption as ourselves, peace, grace, and glory from God the Father and from Christ Jesus our Lord."

After some further preliminary remarks the letter proceeds:—"The greatness of the tribulation in this region and the exceeding anger of the heathen [nations] against the saints, and the sufferings which the blessed Witnesses[a] endured, neither are we competent to describe accurately, nor indeed is it possible to detail them in writing. For with all his strength did the adversary assail us, even then giving a foretaste of his activity among us which is to be without restraint; and he had recourse to every means, accustoming his own subjects and exercising them beforehand against the servants of God, so that not only were we excluded from houses[b], baths, and the forum, but a universal prohibition was laid against any one of us appearing in any place whatsoever. But the grace of God acted as our general against him. It rescued the weak; it arrayed against him men like

---

[a] I have translated μάρτυρες 'witnesses' and μαρτυρία 'testimony' throughout.

[b] Houses of friends and relatives. Olshausen takes them to be public buildings.

firm pillars, who could through patience bear up against the whole force of the assaults of the wicked one. These came to close quarters with him, enduring every form of reproach and torture; and, making light of grievous trials, they hastened on to Christ, showing in reality that the 'sufferings of the present time are not worthy to be compared with the glory that is to be revealed in us[c].' And first they nobly endured the evils which were heaped on them by the populace,—namely, hootings, and blows, draggings, plunderings, stonings, and confinements[d], and everything that an infuriated mob is wont to perpetrate against those whom they deem bitter enemies. And at length being brought to the forum by the tribune of the soldiers, and the magistrates that had charge of the city, they were examined in presence of the whole multitude, and, having confessed, they were shut up in prison until the arrival of the governor.

"After this, when they were brought before the governor, and when he displayed a spirit of savage hostility to us, Vettius Epagathus, one of the brethren, interposed. For he was a man who had contained the full measure of love towards God and his neighbours. His mode of life had been so strict that, though he was a young man, he deserved to be described in the words used in regard to the elderly Zacharias, 'He had walked therefore in all the commandments and ordinances of the Lord blameless[e].' He was also eager to serve his neighbour in any way, he was very zealous for God, and he was fervent in spirit. Such being the character of the man, he could not bear that judgment should be thus unreasonably passed against us, but was moved with indignation, and requested that he himself should be heard in defence of his brethren, undertaking to prove that there is nothing ungodly or impious amongst us. On this those who were round the judgment-seat cried out against him, for

---

[c] Romans viii. 18.

[d] By 'confinements' in this passage evidently is meant that the populace prevented them from resorting to public places, and thus shut them up in their own houses.   [e] Luke i. 6.

he was a man of distinction; and the governor, not for a moment listening to the just request thus made to him, merely asked him if he himself were a Christian. And on his confessing in the clearest voice that he was, he also was taken up into the number of the Witnesses, receiving the appellation of the Advocate of the Christians [f], and having himself the Advocate, the Spirit [g], more abundantly than Zacharias, which he showed in the fulness [h] of his love in that he had of his own good-will offered to lay down his own life in defence of the brethren. For he was and is a genuine disciple of Christ, 'following the Lamb, whithersoever He goeth [i].'

"After this the rest began to be distinguished [k], for the proto-martyrs were decided and ready, and accomplished the confession of their testimony with all alacrity. But there appeared also those who were unprepared and unpractised, and who were still feeble and unable to bear the tension of a great contest. Of these about ten in number proved abortions; causing great grief and immeasurable sorrow amongst us, and damping the ardour of the rest who had not yet been apprehended. For these, although they suffered every kind of cruelty, remained nevertheless in the company of the Witnesses and did not forsake them. But then the whole of us were greatly alarmed on account of our uncertainty as to confession, not because we feared the tortures inflicted, but because we looked to the end and dreaded lest any one should fall away. Those who were worthy, however, were daily apprehended, filling up the number of the others; so that out of the two Churches all the excellent, and those to whom the Churches owed most of all their establishment and

---

[f] From the heathen judge.   [g] Luke i. 67.

[h] The writer refers to St. John's Gospel (xv. 13): "Greater love hath no man than this, that a man lay down his life for his friends."

[i] Rev. xiv. 4.

[k] This expression seems to refer to what took place in athletic combats. The athletes were tested before fighting, and those in every way qualified were permitted to fight, while the others were rejected. This testing, Valesius supposes, was called διάκρισις.

prosperity, were collected together in prison. Some heathen household slaves belonging to our people were also apprehended, since the governor had given orders publicly that all of us should be sought out. These, through the instigation of Satan, and through fear of the tortures which they saw the saints enduring, urged on also by the soldiers, falsely accused us of Thyestæan banquets[1] and Œdipodean connexions, and other crimes which it is lawful for us neither to mention nor think of; and indeed we shrink from believing that any such crimes have ever taken place among men. When the rumour of these accusations was spread abroad, all raged against us like wild beasts; so that if any formerly were temperate in their conduct to us on account of relationship, they then became exceedingly indignant and exasperated against us. And thus was fulfilled that which was spoken by our Lord, 'The time shall come when everyone who slayeth you shall think that he offereth service to God [m].'

"Then at last the holy Witnesses suffered tortures beyond all description, Satan striving eagerly that some of the evil reports might be acknowledged by them [n]. But in an exceeding degree did the whole wrath of mob, general, and soldiers fall on Sanctus, a deacon from Vienna, and on Maturus, a newly-enlightened but noble combatant, and on Attalus, a native of

---

[1] Lord Hailes, Dr. Routh, and Heinichen, in their notes on this passage, discuss the accusations made against Christians, and their origin. Lord Hailes goes minutely into the matter, apparently drawing his information mainly from a treatise entitled "The Calumnies upon the Primitive Christians accounted for: by Robert Turner, M.A., Vicar of St. Peter's in Colchester. 8vo. London, 1727." He makes a remark on Catiline which I should have made in my Introduction:—"I mean not to affirm that Catiline and his accomplices ever perpetrated a crime so savage. All that is necessary for my purpose is, that the *Thyestæan banquet* of Catiline was popularly reported and popularly believed."

[m] John xvi. 2.

[n] The words here admit of two meanings: that something blasphemous might be uttered by them—such as speaking against Christ and swearing by Cæsar; or that some accusation against the Christians might be uttered by them—confirming, for instance, the reports of infanticide and incest prevalent against the Christians. The latter, in this passage, seems unquestionably to be the meaning.

Pergamus, who had always been the pillar° and foundation of the Church there, and on Blandina, through whom Christ showed that the things that to men appear mean and deformed and contemptible, are with God deemed worthy of great glory, on account of love to Him,—a love which is not a mere boastful appearance, but shows itself in the power which it exercises over the life. For while we were all afraid, and especially her mistress in the flesh, who was herself one of the combatants among the Witnesses, that she would not be able to make a bold confession on account of the weakness of her body, Blandina was filled with such power that those who tortured her one after the other in every way from morning till evening, were wearied and tired, confessing that they had been baffled, for they had no other torture they could apply to her, and they were astonished that she remained in life, when her whole body was torn and opened up, and they gave their testimony ᴾ that one only of the modes of torture employed was sufficient to have deprived her of life, not to speak of so many excruciating inflictions. But the blessed woman, like a noble athlete, recovered her strength in the midst of the confession, and her declaration, 'I am a Christian, and there is no evil done amongst us,' brought her refreshment, and rest, and insensibility to all the sufferings inflicted on her.

"Sanctus also nobly endured all the excessive and *superhuman*ᑫ tortures which man could possibly devise against him, for the wicked hoped, on account of the continuance and greatness of the tortures, to hear him confess some of the unlawful practices. But he opposed them with such firmness that he

---

° 1 Tim. iii. 15.

ᴾ Heinichen construes differently. He makes the 'torturers astonished that Blandina gave her testimony that one kind of torture was sufficient to deprive her of life.' Perhaps the right construction is to make ὅτι mean 'because' or 'for :' 'They were astonished at Blandina bearing her testimony, for one kind of torture was sufficient to have killed her.'

ᑫ The words ὑπερβεβλημένως καὶ ὑπὲρ πάντα ἄνθρωπον naturally go with ὑπομένων, and therefore intimate that Sanctus's endurance was greater than human ; but I doubt if this is intended by the writer.

did not tell them even his own name, nor that of his nation or city, nor if he were slave or free; but, in answer to all these questions, he said in Latin, 'I am a Christian.' This was the confession he made repeatedly, instead of giving his name, his city, his race, and indeed in reply to every question that was put to him; and other language the heathens heard not from him. Hence arose in the minds of the governor and the torturers a determined resolution to subdue him; so that, when every other means failed, they at last fixed red-hot plates of brass to the most delicate parts of his body. And these indeed were burned, but he himself remained inflexible and unyielding, firm in his confession, being bedewed and strengthened by the heavenly fountain of the water of life which issues from the belly of Christ[r]. But his body bore witness to what had happened, for it was all wounds and weals, shrunk and torn up, and had lost externally the human shape. In him Christ suffering wrought great wonders, destroying the adversary, and showing for an example to the rest that there is nothing fearful where there is the Father's love, and nothing painful where there is Christ's glory. For the wicked after some days again tortured the Witness, thinking that, since his body was swollen and inflamed, if they were to apply the same tortures they would gain the victory over him, especially since the parts of his body could not bear to be touched by the hand, or that he would die in consequence of the tortures, and thus inspire the rest with fear. Yet not only did no such occurrence take place in regard to him, but even, contrary to every expectation of man, his body unbent itself and became erect in the midst of the subsequent tortures, and resumed its former appearance and the use of its limbs, so that the second torture turned out through the grace of Christ a cure, not an affliction.

"Among those who had denied was a woman of the name of Biblias. The devil, thinking that he had already swallowed her, and wishing to damn her still more by making her accuse

---

[r] John vii. 38: "He that believeth on Me, as the Scripture hath said, out of his belly shall flow rivers of living water."

falsely, brought her forth to punishment, and employed force to constrain her, already feeble and spiritless, to utter accusations of atheism against us. But she, in the midst of the tortures, came again to a sound state of mind, and awoke as it were out of a deep sleep, for the temporary suffering reminded her of the eternal punishment in Gehenna, and she contradicted the accusers of Christians, saying, 'How can children be eaten by those who do not think it lawful to partake of the blood of even brute beasts?' And after this she confessed herself a Christian, and was added to the number of Witnesses.

"But when the tyrannical tortures were rendered by Christ of no avail through the patience of the blessed, the devil devised other contrivances—confinement in the darkest and most noisome cells of the prison, the stretching of the feet on the stocks[a], even up to the fifth hole, and the other indignities which attendants stirred up by wrath and full of the devil are wont to inflict on the imprisoned. The consequence was that very many were suffocated in prison, as many at least as the Lord, showing his glory, wished to depart in this way. For there were others who were tortured so bitterly that it seemed impossible for them to survive even though they were to obtain every kind of attention, and yet they remained alive in prison, destitute indeed of care from man, but strengthened by the Lord and invigorated both in body and soul, and they animated and consoled the rest. But the new converts who had been recently apprehended, and whose bodies had not previously been tortured, could not endure the confinement, but died in the prison.

"Now the blessed Pothinus, who had been entrusted with the service of the oversight in Lugdunum, was also dragged before the judgment-seat. He was now upwards of ninety years of age and exceedingly weak in body. Though he breathed with difficulty on account of the feebleness of the body, yet he was

---

[a] The holes were placed in a line, so that the further the hole in which one leg was put from the hole in which the other leg was put, the more nearly would the two legs form a straight line, and the greater would be the pain.

strengthened by the eagerness of his spirit on account of his earnest desire to bear his testimony. His body indeed was already dissolved through old age and disease, yet the life was preserved in him, that Christ might triumph through him. When he was brought by the soldiers to the judgment-seat, under a convoy of the magistrates of the city and amid exclamations of every kind from the whole population, as if he himself were the Christ, he gave the good testimony. Being asked by the governor who was the God of the Christians, he said, 'If thou art worthy, thou shalt know.' Thereupon he was unmercifully dragged about and endured many blows, for those who were near maltreated him in every way with their hands and feet, showing no respect for his age, while those at a distance hurled against him each one whatever came to hand, all of them believing that they would sin greatly and act impiously if they in any respect fell short in their insulting treatment of him. For they thought that in this way they would avenge their gods. And Pothinus, breathing with difficulty, was cast into prison, and two days after he expired.

"Upon this a grand dispensation[t] of God's providence took place and the immeasurable mercy of Christ was made manifest, such an occurrence as but rarely happens among the brotherhood, yet one that does not fall short of the art of Christ. For those who in the first apprehension had denied, were imprisoned along with the others and shared their hardships. Their denial, in fact, turned out at this time to be of no advantage to them. For while those who confessed what they really were were imprisoned simply as Christians, no other accusation being brought against them, those who denied were detained as murderers and profligates. They, moreover, were doubly punished. For the confessors were lightened by the joy of their testimony and their hope in the

---

[t] The dispensation is that those who denied were not set free but confined with the others: and that this harsh treatment and sad state of mind confirmed the resolution of those not yet apprehended to confess Christ. Various other explanations have been given, but this seems the most reasonable.

promises, and by their love to Christ, and by the Father's Spirit. But the deniers were tormented greatly by their own consciences, so that when they were led forth their countenances could be distinguished among all the rest. For the confessors went forth joyous, with a mingling of glory and abundant grace in their looks, so that their chains lay like becoming ornaments around them, as around a bride adorned with golden fringes wrought with divers colours[u]. And they breathed at the same time the fragrance of Christ[x], so that some even thought that they were anointed with this world's perfume. But the deniers were downcast, humbled, sad-looking, and weighed down with every kind of disgrace. They were, moreover, reproached even by the heathens with being base and cowardly, and charged with the crime of murder; they had lost the altogether honourable, glorious, and life-giving appellation[y]. When the rest saw this, they were strengthened, and those who were apprehended, confessed unhesitatingly, not allowing the reasoning of the devil to have even a place in their thoughts."

Eusebius omits something, saying that after a little the letter proceeded as follows:—

"After these things, then, their testimonies took every shape through the different ways in which they departed[z]. For plaiting a crown from different colours and flowers of every kind they presented it to the Father. It was right therefore that the noble athletes, after having endured divers contests and gained grand victories, should receive the great crown of incorruption.

"Maturus, therefore, and Sanctus, and Blandina, and Attalus were publicly [a] exposed to the wild beasts—that common spectacle of heathen barbarity; for a day was expressly

---

[u] Psalm xlv. 13.   [x] 2 Cor. ii. 15.   [y] Of Christian.

[z] I have adopted here an emendation of Routh's. The literal version of the common text is, "The testimonies of their departure were divided into every form."

[a] The Greek is εἰς τὸ δημόσιον, was led 'to the public [building]' to the wild beasts. The public [building] is taken to be the amphitheatre.

assigned to fights with wild beasts on account of our people And Maturus and Sanctus again endured every form of torture in the amphitheatre, as if they had had no suffering at all before. Or rather like athletes[b] who had overthrown their adversary several times and were now contending for the crown itself, again they endured the lashes[c] which were usual there, and they were dragged about by the wild beasts, and suffered every indignity which the maddened populace demanded in cries and exhortations proceeding from various parts of the amphitheatre. And last of all they were placed in the iron chair, on which their bodies were roasted, and they themselves were filled with the fumes of their own flesh. But the heathens did not stop even here, but became still more frantic in their desire to overcome the endurance of the Christians. But not even thus did they hear anything else from Sanctus than the utterance of the confession which he had been accustomed to make from the beginning. These then, after life had lasted a long time throughout the great contest, were at last sacrificed[d], after they alone had formed a spectacle to the world, throughout that day, instead of all the diversity which usually takes place in gladiatorial shows.

"Blandina[e] was hung up fastened to a stake and exposed as food to the wild beasts that were let loose against her; and through her presenting the spectacle of one suspended on something like a cross, and through her earnest prayers, she inspired the combatants with great eagerness; for in the

---

[b] The words 'several times' are represented in Greek by διὰ πλειόνων κλήρων, lit. 'through several lots.' When there were several athletes to contend, the pairs were determined by lot. After the first contest the victors were again formed into pairs by lot, until finally there should be but one pair left. See the process at the Olympic games described in Lucian Hermotimus, c. xl. p. 782.

[c] The bestiarii, before fighting with wild beasts, had to run the gauntlet.

[d] Rufinus translates, *jugulati sunt*. Probably, 'killed with the sword.' The term may have been a technical one, being applied to the gladiators or bestiarii, whose death may have been looked on as a sacrifice to a god or a dead hero.

[e] Blandina was a slave: hence the mode of punishment. On this matter see Lipsius, De Cruce.

combat they saw, by means of their sister, with their bodily eyes, Him who was crucified for them that He might persuade those who trust in Him that every one that has suffered for the glory of Christ has eternal communion with the living God. When none of the wild beasts at that time touched her, she was taken down from the stake and conveyed back to prison. She was thus reserved for another contest in order that, gaining the victory in many preparative conflicts, she might make the condemnation of the Crooked Serpent[f] unquestionable, and that she might encourage the brethren. For though she was an insignificant, weak, and despised woman, yet she was clothed with the great and invincible athlete Christ. On many occasions she had overpowered the adversary, and in the course of the contest had woven for herself the crown of incorruption.

"Attalus also was vehemently demanded by the mob, for he was a man of mark. He entered the lists a ready combatant on account of his good conscience, since he had been truly practised in the Christian discipline, and had always been a Witness of the truth among us. He was led round the amphitheatre, a tablet going before him, on which was written in Latin, 'This is Attalus the Christian;' and the people swelled with indignation against him. But the governor, learning that he was a Roman, ordered him to be taken back to prison and kept with the rest who were there, with regard to whom he had written to the Cæsar, and was now awaiting his determination.

"The intervening time did not prove barren or unfruitful to the Witnesses, but through their patient endurance the immeasurable love of Christ was made manifest. For through the living the dead were made alive; and the Witnesses conferred favours on those who were not Witnesses, and the Virgin Mother had much joy in receiving back alive those whom she had given up as dead abortions. For through the Witnesses the greater number of those who had denied returned, as it were, into their mother's womb, and were con-

[f] Lord Hailes remarks that this alludes to Isaiah xxvii. 1.

ceived again and re-quickened; and they learned to confess. And being now restored to life, and having their spirits braced, they went up to the judgment-seat to be again questioned by the governor, while that God who wishes not the death of the sinner[g] but mercifully calls to repentance, put sweetness into their souls. This new examination took place because the Cæsar had given orders that the Witnesses should be punished, but that if any denied they should be set free. And as now was commencing here the fair, which is attended by vast numbers of men assembling from all nations, he brought the blessed up to the judgment-seat, exhibiting them as a theatrical show and spectacle to the mobs. Wherefore also he again questioned them, and whoever appeared to have had the rights of Roman citizenship he beheaded, and the rest he sent to the wild beasts.

"Now Christ was greatly glorified in those who formerly denied, for, contrary to every expectation of the heathen, they confessed. For these were examined separately, under the belief that they were to be set free; but confessing, they were added to the number of the Witnesses. But there were also some who remained without; namely those who had no trace of faith, and no perception of the marriage garment[h], nor notion of the fear of God, but through their conduct caused evil reports of our way of life, that is, sons of perdition. But all the rest were added to the Church.

"Present at the examination of these was one Alexander, a native of Phrygia, a physician by profession. He had lived for many years in Gaul, and had become well known to all for his love to God and his boldness in proclaiming the truth, for he was not without a share of apostolic grace. He stood near the judgment-seat, and, urging by signs those who had denied to

---

[g] Ezek. xxxiii. 11.

[h] Heinichen renders 'the bride's garment,' and explains in the following manner. The bride is the Church, the garment Christ; and the sons of perdition had no idea what garment the Church of Christ should wear, had no idea that they should be clothed with Christ, and be filled with his Spirit. It is generally taken to be the marriage garment of Matt. xxii. 12.

confess, he looked to those who stood round the judgment-seat like one in travail. But the mobs, enraged that those who had formerly denied should now confess, cried out against Alexander as if he were the cause of this change. Then the governor summoned him before him, and inquired of him who he was; and when Alexander said that he was a Christian, the governor burst into a passion, and condemned him to the wild beasts. And on the next day he entered the amphitheatre along with Attalus; for the governor, wishing to gratify the mob, again exposed Attalus to the wild beasts. These two, after being tortured in the amphitheatre with all the instruments devised for that purpose, and having undergone an exceedingly severe contest, at last were themselves sacrificed. Alexander uttered no groan nor murmur of any kind, but conversed in his heart with God; but Attalus, when he was placed on the iron chair, and all the parts of his body were burning, and when the fumes from his body were borne aloft, said to the multitude in Latin, 'Lo! this which ye do is eating men. But as for us, we neither eat men nor practise any other wickedness.' And being asked what name God has, he answered, 'God has not a name as men have.'

"After all these, on the last day of the gladiatorial shows, Blandina was again brought in along with Ponticus, a boy of about fifteen years of age. These two had been taken daily to the amphitheatre to see the tortures which the rest endured, and force was used to compel them to swear by the idols of the heathen; but on account of their remaining steadfast, and setting all their devices at nought, the multitude were furious against them, so as neither to pity the tender years of the boy nor to respect the sex of the woman. Accordingly they exposed them to every terror, and inflicted on them every torture, repeatedly trying to compel them to swear. But they failed in effecting this, for Ponticus, encouraged by his sister[i], so plainly indeed that even the

---

[i] She may have been his sister by birth, as some have supposed, but the term 'sister' would have been applied had she been connected by no other tie than that of a common faith.

heathens saw that it was she that encouraged and confirmed him, after enduring nobly every kind of torture, gave up the ghost; while the blessed Blandina, last of all, after having like a noble mother encouraged her children and sent them on before her victorious to the King, trod the same path of conflict which her children had trod, hastening on to them with joy and exultation at her departure, not as one thrown to the wild beasts, but as one invited to a marriage supper. And after she had been scourged and exposed to the wild beasts, and roasted in the iron chair, she was at last inclosed in a net and cast before a bull. And after having been well tossed by the bull, though without having any feeling of what was happening to her through her hope and firm hold of what had been entrusted to her and her converse with Christ, she also was sacrificed, the heathens themselves acknowledging that never among them did woman endure so many and such fearful tortures.

"Yet not even thus was their madness and their savage hatred to the saints satiated. For wild and barbarous tribes, when excited by the Wild Beast, with difficulty ceased from their rage, and their insulting conduct found another and peculiar subject in the bodies of the Witnesses. For they felt no shame that they had been overcome, for they were not possessed of human reason, but their defeat only the more inflamed their rage, and governor and people, like a wild beast, showed a like unjust hatred of us, that the Scripture might be fulfilled, 'He that is unjust, let him be unjust still; and he that is righteous, let him be righteous still[j].' For they threw to the dogs those who had been suffocated in prison, carefully watching them day and night, lest any one should receive burial from us. They then laid out the mangled remains left by the wild beasts, and the scorched remains left by the fire, and the heads of the rest along with their trunks, and in like manner for many days watched them lying unburied with a military guard. There were some who

---

[j] Rev. xxii. 11. Lardner thinks the passage is quoted from Dan. xii. 10. Credib. part ii. c. 16.

raged and gnashed their teeth at them, seeking to get from them further vengeance. Others derided and insulted them, at the same time magnifying their own idols, and ascribing to them the punishment inflicted on the Christians. There were persons also of a milder disposition, who to some extent seemed to sympathize, yet they also frequently upbraided, saying, 'Where now is their God, and what good have they got from that religion which they chose in preference to their life?' Such was the diversity which characterized the conduct of the heathens. But our state was one of deep sorrow, that we could not bury the bodies. For night aided us not in this matter; money failed to persuade, and entreaty did not shame them into compliance; but they kept up the watch in every way, as if they were to gain some great advantage from the bodies of the Christians not obtaining burial."

Something is omitted. The letter then goes on :—

"The bodies of the Witnesses, after having been maltreated in every way, and exposed in the open air for six days, were burned, reduced to ashes, and swept by the wicked into the river Rhone, which flows past, in order that not even a vestige of them might be visible on earth. And these things they did, as if they had been able to overcome God, and deprive them of their second birth[k], in order, as they said, that 'they may not have hope in a resurrection, trusting to which they introduce some strange and new mode of worship, and despise dangers, and go readily and with joy to death. Now let us see if they will rise again, and if their God can help them and rescue them out of our hands.'"

Eusebius here breaks off his series of continuous extracts, but he makes a few more for special purposes. The first is the account which the Churches gave of the character of the Witnesses :—

"Who also were to such an extent zealous followers and imitators of Christ, who being in the shape of God thought it not an object of desire to be treated like God[l]; that though

---

[k] παλιγγενεσία: the term refers here to the new state of affairs at the end of the world.   [l] Phil. ii. 6.

they were in such glory, and had borne their testimony not once nor twice but often, and had been again taken back to prison after exposure to the wild beasts, and bore about with them the marks of the burnings and bruises and wounds all over their bodies, yet did they neither proclaim themselves witnesses, nor indeed did they permit us to address them by this name; but if any one of us on any occasion, either by letter or in conversation, called them Witnesses, they rebuked him sharply. For they willingly gave the title of Witness to Christ, 'the faithful and true Witness[m],' and firstborn from the dead, and the leader to the Divine life. And they reminded us of those Witnesses who had already departed, and said: 'These indeed are now Witnesses, whom Christ has vouchsafed to take up to Himself in the very act of confession, thus putting his seal upon their testimony through their departure. But we are mean and humble confessors.' And with tears they besought the brethren that earnest prayers might be made for their being perfected. They in reality did all that is implied in the term 'testimony,' acting with great boldness towards all the heathen, and their nobleness they made manifest through their patience and fearlessness and intrepidity. But the title of Witness, as implying some superiority to their brethren[n], they refused, being filled with the fear of God."

After a little they say:—

"They humbled themselves[o] under the powerful hand by which they are now highly exalted. Then they pleaded for all[p], but accused none; they absolved all, they bound none; and they prayed for those who inflicted the tortures, even as

---

[m] Rev. i. 5 and iii. 14.

[n] The Greek is τὴν πρὸς τοὺς ἀδελφοὺς τῶν μαρτύρων προσηγορίαν, generally translated, 'offered to them by their brethren.'

[o] 1 Peter v. 6.

[p] The Greek is πᾶσι μὲν ἀπελογοῦντο. Rufinus translated, 'Placabant omnes, neminem accusabant.' Valesius thought that the words ought to be translated, 'They rendered an account of their faith to all;' or 'they defended themselves before all.' Heinichen has justified the translation in the text by an appeal to a passage in Eusebius, Hist. Eccl. iv. 15.

Stephen the perfect Witness, 'Lord, lay not this sin to their charge ⁿ.' But if he prayed for those who stoned him, how much more for the brethren?"

After other things, again they say :—

"For they had this very great conflict with him [the devil] on account of their genuine love, in order that the Beast being choked might vomit forth those whom he thought he had already swallowed. For they assumed no airs of superiority over the fallen, but with those things in which they themselves abounded they aided the needy, displaying towards them the compassion of a mother. And pouring out many tears for them to the Father they begged life ʳ, and He gave it to them, and they shared it with their neighbours. And departing victorious over all to God, having always loved peace and having recommended peace to us, in peace they went to God, leaving no sorrow to their Mother nor division and dissension to their brethren, but joy and peace, and concord and love."

"The same writing of the fore-mentioned martyrs," says Eusebius, "contains a story worth remembrance.

"For there was one of them of the name of Alcibiades, who lived an exceedingly austere life, confining his diet to bread and water, and partaking of nothing else whatsoever. He tried to continue this mode of life in prison, but it was revealed to Attalus after the first conflict which he underwent in the amphitheatre that Alcibiades was not pursuing the right course in refusing to use the creatures of God, and in leaving an example which might be a stumbling-block to others. And Alcibiades was persuaded, and partook freely of all kinds of food, and thanked God. For they were not without the oversight of the grace of God, but the Holy Spirit was their counsellor."

ⁿ Acts vii. 60.   ʳ Ps. xx. 4.

IV. THE DOCTRINES OF THE LETTER.

God.—There is no discussion in regard to God's nature or character in the epistle. Attalus, in reply to a question, states that God has no name, as man has. He means that the term 'God' is not a proper name, and that He is inexpressible, as we have already seen Justin Martyr maintain. He can be known only by those who are worthy. Mention is made several times of the benefits which God confers on his people. In the commencement a wish is expressed that peace, grace, and glory may come from God the Father to the brethren in Asia and Phrygia. The grace of God fights for his people against the devil, and does not abandon the care of them. He does not wish the death of the sinner, but kindly invites to repentance. Accordingly, He put sweetness into the souls of these, who instead of a second time denying their Lord, confessed Him. He also interfered in a marvellous way, so as to prevent many from denying. This interference is called an economy (οἰκονομία).

The feelings towards Him should be at once fear and love. Those who denied Christ had no notion of the fear of God, while the confessors rejected the appellation of Witnesses, because they were filled with the fear of God. Vettius Epagathus is highly praised for his love to God and his neighbour, and so is Alexander the physician. What is deemed contemptible by this world is deemed worthy of glory with God on account of love to Him. And there is nothing fearful where there is the Father's love. Those who love God are his servants. They have a zeal for God. They can converse with Him in their heart, they pray to Him and thank Him for the food which He supplies. Their sufferings also are a garland of divers colours and flowers presented to the Father. He who suffers for Christ has always communion with the living God; and mention is also made of Christ as the author of the life of God, that is, as producing in men that life which arises from God's ruling in the heart.

Christ.—Jesus Christ is 'our Lord,' and peace, grace, and glory come from God and Him. He identifies Himself with his people. They are his servants and disciples, and what they suffer He suffers. Thus it is said that Christ suffered in Sanctus, and accomplished great glories. He also triumphs through a martyr. And again, it is said that Christ showed through Blandina that the things despised by men are counted worthy of glory with God. He also shows his glory in the departure of the saints from this world. The immeasurable mercy of Christ was manifest in preventing those from denying who might have been inclined to do so, and in the endurance of the Witnesses, and its moral effects on the rest. His grace also turned a torture into a cure. And it was He who gave strength to the sufferers. There was nothing painful where there was the glory of Christ. Christ also was greatly glorified when those who at first denied, confessed. Mention is made also of the art of Christ. The tyrannical tortures are said to be made of no avail by Christ through the patience of the blessed, and converse with Christ and love to Him sustain them in the conflict. He Himself is the great and invincible athlete, and Blandina is said to be clothed with Him. He was crucified for them that He might persuade those who trust in Him, that every one who suffers for the glory of Christ, has always communion with the living God. He has also power over death, for the martyrs leave this life as He wishes them to leave it, and in leaving life they are hastening to Him.

Christ is also the faithful and true Witness, the first-born from the dead, and the leader to the life of God. The martyrs were also said to be "imitators of Him, who being in the shape of God did not deem it an object of desire to be treated like God." This last statement is made in the exact words of Philippians ii. 6, and throws light on the interpretation of the passage. The writers of this epistle did not regard the ὑπάρχων as expressing substantial existence, for they apply the same word immediately to the martyrs, and indeed the word is used frequently in the New Testament itself for a merely temporary state. The writers of this epistle regarded the second part of the extract as denoting an act of humility. The supposition of Lord Hailes, that part of the quotation is omitted, is extremely unlikely. Routh positively affirms that no ecclesiastical author before the period of the Nicene Council can be adduced who has clearly indicated that he understood by the words οὐχ ἁρπαγμὸν ἡγήσατο what our English translators have rendered them, 'did not deem it robbery.' This is the extent of the inferences which we can positively draw in regard to this passage from the mode in which it is quoted. We have no means of determining in what sense they understood μορφὴ θεοῦ or ἴσα θεῷ.

The Spirit.—There are three allusions to the Spirit. In the first Epagathus is said to "have the Paraclete in him, the Spirit more than Zacharias." The words 'the Spirit' may possibly be an interpolation. It is omitted in some manuscripts, and Læmmer, the last editor of Eusebius, discards it. The Paraclete would then be Christ, and not the Spirit. In the second passage the Father's Spirit is spoken of as lightening the minds of the sufferers. In the third 'the Holy Spirit' is said to have been their counsellor.

Devil.—No mention is made in the letter of good or bad angels, or of demons. The devil is frequently introduced. He is sometimes called the Devil, sometimes Satan, sometimes the Wicked One, sometimes the Wild Beast, and once the Crooked Serpent. He is represented as suggesting, contriving, and causing the sufferings of the Christians. Persecutions are attacks of the devil on Christians. He urged on the barbarous tribes to assail them, and the attendants in prison were full of him. He also employs stratagem, devises contrivances, and uses force to compel Christians to deny Christ and utter accusations against the brethren. But the martyrs conquered him and Blandina rendered his condemnation unquestionable. The letter twice speaks of the devil swallowing. In one case he thought that he had swallowed Biblias. In the other case the beast being choked vomited forth alive those whom he thought he had swallowed. Mention is also made of his coming, which was to be without restraint.

Christians.—The Christians are strongly distinguished from the heathen. The heathen are called the nations (ἔθνη) or Gentiles (ἐθνικοί), or the lawless (ἄνομοι). Christians on the other hand are called the holy (ἅγιοι, 'saints'), or servants of God, or servants of Christ, or brothers and sisters, or, in one word, the brotherhood. And Christianity is called 'the truth with us.' The brethren in Asia and Phrygia have the same faith and hope of redemption as the servants of Christ in Vienna and Lugdunum of Gaul.

The letter throws no light on the constitution of the Church, though some passages have been made subjects of keen dispute. Mention is made of two Churches. Therefore, says Valesius, there must have been two bishops. But, says Massuetus, no notice is taken of the bishop of Vienna in the letter, and, as this is scarcely what we could expect, there must have been no bishop of Vienna, but one bishop must have ruled both Churches [s]. Both opinions are mere conjectures.

The only reference to the office of bishop is in the words descriptive of Pothinus, "who had been intrusted with the service of the oversight in Lugdunum" (ὁ τὴν διακονίαν τῆς ἐπισκοπῆς πεπιστευμένος).

Reference is once made to the office of deacon. Sanctus is said to be a "deacon from Vienna." The letter says that he was a deacon and that he was from Vienna, but it does not say whether he was a deacon in the Church of Vienna or in the Church of Lugdunum. Valesius thinks that he came from Vienna, but was a deacon of the Church in Lugdunum; and Laemmer repeats his opinion as if it were a certainty. Lord Hailes thinks, on the other hand, that he was a deacon of the Church in Vienna. Rufinus wisely leaves the matter doubtful, translating *diaconum Viennensem.*

---

[s] Massuet. Dissert. ii.; De Irenaei Vita, art. i. 14, 15.

The Church is once spoken of as the virgin mother of the Christians, and once simply as the mother. Those who were led to confess Christ, though they at first denied Him, are said to have been "added to the Church." Those who persisted in denying Him are called sons of perdition.

Maturus is called νεοφώτιστος ('newly-enlightened'), where there is probably a reference to his recent baptism as well as his conversion, and the word νεαροί evidently refers to Christians at the same stage.

The Christians of Vienna and Lugdunum deemed it unlawful to eat the blood of animals. Commentators quote passages to the same effect from Tertullian, Minucius Felix, and Clemens Alexandrinus, and remark that the Eastern Church is still of this opinion. Augustine held a different opinion.

The letter, of course, frequently mentions the martyrs or Witnesses. They are called 'the blessed Witnesses,' 'the holy Witnesses.' Mention is also made of the protomartyrs, or foremost martyrs.

We can gather from this letter that there was already a tendency to exalt those who suffered for Christ's sake, and to expect blessings from them. But there is no clear proof that any of the assumptions which characterized the martyrs of the next century were displayed by the Christian witnesses of Vienna and Lugdunum, or that they pretended to confer privileges which later martyrs assumed the right of conferring. The statement that "the Witnesses bestowed favour on those who were not Witnesses," is interpreted by Valesius to mean that they interceded for those who had fallen off, as the martyrs in Cyprian's day did. But this is giving far too precise a meaning to the words. The context shows that all that is meant is that they exhorted and inspired with courage those who were not martyrs. They helped to inflame their piety and attachment to Christ. This alone can be the meaning, if we adopt an emendation proposed by Routh, and embodying Rufinus's translation, "The Witnesses bestowed their gifts on those who were *not yet* Witnesses," and thus made them Witnesses also.

Valesius thinks that the economy of God, which I have discussed in a note to the passage, refers to the Church pardoning the lapsed: but this is an unquestionable mistake.

One of the concluding fragments of the epistle informs us that the Witnesses refused the name of Witnesses. They wished to be called Confessors. We have here an indication of how the word μάρτυς came to signify one who had died for Christ. It originally signified simply a witness. It is used in the New Testament for living witnesses. It was used in the time of the Viennese and Lyons martyrs for living witnesses; and it was used some years after by a bishop as a designation of himself at the commencement of a letter. It was not till a century later that the term 'martyr' was confined to him who had sealed his testimony by his death[t].

Mention is several times made of the κλῆρος τῶν μαρτύρων. Some have inferred from this expression that the martyrs were regarded as a separate and privileged class[u]. But Valesius explains the expression much more successfully by showing that it is borrowed from the language of the games.

Future State.—We have already seen that the letters speak of the martyrs going to Christ. They are also spoken of as going to God. They are also said to have communion with God for ever. They receive after death the crown of incorruption; and mention is made of the παλιγγενεσία, or restoration or renovation of all things, and it is connected with the resurrection.

Biblias was reminded by her temporary suffering "of the eternal punishment in Gehenna." This is the only allusion to the punishment of the wicked. The word used for eternal is αἰώνιος.

Scriptures.—Frequent quotations of Scripture occur in the letter, but there are only two express references to it. One passage is quoted from the Gospel of John with the words "That which was spoken by our Lord was fulfilled."

[t] See Routh's note, and the part of Pearson's Vindiciæ referred to by him, part ii. c. ix. p. 115.
[u] Olshausen's Eccl. Hist. Monumenta, p. 58, note.

Another passage is quoted with the words, "That the Scripture might be fulfilled;" but it is matter of doubt whether the quotation is made from the last chapter of Daniel or the last chapter of the Revelation of John.

Morality.—The letter sums up morality in love to God and to one's neighbour. In the extract regarding Alcibiades the right of Christians to use all the creatures of God as food is asserted, and their wisdom in so doing is commended. We also learn from the letter that some of the Christians of Vienna and Lugdunum had slaves in their possession.

INDEXES.

I. LITERARY INDEX.

A.

Abraxas, ii. 56.
Academics, ii. 27.
Accusations against Christians, ii. 13, 154.
Ackermann, ii. 50.
Ado, iii. 256.
Advantages of a study of early Christian literature, i. 3.
Æons, iii. 16, 19.
Æschylus, ii. 19, 96.
Æsop, iii. 30.
Africanus, Julius, i. 18; ii. 102.
Agrippa Castor, ii. 55.
Alcibiades the Christian, iii. 279.
Alcibiades the Montanist, iii. 250.
Aldrich, i. 200.
Alexander the Christian physician and martyr, iii. 274.
Alexander the prophet, ii. 21, 152.
Alexander, Dr.W.L., his Anglo-Catholicism not Apostolical, i. 60.
Alexandrian Chronicle; see Chronicon Paschale.
Alexandrian Philosophy, i. 214.
Allegorical interpretation, i. 82; prevalent among the Greeks, i. 83; in Barnabas, i. 220.
Amastris, Church in, iii. 215.
Ambrose, ii 93.
Ammonius, iii. 26.
Amphilochus, ii. 22.
Anastasius Bibliothecarius, i. 20, 99.
Anastasius Sinaita, i. 20; iii. 228, 233.
Anaxagoras, i. 83.
Ancients uncritical, i. 12; their translations, i. 23.
Andreas Cæsariensis, i. 318.
Anencletus, i. 91.
Anicetus, i. 156 158; ii. 84; iii. 183.

Anger, i. 307.
Antinous, ii. 76, 85; iii. 183.
Antipas, ii. 150.
Antoninus Pius, i. 159; ii. 6, 8, 9, 10, 78; iii. 231.
Antonius, iii. 62.
Aphrodite, ii. 285.
Apollinaris of Hierapolis, his life, iii. 239. His writings, iii. 239-248. Opinions attributed to him, iii. 249.
Apollinaris of Laodicea, iii. 249.
Apollo, ii. 285.
Apollonius the Christian, iii. 65.
Apollonius the Egyptian, iii. 81.
Apollos, ii. 138.
Apologists, ii. 3-15; their work, ii. 16-22; their position, ii. 26; argument from miracles, ii. 32; from teaching of Christ, *ibid.*; their relation to heresies, ii. 35; did not conceal their opinions, ii. 38, 169; their theological doctrines, ii. 38; opinions on morals, ii. 47.
Apostolical Fathers: their name, i. 81; character, i. 82; their relation to Judaism, i. 82, 83; their doctrines, i. 86.
Apuleius, ii. 20, 21.
Aratus, iii. 71.
Archelaus, ii. 150.
Aristarchus, i. 12.
Aristides, ii. 4, 54.
Aristion, i. 313.
Aristippus, iii. 29.
Aristobulus, i. 83; ii. 107.
Ariston, i. 160.
Aristo Pellæus, ii. 56.
Aristophanes, iii. 5.
Aristotle, ii. 25, 27, 116, 117; iii. 29, 121.
Arsinous, iii. 207.

290   LITERARY INDEX.

Art, ancient, i. 9.
Artemis, iii. 7.
Artemon, iii. 238.
'Αρχαῖος and ἀρχή, i. 108 ; ii. 61.
Ashton, ii. 146.
Asklepios, ii. 234, 286.
Assyria, iii. 3.
Astrology, iii. 28.
Athanasius, i. 258.
Atheism of Christians, ii. 12, 154.
Athena, ii. 285.
Athenagoras, ii. 4, 123. Concerning his life, iii. 107. Information derived from the fragment of Philip of Sida, ibid.; from the inscription on the MSS. as to the date, iii. 108. The works of Athenagoras, iii. 114. The Novel attributed to him, iii. 115. The character of Athenagoras and his writings, ibid. Their superior literary style, ibid. Explanation of the persecutions of the Christians, iii. 118. His treatment of mythology and of philosophy, iii. 120. His Platonism, iii.122. His defence of Christianity, iii. 124. Abstract of the Apology of Athenagoras, iii. 125. Abstract of the treatise on the Resurrection of the Dead, iii. 131. The doctrines of Athenagoras in regard to God, iii. 142 ; the Logos and the Spirit, iii. 149 ; angels, iii. 155 ; the constitution of man, iii. 159 ; sin and salvation, iii. 165 ; the future state, iii. 169 ; the Scriptures, iii. 171 ; morality, iii. 173. Literature—manuscripts, editions, and translations, iii. 176.
Athenogenes, iii. 114.
Athens, Church in, iii. 215.
Atonement, Day of, i. 223.
Attalus the martyr, iii. 257, 273.
Aubé, ii. 73, 82.
Augustine, i. 62 ; ii. 39 ; iii. 284.
Aurelius, Marcus, i. 181 ; ii. 6, 78, 83 ; iii. 22, 109, 119, 231.
Autolycus, iii. 64.

B.

Bacchylides, iii. 215.
Barbeyrac, i. 73 ; ii. 48, 336.
Barchochebas, or Barcochba, ii. 73, 85, 136.
Barecroft, i. 33.
Barnabas, Epistle of, i. 82. Authorship, i. 201. External evidence, i. 202 ; internal, i. 204. Objections to his supposed authorship, i. 205. To whom was the epistle addressed, i. 211 ; not to Jewish Christians only, ibid. Evidence for an Alexandrian origin, i. 214. Date, i. 216. Integrity, i. 221. Its religious character, i. 222. Abstract, i. 223. Doctrines in regard to God, i. 232 ; Christ, i. 233 ; Holy Spirit, angels, and devil, i. 236 ; on man, i. 237 ; future state, i. 240 : on Scriptures, i. 241. Literature, i. 251.
Baronius, iii. 254.
Barth, i. 311.
Basilides, ii. 55 ; iii. 207.
Basilidiani, ii. 179 ; iii. 196.
Bauer, Bruno, i. 38.
Baur, Ferdinand, i. 36, 55, 88, 101, 127, 159, 176, 267 ; ii. 50, 86, 185 ; iii. 188, 197, 202, 247.
Bekker, i. 19, 20.
Bellarmine, i. 28, 261.
Bellerophon, ii. 285.
Bennet, Dr. James, i. 63 ; ii. 138.
Bernardus, i. 101.
Bernays, i. 17.
Berosus, iii. 83.
Bessarion, iii. 61.
Betty, Joseph, iii. 106.
Biblias, iii. 268.
Bickersteth, i. 35.
Bigne's Library of the Fathers, i. 34.
Bignonius, i. 102.
Biographia Ecclesiastica, i. 32.
Blandina, iii. 275.
Blondellus, i. 266 ; iii. 251.
Blunt, Professor, on the Right Use of the Fathers, i. 68, 71 ; ii. 315. On the Fathers against Roman Catholic practices, i. 24.
Bobbio, iii. 204.
Boehl, ii. 147.
Boisius, i. 121.
Book of the Fathers, i. 33.
Books, Small, on Great Subjects, i. 76.
Braun, ii. 83, 146, 164.
Brewster's Life of Sir Isaac Newton, i. 71.
Brown, Rev. H., ii. 146.
Brunn, N. von, ii. 146.
Bucolus, i. 160.
Bull, Bishop, i. 69, 71, 268, 287 ; ii. 211, 223 ; iii. 42, 44, 189.
Bunsen, Baron, i. 75, 138, 185, 269, 286 ; ii. 69, 136, 138, 147 ; iii. 204, 207, 234.

Burton, Dr., i. 70.
Burton, W., i. 141.

C.

Cabbala, iii. 20.
Cæcilius, ii. 60.
Cæsar, Julius, iii. 213.
Caius, iii. 204.
Canisii, Antiquæ Lectiones, i. 34.
Capitolinus, iii. 109.
Carpocratians, iii. 196.
Cassian, iii. 14.
Cassiodorus criticized, i. 16, 17.
Catena of Victor of Capua, i. 185.
Catholicism, i. 40.
Catiline, ii. 14; iii. 266.
Cave, his Historia Literaria, i. 32; iii. 65, 108, 179, 221.
Cedrenus, Georgius, i. 19; ii. 73.
Ceillier, his History of Ecclesiastical Writers, i. 29; ii. 56.
Celsus, ii. 4, 57; iii. 107.
Celsus, in the Dialogue of Papiscus and Jason, ii. 59.
Cerdo, i. 84; ii. 84.
Cerinthus, i. 155.
Chanutus, ii. 146.
Chevallier, Temple, i. 122; ii. 146.
Christian Church: its liberality, i. 52; ii. 183. Its progress during the age of the Apologists, ii. 32. Cause of progress, ii. 35. Its institutions, ii. 47.
Christian religion: how designated, iii. 33.
Χριστιανισμός, i. 180.
Christianity: its earliest form, i. 48. Its intense morality, i. 50. No system, ibid. Indifference in regard to outward forms, i. 51. Its early spread, ii. 32.
Christians: their trials, ii. 11. Accusations against them, ii. 12; iii. 28. Creed of, ii. 71. Meeting-place, ibid.
Chronicles, Greek, i. 19.
Chronicon Paschale, or Alexandrian Chronicle, i. 19; ii. 58, 73; iii. 11, 184, 234, 247.
Χρόνος, iii. 238.
Chryseros, iii. 64.
Chrysophora, iii. 217.
Church, the Catholic, iii. 212. History of the, what it should be, i. 4. Its unity in doctrines, i. 155.
Circumcision, i. 209.
Clarisse on Athenagoras, iii. 108.

Clarke, Dr., on the Trinity, i. 71.
Clarke, Dr. Adam, his Concise View, i. 33.
Clemens Alexandrinus, i. 8, 13, 92, 100, 202, 255; ii. 57, 106, 331; iii. 3, 10, 13, 15, 16, 18, 107, 224, 284.
Clemens Romanus, i. 85. Life, i. 90. Overseer of Roman Church, i. 91. Order in line of succession from apostles, i. 91-94. Is he the person mentioned in Philippians? i. 95. Death of Clemens, i. 96. Of what nation, ibid. Attempts to prove him a Roman, i. 97. Date of letter, i. 99. Epistle to Corinthians, ibid. When discovered, ibid. Source of information in regard to Clemens, ibid. Writings of Clemens, ibid. The letter ascribed to Clemens by Dionysius, i. 100. Subsequent writers unanimous, ibid. Is the letter spoken of by Irenæus the one we now possess? ibid. Have we the whole of it? i. 102. Doubts on the 40th and 41st chapters, i. 103. Letter well known in early times, i. 104. Date of letter, i. 105. Arguments for A.D. 68, ibid. Arguments from Epistle to the Hebrews, i. 108. Circumstances of Corinthian Church, i. 109. Resemblance to New Testament, i. 111. Clemens on order and harmony of the world, i. 112. His theology, i. 113. Various opinions, i. 114. Abstract of letter, ibid. Writings ascribed to Clemens, i. 118. Supposed authorship of Epistle to the Hebrews, i. 119. Editions and translations of letters of Clemens, i. 121. Theology of Clemens, i. 122. On God, ibid. On Christ, i. 124; His life, i. 127; His work, ibid.; His death, i. 128; His second coming, i. 130. On the Holy Spirit, i. 131. On the Trinity, ibid. On angels, ibid. On the devil, i. 132. On man: his original state, ibid. On salvation, ibid. On the Church, i. 135. Identity of overseers and elders, i. 139. On Jewish Church, i. 140. On the three orders in the Church, ibid. On rites of Church, i. 142. On future state, ibid. On martyrs, i. 143. On prayers to saints, ibid. On the Scriptures, i. 144. On liberties with text of Old Testament, i. 145. Passages

quoted by Clemens not now found in Old Testament, i. 146. On inspiration, i. 147. On New Testament, *ibid.* On interpretation of Scripture, i. 151. On morality, i. 152. Clemens mentioned in Hermas, i. 264 ; ii. 138.
Clementines, i. 94, 99 ; ii. 44.
Cleobius, iii. 195.
Cleopas, iii 201.
Clericus, i. 87 ; iii. 255.
Clinton, iii. 110.
Clymenus, iii. 81.
Codex Alexandrinus, i. 99.
Colomesius, i. 121.
Columban, iii. 204.
Commodus, iii. 109.
Congreve, ii. 8.
Constitutions, Apostolical, i. 99, 119.
Contogones, History of the Fathers, i. 30. On Clemens, i. 90.
Cooper, Basil, ii. 147.
Corinthian Church, i. 109 ; iii. 182, 214.
Cornwallis, Miss, her Small Books on Great Subjects, i. 76.
Corruptions of ancient writings, i. 23.
Cossartius, i. 121.
Cotelerius, on Pastor of Hermas, i. 268, 302, 305. Edition of Apostolical Fathers, edited by Joannes Clericus, i. 87.
Coustantius, i. 122.
Cox, Lives of the Fathers, i. 33.
Cramer, iii 199.
Cra'es iii. 29.
Credner, iii. 206, 211.
Crescens, ii. 68 ; iii. 9, 30.
Crete, Churches in, iii. 215.
Critical study of writings, advantages and disadvantages of, i. 4.
Crit'cism, Principles of, i. 10.
Cross, i. 208.
Cudworth, ii. 24.
Cunningham, Dr., his Historical Theology, i. 64
Cureton, ii. 93 ; iii. 234.
Cynics, ii. 163 ; iii. 6, 9, 30.
Cyprian, suspects tampering with his letters, i. 22 ; iii. 212.
Cyrenius, Christ born in time of. ii. 85.
Cyril of Alexandria, ii. 107, 109.

D.

D'Abbadie, i. 311.
Dachery, i. 252.
Dähne, ii. 108.
Daillé, i. 15, 16, 24, 58, 59, 184.
Danaids and Dircæ, i. 97.
Daniel, iii. 3, 5, 8, 14, 26, 42, 45, 53, 58, 61.
David, date of, ii. 152.
Davidson, Dr., i. 316.
Davis, ii. 341.
Dechair, iii. 177.
De la Guilletiere, ii 55.
Democritus, iii. 30, 33, 118.
De Quincey on Malalas, i. 19. Uses the word 'Epi-Christian,' i. 81. Essenism. i. 111 ; iii. 201.
Deucalion, ii. 104.
Development of doctrines, what it means, i. 5 ; various opinions on, i. 55.
Diagoras, iii. 8.
Διγαμία, ii. 340.
Δικαιῶ, meaning of, i. 77.
Dindorf, Louis, his edition of Chronicon Paschale and of Malalas, i. 19.
Dindorf, Wilhelm, his edition of Syncellus and Nicephorus. i. 19 ; of Pastor of Hermas, i. 307.
Dio Cassius, iii. 242.
Diogenes, iii. 29.
Diognetus, the Epistle to, ii. 126. No external testimony : its doctrines on God, Christ, ii. 127 ; on man converted, ii. 133. The style of the letter, ii. 134 ; its date, ii. 135. The character of the writer, ii. 136. Theories regarding him, ii. 138. The manuscript, ii. 140. The latter portion of the letter, ii. 142.
Dionysius Bar-Salibi, iii. 25.
Dionysius of Corinth ; his letters mutilated, i. 22. On Clemens, i. 91. On the letter of Clemens, i. 100. His life, iii. 214. His writings, *ibid.*
Dionysius the Areopagite, i. 14 ; iii. 215.
Dionysus, ii. 285.
Disease, iii. 30.
Docetes, i. 83.
Dodwell, i. 17, 108 ; ii. 81 ; iii. 25, 58, 64, 106. 253.
Döllinger on the development of doctrine, i. 57.
Domitian, interview between him and the relatives of Christ, iii. 198.
Dommerich, iii. 181.
Donaldson, Dr., History of Greek Literature, iii. 5.
Dorner, i. 127, 267, 270 ; ii. 182 ; iii. 154, 202.

LITERARY INDEX. 293

Dressel, i. 88, 90, 301.
Ducæus, iii. 61.
Duncker, ii. 181.
Dunlop's History of Fiction, iii. 115.
Du Pin, i. 28; ii. 82.

E.

Ebionites, i. 219, 267.
Ebionitism, i. 39; ii. 190; iii. 189, 197.
Ekker, Ecco, on the Epistle to the Corinthians by Clemens Romanus, i. 101.
Eleutherus, iii. 183, 251.
Elias, Revelation of, i. 146; iii. 203.
Elpistus, iii. 215.
Empedocles, iii. 29.
Encrateis, or Encratites, iii. 10, 11, 12, 27, 220, 244.
English Church, treatment of the Fathers, i. 67.
Ennius, ii. 21.
Ep-Apostolic, i. 81.
Ephrem Syrus, iii. 26.
Epi-christian, i. 81.
Epicurus, ii. 286; iii. 8.
Epiphanius, i. 17, 95; ii. 73, 331; iii. 3, 10, 12, 24, 27, 114, 193.
Essenes, iii. 201.
Euhemerus, ii. 19, 21, 23, 95; iii. 70, 73, 75.
Euripides, ii. 20, 96; iii. 121.
Eusebius, i. 8, 13, 18, et passim.
Eutychis, iii. 60.
Evangelical theology, i. 60. Evangelical treatment of the Fathers, i. 59.
Evans, Rev. R., Biography of the Early Church, i. 15, 33.
Evidence, Historical, i. 10; Internal, 21.

F.

Faber, his edition of Polycarp's letter, i. 200; of the Pastor of Hermas, i. 311.
Fabricius, his Bibliotheca Ecclesiastica, i. 16. His Delectus Argumentorum, ii. 49. His Bibliotheca Græc., ii. 147; iii. 64, 181.
Fate, Stoic belief in, ii. 162.
Fathers, Library of the, ii. 146.
Fell, Bishop, edition of Clemens Romanus, i. 121; of Barnabas, i. 253; of Pastor of Hermas, i. 311; of Cyprian, ii. 59, 60. On Justin's Apology, ii. 81. Edition of Theophilus, iii. 105; of Athenagoras, iii. 177.
Florinus, letter to, i. 154.
Florius, iii. 257.
Flower, Rev. W. B., his translation of Theophilus, iii. 106.
Forbes of Corse, i. 66, 67.
Forgeries in early Christian literature, i. 22.
Francklin, iii. 4.
Freppel's Les Pères Apostoliques, i. 83, 89. His Les Apologistes, ii. 49; iii. 235.
Frey, i. 87.
Friday, ii. 164.
Friedländer, i. 85.
Frisius, iii. 60, 105.
Fronto Ducæus, iii. 181.
Fumée, M., de S. Genillac, iii. 115.
Fundanus, iii. 231.

G.

Gaius, i. 174.
Gale, Thomas, iii. 180.
Galileans, iii. 201.
Gallandi, his Bibliotheca Patrum, i. 34.
Galliccioli, ii. 146.
Gasparin, Count de, i. 51, 268.
Gellius, Aulus, iii. 22.
Γευσέ, meaning of, i. 108.
Genoude, i. 35.
Gesner, iii. 23, 60, 61, 177.
Gfrörer's Philo, i. 83; ii. 108, 323.
Giles, Rev. Dr., i. 35.
Gilly, Dr., on Jerome, 16.
Gilse on the Morality of the Apostolic Fathers, i. 89.
Gladiatorial shows, iii. 99.
Gnosis, i. 103.
Gnossians, iii. 216.
Gnostics, ii. 14, 35, 36; iii. 20.
Goarus, i. 19.
Gobarus, Stephanus, ii. 98; iii. 185, 202.
Godwin, Professor, his Essay on the Earliest Form of Christianity, i. 48, 49.
Goode, Rev. William, his Divine Rule of Faith. i. 60.
Gorthæus, iii. 195.
Gortyna, iii. 215.
Göz, ii. 146, 147.
Grabe, i. 120; ii. 82, 86, 89, 97, 146, 223; iii. 67.
Granianus, Serenus, ii. 53.

Grant, Sir Alexander, ii. 29.
Γραφεῖον, meaning of, i. 147.
Grapte, i. 264.
Gratz, i. 270.
Graul, ii. 32, 49.
Gregory of Tours, iii. 261.
Gualtherus, Cornelius, iii. 213.
Gundert, i. 109.

H.

Hades, ii. 116.
Hadrian, ii. 6, 9, 53, 54, 56; iii. 231.
Hailes, Lord, i. 72; iii. 263, 282, 283.
Halloix, i. 200; ii. 164; iii. 193.
Hamilton, Sir W., i. 6; iii. 41.
Hase, iii. 61.
Hebrews, Epistle to, i. 108, 119, 220, 259.
Hefele, i. 87, 105, 174, 203; ii. 147.
Hegel, i. 7, 36.
Hegesippus, i. 90, 99. His descent, iii. 182. The period at which he lived, iii. 183. His "Notes or Recollections," iii. 184. His agreement in doctrine with the Churches in Greece and Italy, iii. 186. An account of his Fragments: on the death of James, iii. 190; appointment of a successor to James, iii. 195; interview of the relations of our Lord with Domitian, iii. 198; the martyrdom of Simeon, iii. 200; the seven heresies of the Jews, iii. 201. The Latin History of Josephus or Hegesippus, iii. 213.
Heinichen, iii. 26, 217, 241, 266, 267, 274, 278.
Helena, ii. 179.
Hemerobaptistæ, iii. 201.
Henke, i. 202.
Heraclitus, ii. 157, 163, 286; iii. 29, 118.
Herakles, ii. 286.
Herbig, ii. 122.
Heretics, i. 83; ii. 35.
Hermas, i. 85; iii. 207. Pastor of, i. 255. External testimony. *ibid.* Its authorship, i. 258. Internal evidence, i. 261. Date, i. 264. Place, i. 266. Its supposed Judaistic tendency, *ibid.* Heresies attributed to it, i. 269. Object of the work, i. 270. Abstract of it, i. 272. Doctrines of Hermas—On God, i. 281; on Christ, 283; Holy Spirit, 287; angels, 289; devil, 291; man, 292; salvation, 293; conduct of Christians, 296; on the Church, 301: on a future state, 305; Scriptures, 306. Literature, *ibid.*
Hermes, ii. 234.
Hermes Trismegistus, ii. 108.
Hermias, ii. 4. Life and writings, iii. 179. Literature, iii. 180.
Hermias Sozomenus, iii. 179.
Hermogenes, iii. 68.
Herodotus, i. 98; iii. 70, 120.
Heroldus, iii. 61, 105, 177.
Hesiod, ii. 17, 20; iii. 70.
Heyns, i. 89.
Hierapolis, iii. 240.
Hieromus, or Hiram, iii. 82.
Hilary, ii. 135.
Hilgenfeld, i. 89, 97, 108, 114, 127, 159, 176, 182, 214, 217, 268; iii. 211, 224, 246.
Hinds, Dr., i. 89.
Hippolytus, iii. 11, 12, 14, 203.
Hodius, i. 19.
Homer, ii. 17, 20, 22, 103, 116, 117, 118, 124, 160; iii. 39, 70.
Homilies of Clemens, i. 90, 119.
Honorius Augustodunensis, iii. 223.
Horace, ii. 21.
Hornemann, i. 87.
Horsley, Bishop, i. 72.
Hort, ii. 73, 86.
Hosmann, iii. 63.
Huber, i. 8.
Human sacrifices, iii. 7, 29.
Humphreys, David, iii. 178.
Humphry, Dr., his edition of Theophilus, iii. 105.
Hutchin, ii. 146.
Hystaspes, ii. 288, 320.

I.

Ireland, Dr., Lectures, ii. 49.
Irenæus, i. 84, 91, 100, 154, 181, 255; iii. 8, 12. Letter on Passover, i. 156, 157. Statements of Irenæus with respect to Polycarp misinterpreted, i. 157.
Isidorus, ii. 56.
Ittigius, his edition of the Apostolical Fathers, i. 87.

J.

Jachmann, i. 270, 286, 300.
Jacobson, Dr., i. 87.
James the Apostle, iii. 190.
James grandson of Judas, iii. 200.
James, Rev. Thomas, on Corruptions, i. 23.
Jamieson, Dr., i. 72.

Jebb, ii. 146.
Jeremie, Dr., ii. 50.
Jerome, i. 15, 18, 23, 93, 157, 202, 258; ii. 53, 56; iii. 5, 11, 12, 14, 18, 64, 68, 189, 207.
Jerusalem, Church in, iii. 190.
Jethro, ii. 150.
Jews, ii. 10, 33, 43, 59, 60, 155, 174, 178, 203; iii. 201.
John the Apostle, i. 154, 156, 157, 312.
John the Presbyter, i. 313.
John of Damascus, i. 20; ii. 90, 96, 119; iii. 11.
Jonsius, ii. 101.
Jortin, i. 164.
Joseph, reputed father of Jesus, iii. 201.
Josephus, i. 209.
Journal of Classical and Sacred Philology, ii. 73; of Sacred Literature, i. 254.
Jovinian, iii. 14.
Judas, death of, i. 317.
Judas, the brother of the Lord, grandsons of, iii. 198.
Julian, ii. 135.
Junius, i. 89, 102, 121.
Jupiter Latiaris, iii. 7, 80.
Justin Martyr, i. 219; ii. 4, 22, 33; iii. 8, 9, 11. His birth, ii. 62. His conversion, ii. 63. His subsequent life, ii. 67. His martyrdom, ii. 68. General account of his writings, ii. 74. The Apologies, their genuineness, ii. 75. The so-called second Apology's claim to be the second, ii. 76. The date of the first Apology, ii. 83. Dialogue with Trypho—its genuineness, ii. 86; its form, ii. 88; its date, ii. 89. The Discourse to the Greeks—its genuineness, ii. 90; the Syriac translation, ii. 93; abstract of it, *ibid*. On the Monarchy of God—its genuineness, ii. 94; abstract of it, ii. 96. Hortatory Address to the Greeks—its genuineness, *ibid.*; external testimony, *ibid.*; internal evidence, ii. 98; references to ancient writings, ii. 101; its doctrines, ii. 110; abstract, ii. 116. Fragment on the Resurrection—its genuineness, ii. 119; abstract of it, ii. 123; doctrines, ii. 125. The spurious works, ii. 142. Literature, manuscripts, and editions, ii. 144. His character, ii. 147. His acquaintance with Hebrew, ii. 148. His critical powers, ii. 149. His mistakes, ii. 150. His intense hold of Christianity, ii. 152. His boldness, ii. 153. His defence of Christians, ii. 154. His attacks on heathenism, ii. 155. His liberality, ii. 156. His fondness for Socrates and Plato, ii. 157. His obligations to Plato, ii. 158. His relation to the Stoics, Epicureans, Cynics, and poets, ii. 161. His presentation of Christianity, ii. 165. Christ, *ibid*. His teaching, *ibid*. Miracles, ii. 167. Argument from miracles, *ibid*. Expulsion of demons, ii. 169. Argument from prophecy, ii. 170. His mode of dealing with Jews, ii. 174; with heretics, ii. 179. His position in regard to Christian doctrine, ii. 180. His obligations to Plato, *ibid*. The novelty of his opinions, ii. 181. The doctrine of the Logos, *ibid*. His relation to his fellow-Christians, ii. 183. His liberality, *ibid*. Abstracts of the Apologies and Dialogue with Trypho, ii. 190. Justin's doctrines in regard to God: His character, ii. 208; His immateriality, ii. 210; creation and providence, ii. 214. Christ, ii. 218; the Logos, ii. 219; His divinity, ii. 226; His Incarnation, ii. 231; His miraculous birth, and earthly life, ii. 235; His descent into Hades, ii. 239; His character, ii. 240; the object of his Incarnation, ii. 241; His teaching, ii. 243; His suffering, ii. 245; His death, ii. 247; His sacrificial character, ii. 248; His being accursed, ii. 249; His kingdom, ii. 252; Lawgiver, ii. 254; Priest, ii. 255; His second coming, ii. 256; His personal reign on earth, *ibid.*; Judge, ii. 263. Holy Spirit, meaning of term, ii. 264. Difference of Apology from Dialogue with Trypho, *ibid*. The Logos and Spirit, ii. 266. The Spirit worshipped, ii. 268; His subordination, ii. 269; His nature, ii. 270; His work, ii. 272; the Spirit as a gift, ii. 273. Angels: their reality, ii. 275; their habitation and food, ii. 276; their position, ii. 278. Worship of angels, *ibid*. Devil, ii. 280. Evil angels,

ii. 281. Demons, ii. 282; their actions, ii. 283; efforts to defeat Christianity, ii. 285; caused persecutions, ii. 287; assisted heretics, ii. 288; watched the souls of Christians at death, *ibid.* Man—a voluntary agent, ii. 289; terms of free-will, ii. 291. Fall of Man, ii. 293. Universal sinfulness, ii. 295. Conversion, ii. 296. Salvation, ii. 299. The Church, ii. 303; its officers, ii. 304. Procedure on Sunday, ii. 305. Baptism, ii. 307. Nature of it, *ibid.* Administration of it, ii. 308. Thanksgiving, or Eucharist, ii. 311. Its main objects, *ibid.* Peculiar statement of Justin, ii. 314. State after death, ii. 316. Resurrection, ii. 319. Judgment, ii. 322. Scriptures, *ibid.* Portions quoted, *ibid.* Inspiration, ii. 324. Mode of quoting, ii. 326. Mode of interpretation, ii. 327. New Testament, ii. 329. Portions quoted, *ibid.* The Memoirs of the Apostles, *ibid.* Inspiration, ii. 332. Morality, ii. 333. Eternal principles, ii. 334. Eagerness for martyrdom, ii. 335. Suicide, ii. 336. Swearing, ii. 338. Marriage, *ibid.* Polygamy, ii. 342. Self-mutilation, ii. 343. Exposure of children, ii. 344. Payment of taxes, *ibid.* Slavery, *ibid.*

Justus, surnamed Barsabas, i. 317.
Juvenal, i. 84.

K.

Kallistion, iii. 9.
Kaye, Bishop, ii. 88, 113, 187, 223, 233, 331, 338.
Keil, iii. 227.
Kestner, i. 111; iii. 262.
Killin's Ancient Church, i. 64.
Kiss to be used with discretion, iii. 173.
Knox's theology, i. 61.
Koepke, ii. 14.
Kore, ii. 286.
Kortholt, iii. 62.
Köstlin, i. 114.
Krenkel, ii. 147.

L.

Labbé, Dissertations, i. 28, 121; iii. 227.

Lacedæmonian Christians, iii. 215.
Lactantius, iii. 64.
Læmmer, iii. 282, 283.
Λαικός, use of word, i. 104.
Lambecius, iii. 179.
Lange, i. 89.
Lardner, Dr., i. 73, 90: ii. 329; iii. 189, 217, 247, 263, 276.
Laurence, Dr., ii. 323.
Lechler, i. 89.
Lee, Dr. Robert, ii. 331.
Lehmann, iii. 5.
Le Moyne, i. 156, 211, 253; iii. 115.
Lequien, iii. 61.
Lewis, Sir George Cornewall, On Historical Evidence, i. 11.
Libraries of the Fathers, i. 34.
Lindner, iii. 177.
Linus, i. 91.
Lipsius, i. 90, 96, 109, 113.
Lobeck, ii. 20, 107.
Locke, opinion of Christ's divinity, i. 71.
Löffler, ii. 50.
Λόγος, meaning of, ii. 40.
Longuerue, iii. 42.
Lucian, ii. 21, 167; iii. 4, 5, 272.
Lucius, i. 167.
Lücke, i. 47.
Lugdunum, Letter of Churches in Vienna and:—The Letters of the Martyrs, iii. 250. The date of the persecution, iii. 251. Authorship of the Letter, iii. 256. Objections considered, iii. 257. Literature, iii. 262. Translation of the Letter, iii. 263. Doctrines of the Letter in regard to God, iii. 280; Christ, iii. 281; the Spirit, iii. 282; devil, *ibid.*; Christians, iii. 283; future state, iii. 285; Scriptures, *ibid.* Morality, iii. 286.
Luke, work ascribed to, ii. 57.
Lumper's Historia Theologico-Critica, i. 29; iii. 257.
Luther's theology, i. 61.
Lysis, iii. 121.

M.

M'Crie, i. 61.
Mader, i. 121.
Maine, Henry Sumner, ii. 18.
Maitland, Dr., on Jerome, i. 16.
Malalas, i. 19; iii. 27.
Manetho, iii. 82.
Manichæus, iii. 13.
Maranus, ii. 90, 128, 145, 224, 233,

260, 262, 274, 277 ; iii. 22, 31, 105, 179, 181.
Marciani, ii. 179 ; iii. 196.
Marcion, i. 84, 156, 183 ; ii. 84, 138, 139, 179, 288 ; iii. 9, 11, 12, 13, 68, 207, 215, 219.
Marcus Aurelius ; see Aurelius.
Markland, ii 146.
Marsh. ii. 329.
Martial, i. 84.
Martyr, meaning of the word, iii. 285.
Martyrdom—the birthday of the martyrs, i. 168. Its privileges, ii. 59 ; iii. 284.
Martyria, formation of, i. 175, 176.
Martyrium of Polycarp, i. 160, 177. See Polycarp.
Mary—Maries of the New Testament, i. 317.
Masbotheans, iii. 201.
Masbotheus, iii. 195.
Massuetus, iii. 283.
Maturus, iii. 266.
Maumont, ii. 146.
Maurice's Ecclesiastical History, i. 76.
Maximus, i. 14, 185 ; ii. 57.
Meletine legion, iii. 242.
Meletius, iii. 236.
Melito, ii. 4. His life, iii. 221. His writings, iii. 223.
Menander the Comic Poet, ii. 96, 164.
Menander the Ephesian, iii. 82.
Menander the Heretic, ii. 179, 288.
Menandrians, iii. 196.
Menardus, H., i. 252.
Merivale, i. 12.
Μεταμέλεια, i. 294.
Μετάνοια, i. 293.
Methodius, ii. 119, 331 ; iii. 114.
Metrodorus of Lampsacus, i. 83.
Migne, J. P., his Patrologiæ Cursus Completus, i. 34.
Mikropresbytikon, iii. 177.
Mill, iii. 26.
Miltiades, iii. 207.
Milton, on the Fathers, i. 58. Opinion of Christ's divinity, i. 71.
Minucius Felix, iii. 113, 284.
Minucius Fundanus, ii. 53.
Miracles, Justin's views on. ii. 167.
Mithras, ii. 286.
Modestus, iii. 219.
Moehler, ii. 135 ; iii. 66. On Jerome, i. 16. His Patrologie, i. 30. On early Christian theology. i. 51. On Clemens, i. 81.

Mommsen, iii. 110.
Montanism, iii. 114, 222, 227, 240, 244, 250.
Montfaucon, iii. 60.
Morality of the Apostolical Fathers, i. 84. Works on, i. 89. Of Justin, ii. 333 ; of Athenagoras, iii. 173.
Morell, ii. 145.
Morgan, Cæsar, ii 50.
Moses, books of, supposed to be the source of much of the wisdom of the Greeks, ii. 97, 110, 156. Older than any Greek writings, ii. 103, 117 ; iii. 21, 32, 81, 82.
Moses Chorenensis, his account of Aristo of Pella, ii. 57.
Moses, Rev. Thomas, ii. 147.
Mosheim, i. 74, 102 ; iii. 109, 122.
Muralto, i. 87.
Muratori, i. 259.
Muratorian fragment, iii. 203 : an account of it, *ibid.* ; its authorship, iii. 207 ; its character, iii. 210 ; its date, iii. 212.
Musanus, iii. 219.
Music, study of, iii. 30.
Musonius, ii. 163, 286.
Mythology, Greek and Roman, ii. 16 ; ancient explanation of, ii. 23.

N.

Nannius, iii. 177.
Neander, i. 103, 214 ; ii. 82, 234, 249, 271. His history of Christian dogmas, i. 55. His treatment of the Fathers, i. 75. Works on Philosophy and Christianity, ii. 50.
Nelson on Petavius, i. 70. Life of Bishop Bull, i. 71.
Neo-Platonism, ii. 30.
Newman, his Essay on Development, i. 56 ; on Bull, i. 69.
Newton, Sir Isaac, his opinion of Christ's divinity, i. 71.
Nicephorus, i. 16, 306 ; iii. 107, 223.
Nicetas, i. 166.
Nicomedian Christians, iii. 215.
Noah, ii. 164.
Nourry, i. 29 ; iii. 61.

O.

Œcumenius, i. 317 ; iii. 2.
Oehler's Corpus Hæreseologicum, i. 18.
Olshausen, ii. 147 ; iii. 15, 285.
Opsimus, iii. 121.
Orelli's Inscriptions, iii. 110.

Origen, i. 13, 51, 92, 93, 100, 119; ii. 59; iii. 14, 16, 65, 221.
Orosius, iii. 252.
Orpheus, ii. 96, 117; iii. 70, 120.
Orphic Hymns, ii. 106.
Otto, ii. 87, 100, 120, 126, 135, 145, 147, 222, 224, 233, 236, 237, 274, 293, 303, 326, 327, 329; iii. 5, 15, 61, 62, 67, 105, 177.
Oudin, i. 28.
Οὐσία, iii. 239.

P.

Pagi, ii. 82; iii. 253.
Palmas, iii. 216.
Pantænus, iii. 107.
Papebroch, ii. 69, 82.
Papias, i. 85. Life of, i. 312; death, 313. Opinions on millennium, i. 315. Miracles related by, i. 317.
Passover, i. 156-159; iii. 223, 224.
Paul the Apostle, i. 9, 106, 150, 199; ii. 185; iii. 179, 202, 216.
Paul, Ludwig, iii. 177.
Paulus Servilius, iii. 223.
Pausanias, ii. 20; iii. 69.
Pearson, Bishop, i. 15, 99, 318; ii. 81; iii. 252, 285.
Πεποίθησις, i. 133.
Peripatetics, ii. 63; iii. 123.
Permaneder, Bibliotheca Patristica, i. 27.
Persecutions, ii. 6, 10, 154, 287; iii. 27, 118, 230.
Persephone, ii. 285, 286.
Perseus, ii. 285.
Persius, i. 84.
Petavius, i. 55, 69; iii. 145, 193.
Peter the Apostle, i. 91, 106, 150, 316; iii. 216.
Pharisees, iii. 201.
Philastrius, i. 18; iii. 11.
Philemon, ii. 96.
Philip the Apostle, i 317; iii. 215, 218.
Philip Sidetes, iii. 107.
Philippians, letter of Polycarp to, i. 181.
Philo, i. 82; ii. 42, 164, 182; iii. 123.
Philocalia, i. 94.
Philolaus, iii. 121.
Philomelium, Church in, i. 164, 170.
Philosophy, ancient, ii. 25, 64, 113; iii. 29, 70.
Philosophy of the Fathers, i. 8.
Phœnix, i. 97, 98.
Photius, i. 20, 124; ii. 54, 90, 98; iii. 108, 114, 243.

Photographic facsimiles of the epistles of Clemens, i. 122.
Pierius of Alexandria, iii. 249.
Pilate, acts of, ii. 149, 171.
Pindar, ii. 19.
Pinytus, iii. 216, 218.
Pionios, i. 174, 183.
Piper, iii. 230.
Πίστις, i. 133.
Pius, Bishop, i. 260.
Plato, i. 83; ii. 18 22, 23, 26, 27, 46, 66, 98, 100, 110, 112, 117, 118, 157, 158-161, 180, 208, 214, 268, 319; iii. 29, 69, 70, 71, 81, 121-123, 128, 147.
Platonic philosophers, ii. 64.
Platonism, ii. 121.
Plautus, ii. 21.
Pliny the Elder, i. 98; ii. 20; iii. 116.
Pliny the Younger, ii. 5.
Plutarch, ii. 20, 23, 30. Pseudo-Plutarch de Placitis Philosophorum, ii. 101.
Poets, Greek, ii. 163; iii. 70, 121.
Polycarp, i. 83, 84, 85, 105, 211; iii. 225. Life, i. 154. Sources of information, i. 156. The Martyrium, i. 160. Discussion as to its genuineness, i. 161. Discussion on supposed voice from heaven, i. 162. On his death, i. 164. On the history of his body, i. 166. Discussion as to truth of narrative, i. 167. Probable date of letter, i. 170. Interpolated passages, ibid. Prayer, i. 172. On chapter xx., i. 173; on concluding sentences of Martyrium, i. 174. On worth of letter, i. 176. Abstract of Martyrium, i. 178. On age of Polycarp, i. 180. On his writings, i. 181. Letter of Polycarp to Philippians, ibid. Supposed date, i. 185. Other letters, ibid. Value of letter, i. 187. Abstract of letter to Philippians, i. 188. Doctrines of letter, i. 189; on God, ibid.; on Christ, i. 190; on Spirit, i. 193; on angels, ibid.; on sin, ibid.; on salvation, ibid.; on the Church, i. 194; on a future state, i. 196; on Scriptures, ibid. Quotations from New Testament, i. 197; on morality, i. 199. Literature of the letter, i. 199.
Polycrates, iii. 221.
Polytheism, origin and character of, ii. 95, 110, 155, 284, 286; iii. 28, 48, 70, 120.

Polygamy, ii. 48, 328, 342; iii. 16.
Pompeius, Marcus, ii. 89.
Ponticus, iii. 275.
Pontus, Churches in, iii. 215.
Porter, Richard, iii. 178.
Possevinus, i. 27.
Pothinus, iii. 269.
Pressensé, i. 86; ii. 32, 138; iii. 32.
Priestley, his Corruptions of Christianity, i. 72.
Primus, iii. 182.
Procopius of Gaza, ii. 119.
Prophets, the, ii. 26, 118.
Protestant historians of the Fathers, i. 32; treatment of the Fathers, i. 57.
Protestants, Gnostics called. ii. 57.
Proteus, or Peregrinus, iii. 22.
Ptolemy, king of Egypt, ii. 150.
Publius, iii. 215.
Pythagoras, ii. 96, 117; iii. 118, 123.
Pythagoreans, ii. 63.

Q.

Quadratus, ii. 4, 51; iii. 215.
Quirinus, ii. 171.

R.

Rechenberg, iii. 177.
Recognitions, i. 94, 99, 119.
Reeves, ii. 146.
Reithmayr, i. 30. 87; ii. 55.
Reminiscence, Platonic doctrine of, ii. 65; iii. 160.
Renan, iii. 234.
Reuss, i. 86, 89; on theology of Clemens, i. 113
Rhetoricians, iii. 5.
Rhodon, iii 9, 23, 107.
Riddle's Christian Antiquities, i. 33.
Ritschl, i. 39, 44, 128, 269.
Ritter, History of Philosophy, i. 8; ii. 341.
Roman Catholics, accused of corrupting the texts of the Fathers, i. 23. Works on the Fathers, i. 27, 30; their ideas of the development of theology, i. 55.
Rome, the Church in, i. 92; iii. 216.
Rössler, i. 34 : ii. 146.
Rothe, i. 88, 301.
Routh, i. 190, 200; ii. 57; iii. 113, 199, 249, 282, 284, 285.
Rufinus, i. 16, 23, 94; iii. 5, 27, 189, 221, 223, 278, 284.
Ruinart, ii. 69; iii. 254.

Russel, Richard, i. 87.
Rusticus, ii. 70.

S.

Sadducees, iii. 201.
Sagaris, iii. 223.
Salmasius, iii. 255.
Samaritans, iii. 201.
Sanctus, iii. 257, 267.
Sandius, i. 70.
Sappho, iii. 39.
Sardanapalus, ii. 286.
Saturniliani, ii. 179; iii. 196.
Saturninus, iii. 9.
Scaliger, his Thesaurus Temporum, i. 19; ii. 82; iii. 192, 242.
Schenkel, i. 211, 214.
Schleiermacher, ii. 329; influence of, i. 75.
Schliemann, i. 83; ii. 184.
Schmidt, i. 85.
Schwartz, ii. 16.
Schwegler, i. 12, 23, 39-45, 88, 101, 114, 182; ii. 331.
Scultetus, his Medulla Theologiæ Patrum, i. 66.
Seiler, Raphael, iii. 181.
Semisch, ii. 86, 101, 119, 122, 149, 171, 189, 211, 222, 231, 239, 251, 264, 271, 272, 278, 293, 323, 325, 327, 329.
Semler, iii. 115; treatment of Fathers, i. 74.
Seneca, ii. 20.
Septuagint, ii. 88, 113.
Serapion, iii. 244.
Severiani, iii. 11, 12, 220.
Severus the Emperor, iii. 65, 258.
Sibyl, i. 97, 98; ii. 97, 117, 119, 288, 320; iii. 102.
Simeon, son of Clopas, iii. 195.
Simeon Metaphrastes, i. 20; ii. 69.
Simon Magus, ii. 62, 150, 179, 288.
Simonians, iii. 195.
Simonides, i. 308.
Sinaitic Codex, i. 309.
Sirach, Book of, ii. 43.
Sirmond, i. 251.
Slavery, i. 251; ii. 344.
Smith, Thomas, his edition of Ignatius and Polycarp, i. 200.
Smyrna, letter from Church in, i. 154, 155, 157.
Socrates, i. 174; ii. 18, 26, 110, 113, 117, 119, 157, 180, 286; iii. 70, 118.
Socrates the historian, iii. 108, 236, 249.
Solanus, iii. 4.

Sophocles, ii. 96, 117; iii. 121, 239.
Glossary of Later and Byzantine Greek, i. 35.
Sophron, iii. 30.
Soter, iii. 183, 216, 219.
Souverain, ii. 50.
Sprenger's Thesaurus, i. 34.
Stanley, Dean, i. 5; iii. 193.
Staüdlin, ii. 120.
Stephanus, H., ii. 128, 140, 146.
Stephanus, R., ii. 145.
Stückl, i. 8.
Stoics, i. 83; ii 23, 28, 38, 63, 121, 161-163, 181, 289, 320; iii. 6, 30, 58, 121.
Stoughton, his Ages of Christendom, i. 64, 82, 269.
Style, objected to by Theophilus, iii. 69.
Sub-apostolic, i. 81.
Subintroductæ, i. 265.
Suetonius, iii. 253, 254.
Suicer, ii. 340; iii. 228, 239, 259. His Thesaurus Ecclesiasticus, i. 35.
Suidas, i. 160, 185.
Sulpicius Severus criticized, i. 16, 17.
Sylburg, ii. 145.
Syncellus, i. 19, 99.
Syria, iii. 3.

T.

Tacitus, i. 84, 98.
Talmud, i. 207, 208.
Tanis, ii. 281.
Tatian, i. 9; ii. 4, 22, 68. His country, iii. 3. His profession, iii. 4. His conversion, iii. 7. His Christian life, iii. 8. His heretical life, iii. 11. His heretical opinions, *ibid.* Misrepresentations, *ibid.* His opinion of marriage, iii. 14; of another God, iii. 16; of Adam, *ibid.* Explanation of his heresies, iii. 17. His Oration, iii. 20; its genuineness and date, iii. 21. His other works, iii. 22. His Harmony, iii. 24. His heretical work, On Perfection according to the Saviour, iii. 26. His character, iii. 27. His references to persecution, *ibid.* His attitude towards heathenism, iii. 28. His treatment of philosophers, iii. 29. His rejection of all human studies, iii 30. His defence of Christianity, iii. 31. Abstract of the Oration to the Greeks, iii. 34. Doctrines of Tatian—On God, iii. 40; His immateriality, *ibid.;* peculiar notions of creation, iii. 41; the Logos, iii. 42; the Spirit—use of the term, iii. 46; peculiar doctrine of Spirit, *ibid.;* devil and demons — their nature, their continuance, and ultimate state, iii. 48; man—his nature, iii. 52; freewill, iii. 54; salvation, iii. 55; Christians—their mode of life, iii. 56; resurrection, iii. 58; Scriptures, iii. 59; morality, iii. 60. Literature—manuscripts and editions, iii. 60.
Taxes, payment of, ii. 344.
Taylor, Isaac, on Jerome, i. 16. His Ancient Christianity, i. 60.
Teaching in the Church, i. 264.
Tentzel, ii. 82; iii. 110, 179.
Tertullian, i. 9, 81, 93, 158, 219, 258; ii. 123; iii. 12, 222, 284.
Testimony, historical, i. 10.
Thalemannus, ii. 146.
Thales, iii. 128.
Thallus, ii. 105; iii. 83.
Theatre, iii. 29, 99.
Thebuthis, iii. 195.
Theiner, iii. 254.
Theodoret, i. 17; ii. 56; iii. 11, 24, 244.
Theology, early Christian: mode of treatment, i. 46.
Theophilus, ii. 4. His descent, iii. 63. Date of death, iii. 64. Writings of Theophilus, *ibid.* Genuineness of the books addressed to Autolycus, *ibid.;* their completeness, iii. 67. Other works of Theophilus, *ibid.* His style, iii. 69. Estimate of heathenism, *ibid.* Defence of Christianity, iii. 71. Abstract of Theophilus to Autolycus, iii. 72. Doctrines of Theophilus in regard to God, iii. 83; the Trinity, iii. 87; the Logos, *ibid.;* the Spirit, iii. 89; angels, devil and demons, iii. 92; man, iii. 93; salvation, iii. 96; Christianity, iii. 98; the future state, iii. 99; the Scriptures, iii. 102. Literature—manuscripts, editions, and translations, iii. 105.
Theophylact, i. 317.
Θεός, meaning of, ii. 41.
Thiersch, i. 88; ii. 9.
Thirlby, ii. 82, 146, 164, 233, 236, 275, 326.
Thomas à Kempis, iii. 26.
Thönnissen, on Clemens Romanus, i. 101; on his statements in regard to overseers, i. 141.

Thucydides, iii. 70.
Thundering Legion, Miracle of the, iii. 241, 252.
Tillemont, i. 28, 94, 96-177; ii. 135; iii. 112, 114, 254, 259.
Timothy, ii. 138.
Tischendorf, i. 254, 308; ii. 149.
Trajan, ii. 5.
Tregelles, iii. 209, 210.
Trithemius, Joannes, iii. 219.
Trollope, ii. 146.
Trophonius, ii. 22.
Trypho, ii. 89.
Tübingen school, i. 36, 77, 182.
Tulloch, Principal, on Luther, i. 61.
Turner, iii. 266.
Tzschirner, ii. 20, 49.

U.

Uhlhorn, i. 109.
Urbicus, i. 167; ii. 81.
Usher's edition of Polycarp, i. 200; of Barnabas, i. 252.
Usuardus, iii. 256.

V.

Valens, i. 156.
Valentiniani, ii. 179; iii. 196.
Valentinus, iii. 9, 11, 13.
Valerian, iii. 61.
Valesius, i. 169; ii. 80, 81; iii. 4, 258, 278, 283, 284, 285.
Valla, iii. 177.
Van Mildert's Life of Waterland, i. 71.
Vaughan, Dr., his Causes of Corruption of Christianity, i. 64.
Venus, ii. 104.
Verus, Lucius, ii. 83.
Vespasian, iii. 192.
Vettius Epagathus, i. 167; iii. 264.
Victor of Capua, i. 185; iii. 26.
Vienna, iii. 258.
Vigilius, ii. 60.
Villemain, ii. 20.
Virgil, ii. 21.
Virginity, letters on, i. 119.

Visions of the Pastor of Hermas, i. 273, 274.
Volkmar, ii. 86, 331; iii. 206.
Vossius, i. 253; ii. 101.

W.

Wake, i. 122, 254, 311.
Walch, i. 11. His Bibliotheca Patristica, i. 27; his History of Heretics, i. 74.
Waterland, on the use of the Fathers, i. 67, 70; life of, i. 71.
Weber, iii. 213.
Westcott, i. 81, 267, 269, 305, 312, 318; ii. 37, 136, 331; iii 213, 217, 249.
Wetstein, ii. 87.
Whiston, iii. 232. His Primitive Christianity Revived, i. 73. Sons of, ii. 57.
Wilson's Popular Preachers, i. 33.
Wisdom, personification of, ii. 43.
Wolf's Prolegomena ad Homerum, i. 12, 83.
Wolfius, Hieron, iii. 181.
Wolfius, Jo., iii. 65, 67, 105.
Woog, iii. 221.
Wordsworth, i. 98.
Worth, iii. 3, 23, 45, 53, 62, 179.
Wotton's edition of Clemens Romanus, i. 121.

X.

Xanthicus, i. 173.

Y.

Young, Patrick; see Junius.

Z.

Zeller, i. 12; ii. 28.
Zeno, iii. 29.
Zeus, ii. 18, 234, 285, 286; iii. 50.
Zoker, grandson of Judas, iii. 200.
Zola, iii. 257.
Zopyrus, iii. 69.

II. THEOLOGICAL INDEX.

A.

ABORTIONS, procuring, sinful, i. 251; iii. 175.
Acts of Pilate, the, or the Gospel of Nicodemus, ii. 149, 171.
Adam, ii. 152, 293; iii. 9, 11, 16, 19, 94, 95.
Adultery, i. 300.
Angels, i. 131, 236, 290; ii. 275-280; iii. 155-180. Worship of angels, ii. 278; iii. 156. Evil angels, ii. 280.
Antichrist, i. 191, 236.
Apocryphal books, i. 146, 197, 202, 241, 245, 306; ii. 323, 330.
Apostles, i. 136, 150; memoirs of, ii. 329, 332.
Asceticism forbidden, iii. 286.

B.

Baptism, i 228, 240, 250, 303; ii. 34, 298, 300, 307-311; iii. 98, 284.
Bishops, or overseers, i. 137, 139, 141, 157, 194, 302; ii. 305; iii. 283.
Blood unlawful to eat, iii. 284.

C.

Castration, probably regarded as meritorious, iii. 222.
Christ: the name, ii. 242. His Divinity, i. 69, 124, 190, 233; ii. 34, 40, 44, 128, 177, 180, 226; iii. 152, 226, 238, 281. Son of God, i. 124, 191, 233, 283; ii. 127, 159, 165, 218; iii. 150. Lord, i. 124, 233, 283. Creator, i. 234, 283; ii. 130, 225; iii. 154. The Logos, i. 126; ii. 40, 45, 111, 125, 127, 129, 157, 180, 209, 219-226; iii. 42-46, 87-89, 149-155. Ascriptions to Christ, i 125, 233; ii. 264. Subjection to God, i. 69, 127, 192, 234; ii. 219, 229, 240. The Messiah, ii. 177. Lord of angels, ii. 275. Relation to the Holy Spirit, i. 284; ii. 270; iii. 153. His real humanity, i. 191, 234; ii. 232. His incarnation, ii. 231-234. His object in becoming man, ii. 130, 131, 241, 242, 245, 246. His miraculous birth, ii. 235-237. Why He was born of a virgin, ii. 120, 245. Effect of His teaching, ii. 166, 245. His earthly life, ii. 237. Possessed of a soul, iii. 249. His sinlessness, i. 191; ii. 165, 241. The effects of His death, i. 128, 191, 225, 235, 283; ii. 39, 247; iii. 281. His descent into Hades, ii. 239. His unity, ii. 232. His resurrection, i. 127, 191, 192, 235; ii. 240. His miracles, ii. 167, His prophecies, ii. 171. His present activity and reign, i. 129; ii. 252-255; iii. 281. His second coming and judgment, i. 130, 235; ii. 72, 131, 256-260, 264. The centre of Christianity, ii. 165. The centre of the Old Testament, i. 151, 243; ii. 172, 177. His power over demons; see Demons.
Christians: their conduct, i. 135; iii. 99, 169. Relation to God and Christ, i. 135. Admonition of each other, i. 136, 239. All of them priests, ii. 304. Their progress, iii. 57. Various names, ii. 281.
Church, i. 135, 301; iii. 98, 225. Offi-

ces in the Church, i. 136, 194, 302; ii. 47, 304. Unity of the Church, i. 301; ii. 303; iii. 283. Sons of the Church, ii. 121.
Consubstantiation, ii. 311.
Conversion, i. 237, 294; ii. 296, 299; iii. 97.
Corinthians, First Epistle to the, i. 147.

D.

Deacons, i. 137, 195, 302; ii. 304, 305, 309; iii. 283.
Death, i. 132, 292; ii. 246, 247, 294.
Demon, i. 287; ii. 154, 155, 169, 246, 247, 252, 281, 283–289; iii. 28, 46, 48–52, 93, 158, 167.
Devil, i. 132, 193, 236, 291; ii. 111, 123, 125, 154, 270, 281, 282, 325; iii. 48, 92, 156, 167, 227, 282.

E.

Elders: identity of overseers and elders, i. 139, 194, 302.
Election, i. 134, 293.
Eucharist, i. 142, 156; ii. 311.

F.

Faith, i. 77. Faith in God, i. 133, 237, 295; ii. 297, 300; iii. 97; in Christ, i. 133, 238; ii. 125, 300; in God and Christ, i. 192.
Fall, the, ii. 293; iii. 52, 95.
Fasting, i. 305.
Flood, the general, iii. 81.
Free-will, i. 292; ii. 162, 281, 289; iii. 54, 95, 165.
Future state, i. 143, 196, 240, 305; ii. 134, 257, 316 322; iii. 53, 58, 59, 97, 99-102, 164, 169–171, 285. Opinions of heathens, ii. 164.

G.

Gehenna, ii. 320; iii. 285.
God: His character, i. 122, 189, 232, 282; ii. 125, 126, 213, 216, 217; iii. 40, 83, 86, 142, 280; Being of God, ii. 208. God immaterial, ii. 211; iii. 40, 85, 145. God corporeal, iii. 228. God capable of suffering—a corrupt reading, ii. 233; in Tatian, iii. 46. God propitiated, i. 124, 282, 296; ii. 217. God creator, ii. 214; iii. 40, 41, 85, 146. God regarded as creator by Plato,

ii. 158. God regarded as judge by ancients, ii. 96. Unity of God acknowledged by ancients, ii. 96, 117; iii 121. Proof of, iii. 142.
Gospels, ii. 329; iii. 103, 189, 204, 243. Harmony of, iii. 24. The Lord's writings, iii. 216, 217.
Gospel according to the Hebrews, ii. 330, 331; iii 25, 182, 189.
Gospel of Nicodemus, ii. 149, 171.
Gospel of Thomas, ii. 331.

H.

Hades, ii. 239, 317.
Heaven, ii. 72, 122, 134, 318; iii. 52: in the New Testament, i. 85.
Hebrews, Epistle to the, i. 119.
Hegrin i. 290.

I.

Idols, on food offered to, ii. 185, 200.
Inspiration, presented in a new shape in this age for solution, i. 7. Inspiration of the Old Testament according to Clemens Romanus, i. 144, 147. No statement in regard to the inspiration of the New by Clemens Romanus, i. 150. Inspiration of the Prophets, i. 196. Opinions of Clemens Alexandrinus, i. 203; Barnabas, i. 243. Inspiration of the Pastor of Hermas, i. 255. The Sibyl inspired, ii. 97, 111, 119; iii. 102, 103. Sibyl and Hystaspes inspired, ii. 149; coupled with the Prophets, ii. 288, 324. Inspiration in the Hortatory Address, ii. 114; in Athenagoras, iii. 171. Theory of inspiration of Scriptures, ii. 324-27. Prophets inspired, ii. 324. Inspiration of the New Testament, ii. 332. Inspiration of the Old Testament, iii. 71, 102. Authority of the Wisdom of Solomon, iii. 207, 209.

J.

John, Revelation of, the Apostle, i. 318; ii. 75, 262, 329; iii. 68, 206, 227, 286. Gospel of, iii. 103, 104, 205, 208, 246, 285. Epistles of, iii. 206.
Judaism, in Barnabas, i. 82, 205, 247;

in the Epistle to Diognetus, ii. 132. Obligation of the Law, ii. 175, 199.
Jude, Epistle of, iii. 206.
Judgment; see Future State.
Justification, ii. 130, 298; by faith, i. 77. Justification according to Clemens, i. 133.

L.

Lord's Supper; see Eucharist.
Luke's Gospel and Acts, iii. 204.

M.

Man: his likeness to God, ii. 122, 131; his sinfulness, ii. 295. Has natural notions of right, ii. 334. Men naturally brothers, ii. 335; iii. 159. His constitution, iii. 46, 52, 94, 159, 161. Purpose of his creation, iii. 93, 163.
Mark, Gospel of, i. 316; iii. 204.
Marriage, i. 300: ii. 48, 120, 338; iii. 9, 11, 14, 60, 173, 217.
Martyrdom, i. 300; ii. 335.
Mary, ii. 293; iii. 238.
Mass, ii. 301.
Matter, eternity of, ii. 214; iii. 41, 146. Not eternal, iii 86.
Matthew, Gospel of, i. 316; iii. 245.
Memoirs of the Apostles; see Gospels.
Michael, i. 290.
Millennium, Papias's idea of, i. 85, 215; Barnabas', i. 236; Justin's, ii. 260.
Miracles, argument from, ii. 32, 167; attested by Quadratus, ii. 51; performed by demons, ii. 288.

N.

New Testament; see Testament.

O.

Overseers; see Bishop.

P.

Paradise, iii. 93.
Paul, Epistles of, i. 99, 119; iii. 18, 26, 104, 172, 206.
Penitence, i. 293.
Perseverance of the saints, i. 239, 293.
Prayer, i. 300.
Presbyters; see Elders.
Prophecy, argument from, ii. 31, 170.

Prophets, ii. 168, 324; iii. 47, 59, 71, 91, 103, 104, 171.
Propitiation, God said by Clemens Romanus to be propitiated, i. 124; 296.

R.

Redemption, i. 129, 170, 222, 237; ii. 130, 247.
Regeneration, ii. 308. See Conversion.
Repentance, i. 294, 296. See Conversion.
Resurrection, i. 142, 192, 196; ii. 123, 319; iii. 58, 100, 131, 142, 169.
Riches, acquisition of, i. 299.
Righteousness, ii. 335.

S.

Sabbath, or seventh day of the week, i. 230, 239; ii. 133, 175, 176, 184, 199, 305-307; iii. 99. Omission of Fourth Commandment in Theophilus, iii. 86, 105.
Sacrifice, Christ's, i. 224, 235; ii. 248. The idea of sacrifice, ii. 132; iii. 121, 144. Offered by the Jews, ii. 135. Sacrifices and offerings of Christians, ii. 256, 304, 312, 313.
Sadness, a sin, i. 272.
Saints, prayer to the, not in Clemens Romanus, i. 143
Salvation, i. 132; iii. 41, 55. Through knowledge of God, iii. 56, 168. Through fear of God, i. 133. Through faith in God, *ibid.* Through love to God, i. 134. By favour, i. 193. Through Christ, ii. 125, 131, 242, 297-303. Through good works, ii. 302; iii. 96.
Satan; see Devil.
Satisfaction, ii. 249, 251.
Scriptures, i. 196, 241, 306; ii. 323; iii. 59, 217. Term supposed to be applied to the New Testament, i. 197.
Self-mutilation, ii. 343.
Septuagint, quoted by Clemens Romanus, i. 145; by Barnabas, i. 241; ii. 148, 326.
Servants; see Deacon.
Sin, original, i. 292; ii. 39, 293; iii. 95, 164.
Solomon, Wisdom of, iii. 207.
Spirit, the Holy, opinions of Clemens Romanus on, i. 131. Prophets

inspired by Him. i. 144, 236. The Holy Spirit in Hermas, i. 267, 286, 287; in the Apologists, ii. 39, 264-275; iii. 46-48, 87, 89-92, 150, 155, 171, 282; in Plato, ii. 112, 150; in the Hortatory Address, ii. 113. Identified in function with the Logos, ii. 226.

Substitution, moral, ii. 130.

Suicide, ii. 337.

Sunday, or first day of the week, i. i. 230, 239, 251; ii. 34, 238, 305, 306; iii. 218, 219, 225.

Supererogation, works of, i. 296

Swearing, ii. 338.

T.

Thanksgiving; see Eucharist.

Testament, New, authorship of, known to us through early Christian writings, i. 7. Interpretation of, *ibid* References to, in Clemens Romanus, i. 147. References to, in Polycarp, i. 197. Authority of, i. 198. Quoted by Barnabas, i. 242, 246. References in Papias, i. 316; in Justin Martyr, ii. 329; in Tatian, iii. 24; in Theophilus, iii. 104. List of the Books of New Testament, iii. 204, 210. See Scripture.

Testament, Old, in Barnabas, i. 82. Passages quoted by Clemens Romanus, i. 144. Interpretation of, by Clemens Romanus, i. 151. Interpretation of Old Testament in Barnabas. i. 243, 247; in the Apologists. ii. 31, 34, 171. Old Testament inspiration and completeness of, ii. 174. Interpretation of, ii. 289, 327; iii. 24, 32, 71, 72, 104. Saints, Old Testament, i. 304. List of the Books of Old Testament, iii. 232. Grace required to interpret Old Testament, ii. 175. See Scripture.

Transubstantiation, ii. 311.

Trinity, the opinions of early writers as stated by Blunt, i. 71. Statement of Clemens Romanus, i. 131. The opinions of Apologists, ii. 45. Trinity, or Triad, in Theophilus, iii. 87; in Athenagoras, iii. 150.

V.

Vicarious suffering of Christ, i. 129

W.

Women, duty of, i. 152, 199.

# CORRECTIONS.

Vol. II. p. 34, l. 31, *read* to *for* as.

p. 43, l. 14, 'Son of Jesus' should be cancelled. The writer has not examined the authorship of the book, and has therefore no opinion on it.

Vol. III. p. 11, l. 34, *after* founder *insert* of.

,, p. 57, l. 7, *insert* comma *after* treasure, *and delete it after* digging.

p. 65, l. 24, *for* are *read* is.

p. 108, in note, *read* Philip *for* Photius.

p. 115, l. 23, *delete* Domini.

www.ingramcontent.com/pod-product-compliance
Lightning Source LLC
Chambersburg PA
CBHW030812230426
43667CB00008B/1174